JOHN WESLEY'S
CONCEPT OF
PERFECTION

JOHN WESLEY'S CONCEPT OF PERFECTION

by
Leo George Cox, Ph.D.

Director of Ministerial Training
Marion College, Marion, Indiana

BEACON HILL PRESS OF KANSAS CITY
Kansas City, Mo.

Printed in the United States of America

To
ESTHER
the queen of my home
whose patient confidence in me
gives continuing inspiration.

PREFACE

The material in this book was prepared as a dissertation in partial fulfillment of the requirements for the doctor of philosophy degree which was granted the author in June of 1959 by the State University of Iowa. It is a careful, thorough, and well-documented study of John Wesley's teaching on perfection. Here is a painstaking and exhaustive endeavor to understand Wesley in the light of his Anglican and Reformed tradition and from the perspective of the movement and teachings that followed him. It will be helpful to every layman with a scholarly turn of mind as well as a purpose to be "endued with every Christian grace and be full of his light, grace, wisdom, and holiness" (*John Wesley's Explanatory Notes upon the New Testament*).

This volume belongs on the reference shelf of every minister seeking to be "approved of God" in his dedicated efforts "to teach, reprove, correct, or train up others" (John Wesley). The ministerial student has here an invaluable commentary on the teachings of God's Word with regard to the doctrine of Christian perfection.

John Wesley's high regard for Scripture and the correct interpretation thereof was expressed as follows: "The Scripture is a most solid and precious system of divine truth. Every part thereof is worthy of God. It is the fountain of heavenly wisdom, which they who are able to taste prefer to all writing of men, however wise or learned or holy."

This volume is published with a deep conviction that it is a distinct contribution to current holiness literature.

THE PUBLISHERS

CONTENTS

CHAPTER I

INTRODUCTION

"There is scarce any expression in Holy Writ," wrote John Wesley in his sermon on "Christian Perfection," "which has given more offence than this. The word *perfect* is what many cannot bear. The very sound of it is an abomination to them." Wesley was not here referring to wicked and ungodly men who opposed this term, but to professing Christians. He knew the terrific force of the opposition raised to the teaching of perfection in his day, and he realized the "offence" it had brought to many.

Some advised Wesley to lay aside these expressions, and many others in his day and since have wished that he had followed this advice. But Wesley persisted in using the terms with the contention that they are found in the "oracles of God." Since they are there, neither he nor anyone else had any authority to set them aside. To be obedient as a minister of Christ, he must declare "all the counsel of God." Rather than set them aside, one should explain these terms and give their true meaning. Wesley spent much of his time over a period of 50 years trying to set forth what he considered the Scriptures meant by Christian perfection.[1]

"In 1729, two young men, reading the Bible, saw that they could not be saved without holiness, followed after it, and incited others so to do."[2] Often Wesley began a treatise or letter with these or similar words. To him perfection, or holiness, was a goal to be sought and found. He saw this ideal in his Bible, and his search along with that of others resulted in a continuous flow of pamphlets, letters, and sermons describing that search, exhorting others to seek perfection, and explaining what the experience meant. Wesley believed wholeheartedly in this experience and, although he was not concerned about opinions and particular expressions, he did want to be heard and understood.

For one who has been an admirer of Wesley for a number of years, this investigation through his many writings has been a distinct pleasure. It is sincerely hoped that the sifting, weighing, and organizing of Wesley's thoughts on perfection in this paper, rather than being an "offence" to anyone, will create an interest in this Christian theme and assist in a clearer hearing and understanding of Wesley.

A. PERFECTIONISM IN CHRISTIANITY

One cannot read Wesley long without becoming aware that he found most of his ideas about perfection in the Bible. Ideals of the perfect life—a life dedicated to God and lived according to God's will—are found in both the Old and the New Testaments. Wesley claimed to be a man of one Book and always sought to found his doctrines on the Word of God. Since he thought that his teaching on perfection was scriptural, he could not understand why others opposed him so. He considered that terms were not important, but he did insist on the reality for which the term stood.[3]

Concepts of perfection are found in the Old Testament, and when the New Testament Church came into existence, it had a literature that was rich with an ideal for God's people. Especially in the prophetic literature of the Old Testament is there exhortation to "moral integrity, wholeness, soundness, sincerity, or perfection." This perfection was expected of all the people of God.[4] New Testament Christians saw themselves as the true Israel, and they looked for a complete redemption in Christ. This ideal of perfection may be more implicit than explicit in the New Testament, but when these Scriptures are taken as a whole, the conviction that this ideal is attainable becomes somewhat clearer.

The fact that Wesley found the doctrine of perfection in the Bible does not mean that every inference he draws from the Scriptures is a valid one. Our only insistence here is that the perfectionist movements in Christianity did not need to look outside the Bible for their inspiration. The ideal of the perfect Christian life began when the Church began. All the ideas may not be clear in the New Testament, and this fact can account for varied interpretations, but the privilege of communion with God was for all.[5]

Did the Early Church of the second and third centuries retain this Christian ideal? It is quite readily admitted there was a departure from the ideal, even before the Church was very old. Wesley sees the "mystery of iniquity" as beginning to work at a very early time.[6] From a very early date there was a defection from the original radiance of the classical spirituality of the Early Church.[7] In the second century the Christian apologists, in their attempt to answer the critics and to make Christianity intelligible, reduced the gospel by making Christianity to be perfect knowledge and perfect being.[8] Gradually the idea of the Church began to take the place of the idea of the Kingdom. This shift of ideas caused a postponement of the great hope of a speedy purification in this life. "The stage is set for the appearance of Augustine, who was to combine the hope of a *Civitas Dei* on earth with a profound conviction that only in the next world could the true blessedness of the Christian be attained."[9]

That Augustine had an ideal is very clear. A man moved as he was by the Christian faith would find a perfection that could be enjoyed now in time, but would reach fullness only in eternity. Before his conflict with Pelagius this perfection was a "home even now for the seeking spirit." But his conflict with Pelagius raised the issue of the possibility of sinlessness in this life and it seems that he denied it. Only Jesus and His mother were sinless. Yet when Augustine got away from the negative definitions, he became more perfectionist and his "leading idea is that of the *Summum Bonum,* which in some measure may be enjoyed in this life."[10] Yet in his writings there are contradictory statements, which need explaining in the light of his retraction. "No one is perfect in this life. There is a perfection in this life." But this perfection is only relative and is for strangers on the earth who are not yet "in possession of their promised home." One should never assign any part of the ideal for this life which lies only beyond the grave.[11]

Whatever influence Augustine's ideas may have had upon the successive generations in the Church, his concept on perfection has stayed with us. In the Middle Ages the ideal was not lost sight of, but it was largely reserved for brave souls. In the Reformation the strong emphasis on salvation by faith alone left man so helpless in his sins that no perfection was expected here and now. In fact the term itself was almost always one of reproach.[12] Various differences between the reformers and Wesley will be expounded in this paper. The Reformation was a reaction against what the reformers looked upon as the "works-righteousness" of Catholicism, which they considered to be perfectionism. There is a relationship between the perfection as held by the Roman Catholic church and that held by Wesley, as will be seen later, but often the polemic of the reformers against "works-righteousness" as they saw it is not valid against Wesleyan perfection.

Even when one admits the defection from the high New Testament ideal both in the Church of the medieval period and in the Reformation churches, he must not allow a complete eclipse of the ideal of holiness. Before the Church was very old, men began to withdraw themselves from society. "Monasticism is the boldest attempt to attain Christian Perfection in all the long history of the church." These men wanted to be perfect. St. Anthony set out to win virtues he had seen in others. He wanted victory over Satan, so he went into solitude. Whether we like the methods used by monks or not, it is evident that the initial motive was for Christian perfection.[13]

In monasticism the ideal was not always shining brightly, but there were periods of revival and reform when monks and friars helped to restore pure religion. One can also see a restoration of this desire for holiness in many of the fringe movements in Christianity. In spite of any heresy they supported, the desire was there for reform and inward holiness. The Waldensians and the Spiritual Franciscans had this ideal of perfection before them. There is a stream of holiness literature flowing from many of these spiritual minds, and with but few gaps it reaches back to the Early Church. With every revival some phase of the truth of freedom from sin has been revived along with special emphasis on the infilling of the Holy Spirit.[14]

Nor was the Protestant Reformation free from these perfectionist movements. There were "spiritual Reformers" who wanted the Reformation to "go all the way" in the religion of heart and life. These men have been little known, but are beginning to be recognized as trailblazers for a spiritual religion. They read and appreciated the mystics and ultimately were historically significant for the development of Quakerism.[15] From these and from the pre-Reformation mystical "friends" and "brotherhoods" came Pietism.[16]

The impulse for this movement came from a desire for personal holiness. This movement was a reaction against a sterile orthodoxy and an objectivity with regard to faith prevailing in the Lutheran churches. The Pietists wanted to attain an individual holiness which was not set as a goal in their churches.[17]

Pietism itself is not the equivalent of perfectionism, but it did amount to a quasi-perfectionism. "It embodied and perpetuated those tendencies which made perfectionism possible and which entered as one main influence into English, and hence American, holiness movements."[18] Wesley was influenced by the Moravians, in whom he saw a holiness that appealed to him, and yet some things he saw he had to reject.[19] From this movement can be traced the sanctification movement of Europe in the nineteenth century.[20]

This is only a brief survey of perfectionism in Christianity to the time of Wesley. Rather than being in the mainstream of the Christian Church, it has been found in the subsidiary groups. This fact does not necessarily militate against any validity of the concept. "Intense and vital perfectionism," wrote Elmer Clark, "was found mainly among revolting sects, heretical parties, and fanatics."[21] These smaller groups have felt it their duty to call the Church back to the purity of religion. Pietism told the Church that the reformers were men of little faith—they had not experienced sanctifying power.[22] Wesley challenged his day with the message of holiness, and his doctrine "exerted the most far-reaching influence of any type of the doctrine ever presented."[23]

B. Wesley's Contribution to the Ideal

After Wesley was 80 years old, he wrote these reflections concerning his early life:

> From a child I was taught to love and reverence the Scripture, the oracles of God; and, next to these to esteem the primitive Fathers, the writers of the first three centuries. Next after the primitive church, I esteemed our own, the Church of England, as the most scriptural national Church in the world. I therefore not only assented to all the doctrines, but observed all the rubric in the Liturgy; and that with all possible exactness, even at the peril of my life.[24]

In Wesley's home he learned to strive for the highest in the Christian life. The discipline was strict, the ritual exact, and rules, habits, and obedience were the great words. The average day was spent in singing psalms morning and evening, reading Scripture, and prayers. The Wesley family was isolated from surrounding families and thus became a church society in itself. In this home were established ideals and habits from which Wesley never departed.[25]

Wesley's parents, even though from a dissenting background, had become high churchmen. From them Wesley received his high regard for the Church of England and his dislike for the dissenters. Although the high churchmen of Wesley's day were Protestants, they prized the name Catholic as well. Though they rejected the Roman Papacy, they held to the undivided Church of the first three centuries and to its creeds, rituals, and practice.[26] Eighteenth-century England was at a low ebb religiously and morally. But there were men in the Church of England who emphasized the life of holiness. Robert Nelson was one of these. He understood religion to be of the heart. For him Christian perfection was not just a perfect outward performance of duties, but there must be a change of mind, a renewal of heart, and a purification and sanctification of the inward affections.[27]

It appears quite clear from the reading of Wesley's journals, especially in the early years of the revival, that the opposition to him from the Church of England was occasioned by his preaching of justification by faith, rather than his preaching of perfection. Of course there was persecution at Oxford when the "Holy Club" was formed, and the few young men who were earnest in their pursuit of holiness were dubbed "Methodists." But this opposition came from careless and carefree youth who had no interest in any spiritual life. It was in 1738 and afterward that Wesley was rejected and not allowed to preach in the pulpits of England. And at that time the occasion was his preaching of a "new doctrine" as they supposed—a free offer of salvation to all by simple faith.[28]

Actually in the Church of England there was very little opposition to Wesley's perfectionist teaching when it was understood. The opposition to this teaching came from the Calvinist groups and the Moravians, who thought Wesley was unfaithful to the "Christ our Righteousness" by his emphasis upon holiness of heart and life. When Wesley explained to the Reverend Mr. Gibson, the bishop of London, what he meant by Christian perfection, the bishop said earnestly, "Why, Mr. Wesley, if this is what you mean by perfection, who can be against it?"[29]

It was through English church channels that Wesley learned his perfectionism, and from the Bible.[30] In 1725, when Wesley was 22, he read Bishop Jeremy Taylor's *Rule and Exercises of Holy Living and Dying.* He was greatly affected by the book, especially by the idea of "purity of intention." Immediately he resolved to dedicate all his life to God because there could be no halfway Christian. Then in 1726, Wesley read Thomas a Kempis' *Christian Pattern.* He now saw inward religion in a stronger light than ever and felt that he must give all his heart to God. If one is to ascend to God he must have "one design" in all he does and "one desire" ruling all his tempers. A year or two after this William Law's *Christian Perfection* and *Serious Call* were placed in his hands. "These convinced me, more than ever, of the absolute impossibility of being half a Christian." In 1729, Wesley began to study his Bible as the only true standard of truth and to state his concept of perfection in scriptural terms. In 1733, five years before his evangelical conversion, he preached a sermon on "The Circumcision of the Heart," in which he set forth his view of perfection. This view he claimed still to hold in 1777 "without any material addition or diminution."[31]

In this account one can see the meeting of medieval mysticism and monasticism with an Anglican mysticism in Wesley. The "ideal of Christian perfection comes theologically and historically from the Catholic stream of Christian thought."[32] Maximin Piette, a Catholic Franciscan, sees in Wesley that "anxious search for spiritual perfection found in the religious orders of the Catholic Church," and a likeness to St. Dominic, St. Benedict, St. Francis of Assisi, and St. Ignatius of Loyola.[33] Especially was Wesley following a Catholic tradition in his view of Christian perfection although he disclaimed that his view was that held by the Romanists.[34]

There were other influences than the Catholic that were

to work upon Wesley. "Catholic and Lutheran, Anglican and Moravian influences were all blended in Wesley."[35] Certain dissenting devotional authors as well as the Moravians entered into Wesley's life and helped shape his ultimate concepts on holiness. The part the Moravians had in acquainting Wesley with Luther and the doctrine of justification by faith is very clear. His trip to Germany to visit the Moravians gave him a clearer concept of how holiness is attained.[36] His experience of conversion in May, 1738, and subsequent experiences convinced Wesley that justification and sanctification are by faith and are instantaneous. He felt that the reformers were clear on justification but weak on sanctification, and that his work was to spread scriptural holiness.[37]

Now this man Wesley, in whom so many Protestant and Catholic streams converge, became t h e leader of the great Wesleyan revival. The effects of this revival have been felt throughout Western Christendom and especially in the English-speaking countries. Not only the Church of England and the Methodists felt the impact of this movement, but it was felt in most of the dissenting churches. Whether his doctrine of perfection was always accepted or not, the doctrine of God's free offer of salvation to all men became almost universal in the evangelical denominations. The impact of Methodism was felt in America as well as in England. There, in its frontier evangelism and in the midst of revival fervor of the first half of the nineteenth century, Wesley's perfectionism took root and flourished.[38]

The influence of Wesley's teaching on perfection was felt outside of Methodism in the various sanctification movements, such as Higher Life, Victorious Life, and Keswick groups.[39] In America as many as 50 sects trace their origin to Methodism and most of them teach some phase of holiness.[40] In the twentieth century there are numerous "holiness" churches connected with the National Holiness Association as well as many individuals within the Methodist church and other churches who adhere to the Wesleyan position on holiness. This association and these churches make Christian perfection the reason for their existence as separate groups.[41]

Does Wesley make any significant contribution to the doctrine of perfection? Many think so, and this paper investigates that question further. Wesley's significance is not that he contributed to a naturalistic or humanistic kind of perfectionism as one would find in Ritschl, Wernle, Clemen, Pfleiderer, or Windisch, however much there may be some likenesses.[42] It would seem that he is most significant in that he made the experience attainable here and now and that it was of a nature that all Christians could reach it.[43] And, more significant still, while doing this he still maintained the "Protestant ethic of grace" which he so ably synthesized with the "Catholic ethic of holiness."[44]

George Cell sees that it "belonged to Wesley's genius . . . to join together the faith of the first Reformers with the valuable element in humanism as represented by Erasmus and Arminius in Holland and by Erasmus and the Oxford Reformers with their successors, the great Anglican divines." His ability to do this is due to "his deep, clear synthetic thought" and a "remarkable quality of mind." This is in contrast to the thought of those who think Wesley was a "superficial eclectic" thinker.[45] Cell believes that the conflict caused at the time of the Reformation, when both sides "put asunder what in the nature of Christianity belongs together," can still be seen in the conflict between Wesleyanism and Calvinism. But these two central ideas of Christianity—justification by faith a n d holiness—are "joined together again in Wesleyanism in a well-balanced synthesis."[46] Franz Hildebrandt is hesitant to call this achievement of Wesley's a "synthesis," because faith-holiness to Wesley was a living unity. He sees Wesley as the mediator of Luther to this generation.[47]

C. PERFECTIONISM AND CONTEMPORARY THOUGHT

If for no other reason, there would be a justification for a study of Wesleyan perfectionism in view of the segment of churches and people in America who claim to follow Wesley in this teaching. "There are perhaps a million members of denominations, missionary societies, and other groups, whose chief reason for existence is the exposition of this emphasis in the Wesleyan message." The literature of these groups is not that of exacting research, but largely of a tractarian nature. "A desire is now frequently voiced for a presentation that will satisfy the canons of discriminating scholarship."[48]

In addition to these "holiness" groups there are many in Methodism at large who have a keen interest in this specific teaching of Wesley. Some of these take active and leading part in the National Holiness Association. There has been an increasing interest in research on Wesley in recent decades. Such names as Sangster, Rose, Peters, Turner, and Lindstrom recall for us very recent studies on Wesley in the area of perfection. Rose sees that there is an increasing interest among Methodists in this doctrine and experience.[49] There are groups outside the Wesleyan tradition who have embraced a teaching on perfection similar to Wesley's, but with some difference. A clearer understanding of Wesley may help to dispel some of these differences.[50]

The whole reaction of the nineteenth-century optimistic and humanistic conceptions of the perfectibility of human nature led by the Neo-Orthodox movement might be another reason why Wesleyan perfectionism may have contemporary relevance. The return to the doctrine of original sin and the pessimistic view taken of human nature as a result of two world wars have some theologians feeling that there is little redemption in this life. Karl Barth in his early writings saw reconciliation in this life for man, but he denied any change in man while in this world.[51] However, when Barth is studied in the light of his total dogmatics, he does not give a "grim disavowal of sanctification." He in particular "wishes to take account of the Reformed doctrine of man's total depravity."[52]

G. C. Berkouwer, from a contemporary perspective, believes there can be a doctrine of sanctification consistent with a right view of sin and grace. Considering the difficulties honestly faced by him in his book, *Faith and Sanctification,* where he tries to find common ground for the Reformed theologians' conflicts on the subject, one is impressed with their need of a clearer conception of Wesley's view.[53] One cannot study this book without recognizing the timeliness of this subject and its relevance for the present time.[54]

Today there is an increasing interest in biblical theology. In reading contemporary theological writings one is impressed with the effort to use the corrective of the Scriptures. Since Wesley placed his teaching so basically on the Bible and challenged others to show him wherein, according to the Scriptures, he might be wrong, it makes his teaching on perfection of special interest to the one interested in a "Theology of the Word." If Wesley's ideal is scriptural, then it should be understood or corrected in the light of the Word.

D. PROBLEMS IN WESLEY RESEARCH

A man whose influence has been as far-reaching as Wesley's always creates many and various problems for the research scholar. William Lecky claimed that Wesley "has had a wider constructive influence in the sphere of practical religion than any other man who has appeared since the sixteenth century."[55] John Bready was forced after careful research to change his views about the cultural heritage of the modern English-speaking world. Rather than the French Revolution and its philosophy, it was the Evangelical Revival, which began with Wesley, that nursed the spirit and character values of the English-speaking world.[56] Umphrey Lee feels that these statements need moderating, which fact indicates that this problem is not easily solved.[57]

Wesley's relationship to the Industrial Revolution was dealt with by Wellman Warner in his book, *The Wesleyan Movement in the Industrial Revolution.* David Thompson wrote on *John Wesley as a Social Reformer,* and John Faulkner studied Wesley as a sociologist and churchman. A study of Wesley's social and political influence was made by Maldwyn Edwards, and John Prince wrote *Wesley on Religious Education.* As the bibliography reveals, many books on Wesley have been written, especially on his life and work, and they deal with various problems from a historial point of view.

Most works on Wesley are only biographies and statements of facts about him. Few of them seek to give form to his ideas.[58] Some have been written from the point of view of religious psychology, but very few have given his theological position a close scrutiny.[59] No one should particularly question the need of further study of Wesley since his "personality and the enduring results of his work justify repeated efforts to fully appraise the man and his work." Few people realize the "many-sided nature" of his activities. "He was an extraordinary leader of men and a constructive religious genius."[60]

That Wesley was a clear and able thinker none ought to deny. He had a keen mind and a variety of interests. "But Wesley was a genius, and sometimes a genius is not best understood by those who stand closest to him."[61] Robert Clark thinks that "Wesley was a free thinker, and yet did his thinking most logically and methodically, reasoning far into the night over any problem of religion or life which he did not quite comprehend."[62] Wesley himself refers to the training he had in logic and how it helped him in controversy.[63] Wesley was constantly writing, and Piette guesses that he wrote and published more than any other one Protestant.[64] With such a mind as Wesley's there would be problems created and a consequent need for research.

One of the problems in Wesleyan study has been the relation of Wesley to Protestantism, both as to how he is related to the reformers and as to his contribution to modern Protestantism. Several recent writers have dealt specifically with this problem. Franz Hildebrandt sees a close connection between Luther and Wesley, not so much as a historical succession but in a close relationship of ideas. He thinks Luther can be understood by modern Lutherans only as they take a look at Wesley also.[65] J. E. Rattenbury in his studies on Wesley considers that Wesley joined the succession of reformers as a result of his contact with the Moravians and his conversion experience.[66]

The Catholic Franciscan, Maximin Piette, traces the rise of Protestantism and shows how Wesley made a great contribution in the evolution of Protestantism. He believes that Wesley and the Methodists have exerted a profound influence within all Protestantism with the renewal of spiritual fervor and of religious experience.[67] G. C. Cell and Umphrey Lee have contributed greatly in the solution of the problem of Wesley's place in Protestantism.[68] Cell's contention is that Wesley's change in 1738 had great significance, and his Reformation was a return to the theocentric "faith of the Reformers."[69] Lee, on the other hand, questions the significance of the conversion experience of Wesley, as does Piette, and sees him more as a prophet of modern religion who combines "mystical experience with the ethical, the rational and the institutional elements in religion."[70]

William Cannon in his book, *The Theology of John Wesley*, gives special attention to the doctrine of justification. He says that Wesley is at one with Calvinism in regard to the conception of the act of justification; yet in the operation of grace, they are not the same.[71] Also the reformers included more in justification as an all-inclusive concept than did Wesley.[72] The relationship of Wesley to the reformers and to Protestantism in general may be a problem as yet not settled, but considerable work has been done in this area.

But in the area of Wesley's theology of perfection, or sanctification, or holiness, much less work has been done. Recently there have been studies made of perfection from a historical viewpoint. Elmer Gaddis has been referred to above. He did his work in 1929 and it is a survey of perfectionism in America. Claude Thompson and Robert Clark have written histories of Christian perfection in American Methodism. Timothy Smith recently (1957) published a book, *Revivalism and Social Reform*, in which, though not a study on Wesley or perfection as such, he does reveal the tremendous influence the teaching had in American reform.[73] In his book, *Christian Perfection and American Methodism*, published in 1957, John Peters discusses Wesley's doctrine of perfection in the process of formation and its final statement as qualified by Wesley. Then he traces its transplanting, development, and modification in America during the nineteenth century. His purpose is primarily historical, and not doctrinal.[74]

The most comprehensive and systematic study of Wesley's doctrine of sanctification was done by Harald Lindstrom, a Swedish theologian, whose work was published in 1946. He writes:

> Sanctification itself in Wesley is rarely presented in its full range. The conception is normally restricted. Sometimes it connotes Christian perfection only, no regard being had to the gradual development of sanctification from its commencement in the New Birth. Sometimes, it is true, the latter is included, but then entire sanctification is minimized. In neither alternative, moreover, has the significance, for Wesley's total view of salvation, of the principle of entire sanctification, been clearly expounded.[75]

The aim of Lindstrom is to provide an "analysis of the function and significance of sanctification in Wesley's conception of salvation." He tries to see "sanctification in its full scope and in its due relation to the conception of salvation as a whole." He discusses the connection between justification and sanctification and the relation each has to final and present salvation. Also he gives a detailed examination of the concept of love.[76]

Mention should also be made of the work of William Sangster and George Turner. Sangster wrote *The Path to Perfection* in England during the Second World War. He tries to show Wesley's ideal as being scriptural and as a goal to be aimed at, but he does not subject all of Wesley's thought to a careful scrutiny. Turner's work is more thorough in that he subjects Wesley's doctrine to the test of Scripture and concludes it is biblical. Albert Knudson calls this a "work of extraordinary merit."[77] Turner's purpose is threefold—to discover the biblical teaching, to ascertain Wesley's distinctive emphasis, and to evaluate the doctrine as to its validity in this utilitarian age.[78]

There are problems still, especially in relation to Wesley's conception of perfection. One of these problems is the relationship between the holiness which Wesley taught as attainable in this life and the concept of continuing sinfulness in the believer who needs the constant efficacy of Christ's atonement. Some writers have believed that Wesley's concept of sin was faulty since he taught a possible, present perfection. R. N. Flew fails to be clear in his criticism of Wesley's concept of sin when he says that Wesley had only one definition of sin and that he looked upon sin as a substance.[79] Even Sangster thinks Wesley rejected the idea of "unconscious sin."[80] Lee considers that Wesley's concept of sin misled him in his teaching on perfection.[81] All of which points to the fact that Wesley's concept of sin has not been made clear in its relation to perfection.

Related to this problem and yet different from it is how a person can be perfect now who is still in this life. There is a perfection toward which one is constantly growing. How then can one become perfect and still be able to grow? In the midst of the growing process of a Christian where he is becoming more and more like Christ, how can he by faith be made perfect and yet, ever afterwards, continue to grow in that perfect love? If in that perfecting experience sin is destroyed, how then can sin ever again be a problem to the believer? Also, in connection with this experience of perfect love, there is the problem of assurance. How can one know when he is perfect?

Growing out of these suggested problems is the greater one concerning the imperfections of the human existence and the constant need of confession of unworthiness before God. It is at this point that Wesley has been criticized most severely. If one is free from sin, and therefore holy, would he not be tempted to pride? Is there not danger of pharisaism for such a professor? Also, are not the mistakes and imperfections of the Christian sins and should they not be confessed as sinful? Not only do Calvinists see this problem in Wesleyan perfection[82] but even some Methodist critics.[83] How can one attain a degree of holiness in himself and not jeopardize the relationship of complete unworthiness before God for justification?[84]

In this paper it cannot be promised that an answer to all these questions can be found that would even be satisfactory to the most sympathetic hearer of Wesley. But they are problems that should be honestly faced and discussed. The aim of this paper is to discover, as far as possible, Wesley's answers to these problems. It is believed that when Wesley's thought is clearly understood many of the objections will vanish.

Our methods of procedure will be as follows: First, Wesley's concept of sin will be summarized and his variations from the reformers will be noted. This approach will involve a discussion of grace along with faith and works. These matters will be discussed in Chapter II. Second, the various stages in perfection will be discussed as they are related to the order of salvation. Then the experience of present perfection as proclaimed by Wesley will be related to these various stages, and what he meant by the "second blessing" can be clarified. Associated with these will be the ideas of assurance, freedom from sin, testimony, and the law of love. This discussion will be in Chapters III and IV.

These first two parts of the discussion will prepare the way for the third, which will deal with the human limitations and imperfections of man in his present existence. What Wesley has to say about these will be presented, and attention will be given to the manner in which he relates these mistakes and failures to perfect love. Also the defects in the Christian who has attained a perfect love will be examined in the light of the unworthy condition of mankind. These "sins" of ignorance that remain will be tested against the perfection Wesley taught.

E. Source Materials

Wesley wrote continually, and fortunately for us many of his writings are available. Quite early in life he began a journal and made it ready for publication at different times during his life. The entirety of this journal is now available in *The Journal of the Rev. John Wesley*, an eight-volume set edited by Nehemiah Curnock. This journal is also found in volumes one to four in *The Works of John Wesley*, which was the authorized edition of the Wesleyan Conference Office in London, England, in 1872. From this 14-volume set most of the quotations for this study are made.

Many of Wesley's sermons were prepared for publication by himself and constitute the most significant of his theological writings. There are 141 sermons in Volumes V to VII of the authorized edition. Not all of these were authorized for publication by Wesley himself. E. H. Sugden edited the two-volume set of his *Standard Sermons* published in 1921.

The remaining volumes of the authorized edition contain miscellaneous writings, including letters, treatises, and some writings of other authors approved by Wesley. Many of these treatises and letters contain valuable material for the subject of perfection. Especially is the treatise *A Plain Account of Christian Perfection* of special interest. In 1931, John Telford edited the eight-volume set of *The Letters of Rev. John Wesley, A. M.* Value is also found in Wesley's *Explanatory Notes on the New Testament*. A recent publication is *A Compend of Wesley's Theology* compiled by Burtner and Chiles. This is a systematic organization of some of Wesley's writings under various theological topics.

During Wesley's lifetime John Fletcher, a leading apologist for the Methodists and a minister in the Church of England, wrote his famous *Checks to Antinomianism*.

Wesley admired Fletcher very highly for his saintly character and for the "strength and clearness" of his arguments in writing.[85] These *Checks,* along with a treatise on Christian perfection as one of the checks, and other writings of Fletcher are found in *The Works of the Reverend John Fletcher,* published in 1835 in four volumes.

Three Methodist theological writers of the nineteenth century in England should be noticed. Adam Clarke was known to Wesley and wrote *Christian Theology,* which was published in 1835. Richard Watson, a close student of Wesley, was author of *Theological Institutes,* published in 1828. W. B. Pope wrote the *Compendium of Christian Theology,* which was published in 1881. All of these English writers had great influence upon American Methodists.

In this study special attention will be given to American theologians who have helped to form the interpretation of Wesley as found among the holiness advocates in America. The names of the leading men are Thomas Ralston, Thomas Summers, Randolph Foster, Samuel Wakefield, Miner Raymond, Daniel Whedon, and John Miley. These men, along with other writers such as Daniel Steele and J. A. Wood, helped to formulate a systematic theology for Methodism, and especially of the doctrine of Christian perfection. Many of their writings are considered "classic" by the advocates of Wesleyan perfection in America at the present time.

Mention has already been made of the more recent scholarly works on Wesley's theology. Various writers within the holiness tradition will be referred to from time to time. Special reference will be made to Orton Wiley's *Christian Theology,* the most recent systematic theology in the Wesleyan-Arminian tradition. The reader is referred to the Bibliography for other materials used in this investigation.

CHAPTER II

SIN AND GRACE

Before one can discuss with any degree of understanding Wesley's concept of perfection, he must come to grips with his idea of sin and grace. It is impossible to understand Wesley's concept of sin without relating his definitions to his understanding of grace. Wesley seems to have had two concepts of sin—one concept of sin as it is related to man after the Fall and apart from any grace of God, and the other concept related to man as he is seen with grace operating in his life. This first concept seems to place Wesley at one with Augustine and the reformers, while the second one seems to fix his thought as somewhat Pelagian.

A theologian's doctrine of sin is basic for all and is related to all of the other articles of faith.[1] As already suggested, many of the critics of Wesley's concept of perfection see him defective in the definition of sin. Certainly Wesley's definition of sin was different, as will be seen, from that of the reformers as well as his concept of grace. Whether those definitions are defective or not will depend on one's point of view, but it is important to know what those definitions are. Wesley's doctrine of perfection will stand or fall within the framework of his teachings on sin and grace.

A. TOTAL CORRUPTION OF MAN

Following traditional thought, Wesley believed in an original state of man that was perfect.[2] Adam fell from this high estate and dragged the human race with him. What happened to the "image of God" in man when he fell? Wesley saw this image as containing two elements. He called the one the natural, and the other the moral, image of God. The natural image is man in his spiritual being endued with understanding, freedom of will, immortality, and dominion over all created things. These elements in the natural image are man's equipment as a human being. They are essential to his being a man.[3]

But, for Wesley, primary significance was given to the moral image, which was Adam's moral likeness to God. This likeness to God is righteousness, or holiness, and is a "right temper or disposition of mind, or a complex of all tempers," and is best summed up in the idea of love. What is very important here is that Wesley considered that salvation is the restoration of the moral image of God in man, and in this way he understood the Apostle Paul in Col. 3:8-12 and Eph. 4:22, 24. "These texts, therefore, do manifestly refer to personal, internal holiness; and clearly prove, that this is the chief part of that 'image of God' in which man was originally created."[4]

However, in the Fall man lost his moral likeness to God. "The life of God was extinguished in his soul. The glory departed from him. He lost the whole moral image of God—righteousness and true holiness."[5] But the natural image was marred, not destroyed. Man is still man. It would be impossible for man to continue in existence without the natural image, at least "in part."[6] But as will be seen later, even this would have been lost had God not shown mercy in continuing the race. So in this sense, apart from grace, man's fall was complete and all was lost.[7] In Wesley, then, there is no "relic" of the image of God in man after the Fall, except through God's grace.[8]

What was true of Adam is now true of all his descendants. A certain amount of the natural image is retained, but none of the moral likeness to God. So man by nature is wholly corrupted, according to Wesley. By "nature" he would not mean man as he exists under a gracious dispensation, but as he is from the natural root, or by birth.

> But here is the *shibboleth*: Is man by nature filled with all manner of evil? Is he void of all good? Is he wholly fallen? Is his soul totally corrupted? Or, to come back to the text, is "every imagination of the thoughts of his heart only evil continually?" Allow this, and you are so far a Christian. Deny it, and you are but an Heathen still.[9]

This natural man, the man as he would have been apart from any grace and therefore the only thing about himself for which he could take credit, is under God's displeasure, is destitute of God's favor, and is a child of wrath. He is very evil at heart and polluted; he is spiritually dead and has no power in himself to awaken himself. He is full of defects and is completely captive to Satan.[10]

> And in Adam all died, all humankind, all the children of men who were then in Adam's loins. The natural consequence of this is, that everyone descended from him comes into the world spiritually dead, dead to God, wholly dead in sin; entirely void of the life of God, void of the image of God, of all that righteousness and holiness wherein Adam was created. Instead of this, every man born into the world now bears the image of the devil in pride and self-will; the image of the beast, in sensual appetites and desires.[11]

Wesley could hardly have spoken in darker tones. This picture is one of total corruption, of a disease that infects all men, and this condition he sets over against the redemption to be found in Christ alone. Man is totally helpless in himself to do anything for himself. There is no way that he can initiate one move toward God by himself. Except for grace man would have been left helpless, lost, and forever apart from God.[12]

Such language as this may sound very strange to those who associate Wesleyan teaching with free will and synergism. To many Methodists of a later generation these were strange words and some have felt, and declared, that Wesley changed his views. Wesley's definitions of sin, as we shall see, and of good works did imply that man must and can do something about his salvation. In their attempt to reconcile Wesley's view of man's ability with his view of man's total corruption, some have taught that Wesley changed his views in later life. How could Wesley have believed one was guilty of Adam's sin when there was no personal participation in it? Adam alone is guilty for his sins, and there is no guilt apart from personal responsibility. Even guilt in the sense of liability to punishment was considered inconsistent with the Wesleyan view.[13]

But it has not been proved that Wesley changed his mind.[14] Wesley did believe in some kind of racial sin and guilt. In some sense each member of the race did participate in the first sin. Men "were so constituted sinners by Adam's sinning, as to become liable to the punishment threatened to his transgression."[15] Wesley agreed that even infants are sinners, and that they suffer because they deserve to suffer.

30

God would not be just in permitting them to suffer if they were not guilty in some special sense, nor would Christ be their Redeemer if they were not sinners.[16]

Wesley's reasoning here raises a problem of consistency. If sin is defined as a voluntary transgression of a known law, as seen later in this chapter, how then can one be guilty of Adam's sin? This idea of being guilty for a sinful nature was rejected by later American Methodist theologians such as Whedon, Foster, and Miley.[17] Are these theologians correct in thinking that Wesley ought to have changed his view to be consistent? Are we right in discarding some sense in which individuals do participate in a racial guilt, or might Wesley have held to a concept here that does have a meaning, although not clearly enunciated?

Wesley did not believe that anyone would be punished with eternal death for any sin but his own personal act. In this sense only Adam could have died eternally for his original sin.[18] So it is clear Wesley believed in two kinds of sin, at least, and in two kinds of guilt. One guilt applies to an act performed by a representative in which we participate, and therefore suffer any consequences of that action.[19] This concept of responsibility for the consequences of sin, even those that remain in the sanctified person, is seen in Wesley's attitude toward mistakes and "sins" of infirmity as needing the merit of Christ's death. This idea will be dealt with at length in a later chapter.

It must be held then that for Wesley every man is totally corrupt in his human nature apart from and before any grace is given and that this total corruption leaves a man completely helpless in himself. Wesley believed that this corruption in man was a result of his own sin in a certain sense. More than that, the natural results of that corruption are penal in a certain sense and therefore in need of the atoning merits of Christ. Only against this background of a complete depravity of man can the true picture of Wesley's Christian perfection be understood. Mankind lost everything in Adam; but all, and more, can be restored in Christ.

B. "SOLA GRATIA"

With the corruption of man's nature as complete and total as Wesley viewed it, then any redemption or recovery must come outside man himself. This very reason—that salvation is wholly from God—constrained Wesley to view man as completely helpless. Still, on the other hand, Wesley has been called a synergist and Arminian. If salvation is all of grace, how then can man have anything to do with his salvation? It would seem on the surface that *sola gratia* and unconditional predestination would stand or fall together. God would elect those whom He chooses to save and then change them with His irresistible grace.

But Wesley did not agree with Calvinism on unconditional election. He believed that one's ultimate destiny is determined by his own choice.[20] Furthermore, Wesley's concept of man's part entered into his view of perfection and final justification, both of which he saw as wholly of God's grace. It is important for one who would understand Wesley to grasp his view of grace.

> All the blessings which God hath bestowed upon man, are of his mere grace, bounty, or favour; his free, undeserved favour; favour altogether undeserved; man having no claim to the least of his mercies. It was free grace that "formed man of the dust of the ground . . ." The same free grace continues to us, at this day, life, and breath, and all things. For there is nothing we are, or have, or do, which can deserve the least thing at God's hand. "All our works, thou, O God! hast wrought in us." These, therefore, are so many more instances of free mercy: and, whatever righteousness may be found in man, this is also the gift of God.[21]

Thus grace is back of every good in man. No man can do any good without this grace. It is absolutely necessary before any motion toward life can originate.[22] Yet it is not an irresistible grace, at least in most instances. A person's salvation is not dependent upon the irresistibility of grace. Wesley did see grace at certain occasions working in an irresistible manner for a moment, but it did not continue as such.[23]

What is the nature of this grace? It does act often in a mysterious manner which is only known to God. We cannot always explain why God works when and as He does.[24] This grace of God is not only the favor of God, but is a power, the power of the Holy Spirit working in the life. It may come at times like a torrent, or as a tender leading, but always with the accompanying sense of worthlessness on the part of the believer.[25] "We do speak of this grace, (meaning thereby the power of God which worketh in us both to will and to do of his good pleasure)," that it is perceptible to the heart. One can know, according to Wesley, that this grace is working within oneself,[26] although it also works in an imperceptible manner.[27] This grace is to be used in our living the Christian life.[28]

Wesley saw fallen man as living, not now under a covenant of works, but under a covenant of grace. This does not mean that the law of works is abolished, for we will be judged according to works, but that from the "very hour the original promise was made" the covenant of grace has been operative.[29] Because of this the "grace or love of God, whence cometh our salvation, is FREE IN ALL, and FREE FOR ALL."

> First: It is free IN ALL to whom it is given. It does not depend on any power or merit in man; no, not in any degree, neither in whole, nor in part. . . . It does not depend on his good tempers, or good desires, or good purposes and intentions; for all these flow from the free grace of God. . . . Whatsoever good is in man, or is done by man, God is the author and doer of it. Thus is his grace free in all; that is, no way depending on any power or merit in man, but on God alone, who freely gave his own Son, and "with him freely giveth us all things."[30]

Wesley also believed this grace is free for all. No one is deprived of it. Those who teach the "decree of predestination" are wrong. If they are right, all preaching is vain. Such a doctrine would undermine the preaching of holiness and destroy the comforts of religion. It tends to destroy the zeal for good works and to overthrow the whole revelation of God.[31] Wesley could love the Calvinists, but he did not love their doctrine of predestination.

Grace for Wesley began with prevenient grace. This is a universal or common grace given to all men. It is not the same as Calvin taught, that universal grace was for restraining evil operations and for limiting man's uncontrolled fury.[32] For Wesley this grace had other purposes.

> For allowing that all the souls of men are dead in sin by *nature*, this excuses none, seeing there is no man that is in a state of mere nature; there is no man, unless he has quenched the Spirit, that is wholly void of the grace of God. No man

living is entirely destitute of what is vulgarly called *natural conscience*. But this is not natural: it is more properly termed, *preventing* grace. Every man has a greater or less measure of this, which waiteth not for the call of man. Every one has, sooner or later, good desires; although the generality of men stifle them before they can strike deep root, or produce any considerable fruit. Every one has some measure of that light, some faint glimmering ray, which, sooner or later, more or less, enlightens every man that cometh into the world. And every one, unless he be one of the small number whose conscience is seared with a hot iron, feels more or less uneasy when he acts contrary to the light of his own conscience. So that no man sins because he has not grace, but because he does not use the grace which he hath.[33]

For Wesley, the very existence of the race was dependent upon God's grace. Had the penalty of Adam's sin fallen without mercy, Adam would have died and the race perished with him.[34] Thus one can conclude from Wesley's view that physical life itself, and all blessings resulting from that life, are a direct result of the grace that has been given to mankind. Also any guilt that may be concomitant with the descent of sin from Adam is mitigated through this grace. "By the merits of Christ, all men are cleared from the guilt of Adam's actual sin."[35] No one will ever perish eternally merely for the sin of Adam.[36]

Furthermore, it is clear that this grace is "in" every man, not in the sense of being born in him, but of being "infused." The heathen in some measure are given a knowledge of God and a conscience that bears witness to right or wrong acts. The "very first motion of good is from above, as well as the power that conducts it to the end." It is God who "infuses every good desire" and who accompanies and follows it. All this good work begins with "preventing" grace and includes the "first wish to please God; the first dawn of light concerning his will; and the first slight transient conviction of having sinned against him." All of these imply a beginning of salvation which is a "deliverance from a blind, unfeeling heart." In one sense here is the beginning of holiness even before justification and regeneration.[37]

Such a natural man may be of a compassionate and benevolent spirit, be courteous, gentle, kind, friendly, do good deeds such as feed the hungry, clothe the naked, and even attend church, and yet not be a Christian. He has prevenient grace but is not under saving grace because he has not believed on Christ.[38] Such a man "stifles" God's grace that would lead to repentance while apparently he uses it to make himself a better man in the eyes of men. But unless he acknowledges the source of these good qualities as being of God by his faith in Christ, such works cannot be good.[39]

In every man then there is that which is common to all others. This can be characterized as the "remains of the image of God," an "immaterial principle, a spiritual nature," a "degree of liberty," and "natural conscience." All men have at least "some desire to please God" though they are not real Christians.[40] "There is something in man besides the attributes of his own nature. He is endowed with a spark of divinity. God works in him . . . in the sense of an abiding presence and a continual indwelling."[41] It is a "supernatural gift of God, above all his natural endowments." It is the "true light" that gives light to all men in the world.[42]

So it is not possible for any man, Christian or sinner, correctly to acclaim any good work as his own. If he had been left to himself, he could have done nothing. Therefore all good deeds are of grace, and man's salvation from its earliest beginnings to eternal bliss is all of grace. Any ability a man has to cooperate with God's grace is of grace. Wesley's picture of the natural man is an abstraction.[43] Wesley admitted that "there is no man that is in a state of mere nature."[44]

As a result of Wesley's understanding of grace he was able to adopt a philosophy of salvation that emphasized the part man is to play and yet to maintain the *sola gratia*. By nature all men are totally corrupt and helpless; by grace all men are restored to a salvable condition. Man by nature and man by grace must go hand in hand. This was Wesley's "way of escape from the theological and psychological dilemma which the doctrine of original sin poses for all who adopt it . . . In this world man exists as a natural man plus prevenient grace."[45] Salvation begins with this grace of God given to all, and the graciously enabled man must now work out his own salvation in cooperation with this grace, or be forever lost. For Wesley, then, all the movement toward God before faith is of grace, and all faith and good works are of grace, and all man's efforts towards his own salvation are of grace, and man would have been helplessly lost without that grace. Thus without an unconditional election, Wesley could still claim "all of grace."

C. Atonement in Christ

That the atonement and the grace of God were closely related in Wesley's thought can be seen again and again. Sometimes the atonement was seen as being provided by God's grace, and sometimes the grace was seen as flowing from the atoning Christ. At no place did Wesley give any systematic treatment of the atonement, nor was there any sermon published specifically on the subject, but his ideas on this theme appeared often in his writings. Although there is no reason to believe that he had carefully thought through his doctrine of the atonement,[46] yet his ideas on sin, grace, justification, and sanctification lead one to believe that a Wesleyan conception of the atonement must differ somewhat from the traditional view.

Wesley claimed to be Arminian, and it will be evident that he made his claim good at several points. He was acquainted with the writings of Arminius,[47] and he quotes from Grotius as well. Whether he was acquainted with the governmental theory of the atonement is not known, but John Miley thought that this theory is the only satisfactory explanation of the Wesleyan view.[48] To get a better understanding of Wesley's view on the atonement will assist in understanding his concept of perfection.

Wesley insisted that on several occasions he had maintained these words from the homilies of the church: "These things must necessarily go together in our justification; upon God's part, his great mercy and grace; upon Christ's part, the satisfaction of God's justice; and on our part, faith in the merits of Christ." Then he further added, "Our justification comes freely of the mere mercy of God. For whereas all the world was not able to pay any part towards our ransom, it pleased Him, without any of our deserving, to prepare for us Christ's body and blood, whereby our ransom might be paid, and his justice satisfied."[49]

Here in traditional terms Wesley saw Christ's death as a payment of a debt owed to God and as a satisfaction to God's justice. He considered that the sacrifice of Christ

made as a man was an offering to God in behalf of sinful
men. As Adam was man's representative in sinning, so Christ
represented man in reconciliation.[50] Wesley did use the
concept of Christ's being punished for us, but this expression
was rare.[51] Usually he called Christ's death passive obedience
or the "sufferings of Christ." Christ's death was an objective
satisfaction to God's justice and was the propitiation for man's
sins. But to say that Wesley believed that Christ's death
paid the penalty for man's transgressions because the penalty
had to be paid is saying too much.

Wesley looked upon the atonement both as objective—
something finished, and subjective—something unfinished.
The finished work of Christ was a satisfaction to justice
but only in the provisory sense. It was now possible for all
men to be saved.[52] Had Wesley believed that Christ actually
bore the penalty for man in reality, then he would have
been forced logically to hold that all men would be saved,
or else that Christ died only for an elect—neither of which
he believed. For the penalty could not be paid twice—
by Christ, and the unbeliever.[53] For Wesley it was necessary
to believe that Christ's death was a satisfaction to God in
such a way that forgiveness could justly be granted on faith
and the penalty be remitted. "So that for the sake of his
well-beloved Son, of what he hath done and suffered for
us, God now vouchsafes, on one only condition, (which
himself also enables us to perform) both to remit the punishment due to our sin, to re-instate us in his favour, and
to restore our dead souls to spiritual life."[54] If the penalty
had been paid on the Cross, how could it now by faith
be remitted?

Wesley insisted on a universal atonement. Christ died for
all men. "He obtained for all a possibility of salvation."
There is no sense in which Christ's death was different for
the believer who will be saved and for the unbeliever who
will be lost.[55] It is at this point that Wesley differed widely
from the Reformed position.[56] For him there is no limited
atonement. What did Christ accomplish then on the Cross?
He satisfied God's justice in such a way that the offer of
forgiveness can be made to all. Grace is actually extended
to all men so that whatever was lost in Adam is regained
in Christ. No one can be sent to hell for Adam's sin. A
sense of life is given to all men.[57] Miley sums up the un-

conditional benefits of the atonement in Wesley's thought as "The Present Life," "Gracious Help for All," "Capacity for Probation," and "Infant Salvation." These come to all men whether ultimately saved or not. The infant salvation would occur only in case of death in infancy.[58]

Another element in the atonement was seen by Wesley in a different manner from the Calvinists. He defined "imputed" righteousness only in the sense that for Christ's sake the believer is forgiven. In Wesley there was no sense in which Christ's righteousness is accounted as ours. He did not separate the active and passive obedience of Christ, but Christ was obedient unto death, which fact is the foundation of our forgiveness. Christ was perfectly obedient to the law, but this obedience was preparatory to the obedience unto death. This righteousness of Christ is "imputed" when one believes. Thus faith and Christ's righteousness are inseparable. "He believes in the righteousness of Christ." The righteousness of Christ is the object of faith but does not become the righteousness of the believer. It is his faith that is counted for righteousness. But this "faith is imputed for righteousness" because it is placed in Christ's righteousness, and one is forgiven for the sake of what Christ has done.[59]

Wesley wanted to guard against any idea that Christ kept the law for us in any sense that would excuse the believer from obedience. He thereby rejected the "active righteousness," in the sense used by Calvinists, that Christ fulfilled the demands of the law for us.[60] He said if Christ's obedience is ours, then we perfectly obey Him. In that case we have no need of pardon any more than Christ did.[61] It would be just as true to say that if Christ paid our penalty there could be no forgiveness, for forgiveness implies the remitting of the penalty. Wesley in fact had to reject both any punishment in Christ's sufferings, except as they are consequences of sin, and any obedience on Christ's part that could be counted the believer's obedience. Wesley was concerned that all still be held responsible for obedience to the law of God.

For Wesley the atonement was not only a foundation for forgiveness, but it was also the basis for holiness. Pardon is the first "end" of Christ's death, but "to extinguish our own hell within us" is the second "end."[62] It is through Christ's "merits alone that all believers are saved: that is, justified—saved from guilt,—sanctified—saved from the nature of sin; and glorified—taken into heaven."[63]

> Shall he be the fountain of an imputed righteousness, and procure the tenderest favour to all his followers? This is also not enough. Though a man should be allowed to be righteous, and be exempt from all punishment, yet if he is as really enslaved to the corruptions of nature, as endued with these privileges of redemption, he can hardly make himself easy; and whatever favour he can receive from God, here or hereafter, without a communication of himself, it is neither the cure of a spirit fallen, nor the happiness of one reconciled. Must not then our Redeemer be . . . one that "baptizeth with the Holy Ghost," the Fountain and Restorer of that to mankind, whereby they are restored to their first estate, and the enjoyment of God?[64]

Here Wesley placed the renewal of man, or sanctification, squarely in the redemptive act of Christ by which provision is made for both reconciliation and sanctification. Through the "obedience and death of Christ" all believers are "reconciled to God" and "made partakers of the divine nature."[65] These blessings of the atonement are provided objectively in Christ's death and come when the conditions are met. This idea of victory and deliverance for the believer is carried out in "Christ's royal office" as King.[66] But they are carried out only for those who believe and obey.[67] But how can man meet such conditions for his salvation? It is important to observe how Wesley answered this question.

D. GRACIOUS ABILITY

We have seen thus far the complete inability of natural man, according to Wesley, to do anything about his own salvation. He can make no motion toward God until God first moves him. But God does move him, and that means all men, toward himself. Unconditionally from God through Christ by the Holy Spirit prevenient grace is given to all men. Christ died for all, so it is possible that all could be saved. Why are they not? Wesley was presented with a dilemma—man is not able to save himself, yet man determines whether he is saved or lost. In interpreting Wesley it is easy for some to decide that Wesley is on the Reformed side—man can do nothing. Others tend to the opposite extreme by saying that Wesley taught natural free will and so was Pelagian.

Cell, in his reaction to the claim that the Wesleyan revival resulted from the "libertarian theology" of Wesley, placed Wesley squarely upon the Luther-Calvin concept of salvation. In the doctrine of grace "he was not a whit behind the early Reformers, nor has he deviated a hair's breadth from the early Reformation doctrine of salvation."[68] Wesley did not deviate "from the conviction of both Luther and Calvin in his doctrine that man's power to co-operate with the divine will is itself moment by moment the pure gift of God." Cell declares that Wesley "stoutly maintained first, last and always with the early Reformers that God is the sole agent in our experience of redemption."[69] He was conscious of being "more strictly *monergistic* in his pure *ethic of grace* than some of the later Calvinists."[70] Wesley did, according to Cell, make faith a condition of salvation, but so did the reformers. Rather than Wesley's reaction being against Calvinism, it was against the "humanist libertarian theology" then in England.[71] In the Wesleyan Reformation the doctrine of saving faith was a "complete renewal of the Luther-Calvin thesis that in the thought of salvation God is everything, man is nothing."[72]

Chiles in an article in *Religion in Life,* 1958, gives the same emphasis as Cell. "Wesley's doctrine of grace is substantially that of Paul, Augustine, and the Reformers." "The transition from free grace to free will is one of the fundamental changes in American Methodism since the time of John Wesley."[73] He thinks this transition occurred largely in the nineteenth century under Whedon and Miley. The active free choice of man was made a philosophical doctrine for moral responsibility. By the time of Albert Knudson free will was made a part of man's nature. Chiles holds that in Wesley man is not able to will for God at all, even with prevenient grace, but can only "still" his own sinful efforts. "Man is only free to submit to the further grace of God by the inactivation of the will through despair." Everything else in salvation is dependent on God's action. Man has no freedom to do good. This position is a long way from Knudson's.[74]

Leland Scott in a recent thesis arrives at about the same conclusion. He says that Nathan Bangs was the first one to use the words "gracious ability." It was in the conflict with Calvinism in nineteenth-century America that this change toward free agency was made.[75] Whedon was the ablest writer who dealt with this problem, and in him the "free will" position was established and became representative of the trend in Methodism.[76] It is significant that Whedon varied from Wesley's view on perfection.[77]

On the other hand it is possible to interpret Wesley almost in Pelagian terms. Some can see little difference between a natural ability and a doctrine of prevenient grace. Calvinists have always found this idea in Wesley hard to grasp.[78] Natural man for most people today is as man is now observed, and this would be Wesley's nature plus grace. Wesley never called a present ability in man to choose the right as "natural ability," while many modern writers do.[79] So it is easy for Wesley's insistence on the free grace of God to be obscured.[80]

However this may be, there is no excuse for making Wesley out to be a Pelagian. As already noted, this is what Warfield did.[81] Niebuhr understands Wesley to have a Pelagian doctrine of sin.[82] Even Turner, who belongs in the Wesleyan rather than the Calvinist tradition, lists Wesley's position as being "semi-Pelagian," and states that he "was Pelagian in insisting on human freedom and the volitional nature of sin."[83] If these judgments were true, one could look in vain for Wesley's agreement with the reformers!

The fact is, neither extreme is true. Wesley was not completely with the reformers on either grace or salvation, nor was he with the Pelagians on free will. Pope called his Arminianism the "purest and best form." Though sometimes it is called "semi-Pelagian," it should not be. Since Wesley believed that all "cooperation with grace is of grace," he was safe from any form of Pelagianism.[84] Spalding writes that "the Pelagians believed all men to be created by God in the same condition as Adam before the fall. There is no essential difference between Adam and all other men."[85] The Pelagian theory is not a "doctrine of original sin, but a denial of it in every form."[86] It is very evident that Wesley's thought cannot be placed into this category.

Is it possible that "free grace" and "freedom of choice" cannot be harmonized? Is it necessary to go either to the Reformed extreme or to the Pelagian extreme? Is there a middle ground on which to stand? Can a synthesis of the two ideas be made? One realizes there is a real problem here, and what Wesley said should be helpful. And it is important to know what he said in order to understand his emphasis on sanctification.

One can find plenty of proof for Wesley's belief in the total corruption and inability of man because of the Fall, as has already been shown. Wesley believed that Adam before the Fall had freedom of will to choose either evil or good. But "since the fall, no child of man has a natural power to choose anything that is truly good."[87] Speaking of the man who tries to break loose from sin, Wesley wrote:

> But though he strive with all his might, he cannot conquer: sin is mightier than he. He would fain escape; but he is so fast in prison, that he cannot get forth. He resolves against sin, but yet sins on: he sees the snare and abhors, and runs into it. So much does his boasted reason avail,—only to enhance his guilt, and increase his misery! Such is the freedom of his will; free only to evil; free to "drink in iniquity like water;" to wander farther and farther from the living God, and do more "despite to the Spirit of grace!"[88]

Certainly man cannot bring himself back to God. He is helpless in the clutches of sin. The first move must be God's. This has been shown in the discussion of prevenient grace. Man is totally dependent upon God's grace.

Especially interesting is the fact that something occurs when grace comes. "Every man has a measure of free will restored to him by grace."[89] With this free will is a "power" to work together with God. God is not the "whole worker of our salvation, as to exclude man's working at all." After God starts to work, then we have power to work.[90] This is a restored liberty, the power of choosing between good and evil.[91] For this power one is dependent on grace, but he has the power nevertheless.

Wesley meant by liberty "an active, self-determining power, which does not choose things because they are pleasing, but is pleased with them because it chooses them." God has this power, and man partakes of this principle.[92] This liberty is a property of the soul and is a power of self-determination. Wesley called it a "liberty of contrariety," which is a power to act one way or the contrary.

> And although I have not an absolute power over my own mind, because of the corruption of my own nature; yet, through the grace of God assisting me, I have a power to choose

and do good, as well as evil, I am free to choose whom I will serve; and if I choose the better part, to continue therein even unto death.[93]

This salvation in Christ is offered to all, and actually saves "all that consent thereto," and forces none since that would destroy their nature.[94]

God's grace to man is to be used;[95] this fact indicates a definite part for man. Since a man can "resist" this offered grace, it is evident that predestination is conditional.[96] Man could not be a proper object of God's justice if he were incapable of choosing good or evil.[97] It is the presence of grace that makes a man guilty in his wrongdoing, for "no man sins because he has not grace, but because he does not use the grace that he hath."[98] So it must follow that, when the grace is used, man need not sin. This fact was basic with Wesley. Yet it is all of grace.

With this grace given to him man can cooperate with God. Wesley sets the truth, "Without me ye can do nothing," alongside the word, "I can do all things through Christ which strengtheneth me." Then he proclaims, "Here the charm is dissolved! The light breaks in, and the shadows flee away." God has joined these two together; let no man put them asunder.[99] Wesley described man's reaction to this power in him as follows:

Hence we may . . . infer the absolute necessity of this re-action of the soul, (whatsoever it be called,) in order to the continuance of the divine life therein. For it plainly appears, God does not continue to act upon the soul, unless the soul re-acts upon God. He prevents us indeed with the blessings of his goodness. He first loves us, and manifests himself unto us. While we are yet afar off, he calls us to himself, and shines upon our hearts. But if we do not then love him who first loved us; if we will not hearken to his voice; if we turn our eye away from him, and will not attend unto the light which he pours in upon us; his Spirit will not always strive: he will gradually withdraw, and leave us to the darkness of our own hearts. He will not continue to breathe into our soul, unless our soul breathes toward him again; unless our love, and prayer, and thanksgiving return to him, a sacrifice wherewith he is well pleased.[100]

Can one still claim Wesley is one with reformers on grace? Here is what Luther said in talking about the bondage of the will. The will is in bondage to either the Spirit or sin.

When in bondage to sin it always craves the wrong, and when in bondage to the Spirit it always craves the good. Nor can the will desire otherwise when held in bondage. Yet he calls this a "willingly" kind of desire and it is not compulsion.

> Thus the human will is, as it were, a beast between the two. If God sit thereon, it wills and goes where God will . . . If Satan sit thereon, it wills and goes as Satan will. Nor is it in the power of our will to choose, to which rider it will run, nor which it will seek; but the riders themselves contend, which shall have and hold it.[101]

This same idea was quoted by Calvin in his *Institutes* as first given by Augustine.[102] He agreed with Luther that man has no choice as to whom he serves.

> It is the election of God, which makes this difference between men. We are not afraid to allow, what Paul very strenuously asserts, that all, without exception, are depraved and addicted to wickedness; but with him we add, that the mercy of God does not permit all to remain in depravity. Therefore, since we all naturally labour under the same disease, they alone recover to whom the Lord has been pleased to apply his healing hand. The rest, whom he passes by in righteous judgment, putrefy in their corruption till they are entirely consumed. . . .[103]

It will have to be said out of all fairness to both Wesley and the early reformers that they did not agree on free grace or free will, and although the difference can be held to a minimum, nevertheless in the operation of grace Calvin and Wesley were far apart.[104] Since man has the ability to stifle the grace of God and to kill it in himself, as Wesley taught, we do have the right to ascribe to him the positive role of cooperator with God. When man can be made the deciding factor in his own salvation, it is no longer passivity but activity.[105] This concept lays stress on man's personal responsibility and makes man himself responsible for his own damnation. This conditional view of election does easily lead to synergistic tendencies.[106]

How active is this "gracious ability" in man? Or is it only "inactivation of the will through despair"? Here are some phrases Wesley used in his sermons: "desire and seek" nothing but God, "ask," "seek," "knock," "press on," "take no denial," and "believe in Christ."[107] He wrote, "Stir up the spark of grace which is now in you, and he will give you more grace." "God works; therefore you *can* work: . . . God works, therefore you must work." God "will not save us, unless we 'save ourselves' . . . 'fight the good fight of faith' . . . 'agonize to enter in' . . . 'deny ourselves' . . . and labour by every possible means to 'make our own calling and election sure.' "[108]

Emil Brunner, from the neo-Reformed tradition, would see man's moral effort as his worst enemy, and, since it is the effort of man, it is selfish. It can lead only to a "terrifying adverse balance or 'debt' which cannot be paid." Man's worst state is that in which he has complete confidence in himself.[109] But Wesley did not see this effort as put forth by man himself since all the good works of man are of grace. It is right at this point that Wesley's concept of grace must be seen. This effort, this gracious ability, is of grace and is not from natural man. It is God working in man as he yields to God's grace. This activity is wholly dependent upon God's continuing activity in the soul. However, man must acknowledge the works as of God, and he must not have any confidence in the flesh.

Is this then synergism or monergism? Possibly the best answer is that it is both. Initially it is monergism—God works—and then it is a synergism born of the monergism—man is enabled to work. John Miley may have been true to Wesley when he wrote:

> This primary choice of the good is not the realization of a new spiritual life in regeneration, but is only, and can only be, the election of its attainment. The choice of such an end and its attainment are clearly separable facts. A new spiritual life in regeneration, if chosen as an end, still has its own mode of effectuation, and in itself must be entirely from the divine Spirit. The sphere of *synergism* lies back of this, where, through the help of grace and a proper use of the powers of our spiritual agency, we may choose the good; while that of the divine *monergism* is specially in the work of moral regeneration. Here the doctrine of the most rigid monergist is the reality of truth; while synergism within its own sphere is equally a truth.[110]

A final question to be asked is whether Wesley's synergism came only from Arminius and the Anglicans, or could it also stem from the reformers? There is at least a possibility here. Clyde Manschreck holds that Melanchthon could not find determinism in the Bible. He believed in some sense that man is an active concurrent in his conversion. "The Gospel," wrote Melanchthon in the *Loci*, "is the power of God to salvation to one not opposing, but consenting and believing." Manschreck believes that Luther never charged Melanchthon with departing from his own true teaching, and that Luther let his own early view as expressed to Erasmus drop into the background. Melanchthon "consciously steered a course between Pelagius and Augustine because he did not think either had remained true to Scripture or to experience." He was "misunderstood and caricatured," but "his doctrine was evangelical and Biblical, and was eventually to emerge in the evangelical churches, even in Wesleyanism!"[111]

So, for Wesley, even though man is totally corrupt and unable in himself to make one move toward God and salvation, he is enabled by grace to have a part in his own salvation. God does the redeeming and changing, but the changing man can act—yes, *must* act—in order for God's redeeming act to be accomplished within him. This concept of "gracious ability" did influence the definitions of sin and faith and good works.

E. Voluntary Sins

A constant and clear teaching of Wesley and Wesleyans has been that the believer does not commit sin. This declaration appears very shocking to any who have been taught that sinning is a daily necessity, while to the Wesleyan the assertion that the believer continues to sin is equally shocking. Very likely the real difference is found in the definition of sin.

If the reformers made any distinction between sin as an act and sin as a state, that distinction did not carry the same importance as it did for Wesley. A brief survey of much writing on the doctrine of sin soon reveals this fact. When Luther wrote that the righteous "are sinners, inasmuch as they do not fulfill the law, and still have sinful lusts," he does not distinguish between the believers' "sinning" now, and what it was before justification. He spoke of them as beginning to be healed but does not suggest an area, in relation to sins, in which they are fully healed.[112] The

Christian "is always in sin and always in justification. He is always a sinner, but also repentant and so always righteous."[113] Luther defined a Christian, not as one who has no sin, but as one "to whom God imputeth not his sin."[114] Since the word "impute" means to "reckon" or "account," Luther was saying that God does not reckon one as a sinner, or as having sin, when in reality he is still a sinner and has sin. Wesley's answer to this would have been that God never reckons a person to be what He does not really make him.[115] God reckons the believer no longer a sinner because he is no longer a sinner. This teaching of Wesley will be more fully discussed later.

Calvin did not distinguish between sin that is necessary and voluntary, for necessary sin is justly accounted as guilt as much as voluntary sin. Before God there is no difference.[116] So it is with contemporary Reformed theologians. Emil Brunner follows the same concept when he writes, "The believer is always the unbeliever, the sinner. *Simul justus, simul peccator.*" He does not make any difference in the sins of the sinner before and after he believes. The sinning is of the same nautre.[117] Since Reinhold Niebuhr considers sin to be "inevitable" in human existence, his concept cannot be squared with Wesley's. Wesley considered sins over which a man has no power "improperly so-called." But Wesley saw a further fact about sin over which one may exercise control by grace, and for which he is personally responsible.

Benjamin Warfield called this concept of the sinner-Christian the "gospel of the miserable sinner."

> Though blessed with every spiritual blessing in the heavenlies in Christ, we are still in ourselves just "miserable sinners": "miserable sinners" still, deserving in ourselves nothing but everlasting wrath. That is the attitude which the Reformers took, and that is the attitude which the Protestant world has learned from the Reformers to take toward the relation of believers to Christ.[118]

This in the believer is a "continued sinfulness in fact and in act." Wesley could have agreed that in the believer continues a condition of sinfulness, as we shall see, but to say a believer is sinful in act would be unscriptural for Wesley.

Is there in Reformed theology any sense at all in which a person ceases to sin when he believes? Karl Barth is very clear on this point when he writes:

> Exactly as I am in my present situation, in my present circumstances, on the road along which I have come and on which I have still to travel, I am regarded and acknowledged by God, yes, infinitely far from Him as I am. Not as a second God but as a man who has sinned, is sinning, and will sin, and who can recognize himself as nothing else than lost. . . .[119]

It seems safe to conclude that, from a Reformed point of view, all acts of a sinner are sin because they proceed from the evil heart, and since the believer still is sinful in nature all his acts are tainted with sin, so therefore he sins. There does not appear to be any sense in which it can be said that one ceases to sin when he believes.[120] The nearest to such a distinction is found in Charles Hay, who claimed that Luther made such a distinction. One kind he called "sins of ignorance," which come suddenly and do not obliterate faith. The other kind is knowingly and voluntarily, with an evil purpose, doing wrong against God, such as adultery. In this second case the Holy Spirit departs from the believer, and one so acting is under God's wrath.[121] This would seem to indicate that Luther had in mind a distinction similar to Wesley's, but his mind was not clear on it.

There are those who have concluded, because Wesley talked about voluntary sins as being the only "properly-called" sins, that he had no doctrine of man's sinfulness. The untruthfulness of this conclusion is already evident in this paper. Lindstrom can see the inherent sinfulness of man's nature as being the most prominent part of Wesley's concept of sin.[122] Wesley did not minimize the awfulness of man's sinful nature to make room for willful sin. Man by nature he claimed is all "earthly, sensual, devilish." He "cannot of himself think one good thought; who is indeed all sin, a mere lump of ungodliness, and who commits sin in every breath he draws; whose actual transgressions . . . are more in number than the hairs of his head."[123] A careful reading of Wesley's sermon on the "Spirit of Bondage and Adoption" shows clearly how sin binds man who "willingly sins" while in this state.[124] He likened the lives of sinful men as branches growing from an evil root and as fruit from the evil branch. What else can be expected from such a source?[125]

It is not necessary to tarry on this point longer. Wesley did teach there was an evil nature in man and that this evil made man blind and deaf to spiritual things. He also taught, as we shall see, that this evil nature still remained in the believer and resulted in "sins of the heart." If this were all that the reformers meant by the believer's being a "miserable sinner," then Wesley was in agreement. But he would have taught that they seemed to mean more because they were not clear as to what happened to sin and sinning at justification. The "sin in believers" is not the same as the sins of the unbeliever. The "sins" of the unbeliever cease.

One way to get at this problem is to revert again to Wesley's concept of guilt. It will be recalled that Wesley held that the guilt of Adam's sin was personal to Adam, while his descendants were guilty in the sense of liability to punishment.[126] And yet these children of Adam suffered because they deserved to suffer. Also Christ's death freed all men from the guilt of Adam's sin. Yet Wesley did not hold that anyone is freed from the guilt of his own sin until he believes. Apparently Wesley conceived of two kinds of guilt—one that is personal to a free agent, and one that is representative, or racial. Wesley did not give this kind of guilt a sharp definition in such terms as "racial" or "corporate," but he did have a kind of guilt different from the personal guilt. His use of the term guilt in this second sense, as inherited from Adam, is very different, however, from the Calvinistic use. It cannot result in eternal death until a free agent accepts and makes it his own.[127] When he does this, the guilt is then personal.

Not only is this second kind of guilt—that which attaches to the inherited nature—seen when Wesley discussed guilt in children and the guilt removed by prevenient grace, but also it is seen when he discussed repentance in believers. "A conviction of their *guiltiness* is another branch of that repentance which belongs to the children of God. But this is cautiously to be understood, and in a peculiar sense." They can have no condemnation for it, but they, because of their sinfulness, cannot "bear the *strict justice* of God." They would be condemned for this "sin in believers," and they are still *"worthy of death,"* but the blood of Christ atones for them.[128] So Wesley did assert the existence of a guilt, a peculiar kind, that does cling to the believers because of remaining sin, but it does not condemn. In speaking of mistakes, even those that spring from perfect love, Wesley said that they cannot "bear the rigour of God's justice" but need "the atoning blood."[129] This same "peculiar" guilt clings even to the sanctified in their "sins" of ignorance.

But for Wesley men will be punished ultimately only for their own personal sins. In speaking of the punishments in this world and the next, he wrote, "That all men are liable to these for Adam's sin alone, I do not assert; but they are so, for their own outward and inward sins, which, through their own fault, spring from the infection of their nature."[130] Note here that men can be punished only for those sins that spring from an infected nature "through their own fault." Here is guilt, or condemnation, that comes from personal agency. These sins are open rebellion.

> The wilful sinner is not ignorant or surprised, but knowingly fights against God's express commandment, and the lively, full, and present conviction of his mind and conscience; so that this is the very standard of iniquity.[131]

It is this "wilful sinner" that is pardoned—this sinner who has yielded to his sin. The guilt that clings to this sinner is the guilt of his own acts, his own rebellion, his own wrong choices. The pardon is "remission of the sins that are past." It is not pardon for a condition or state that is inherited, but for iniquities that have been committed. "It is only sinners that have any occasion for pardon"; it is the "sinner that is forgiven." God saves from the guilt of sin those who are lost.[132] When asked if this definition of sin—"a voluntary transgression of a known law"—were a proper one, Wesley replied, "I think it is of all such sin as is imputed to our condemnation. And it is a definition which has passed uncensored in the church for at least fifteen hundred years."[133] It is then this willful sin that is pardoned because it alone can bring condemnation from God.

This willful, personal sin is the sin that "through almighty grace we may avoid."[134] "By the grace of God we may cast away all transgressions: Therefore, if we do not, they are chargeable to ourselves." Man is inclined to evil by Adam's sin, but by "grace we may conquer this inclination; or we may choose to follow it, and so commit actual sin."[135] Man, then, reaches an age of accountability for his sins, and failure to use God's grace subjects him to condemnation. Man is responsible. He is not as the beasts, who cannot help themselves, but he chooses and has a will. There can be no vice but "where such a being knows, loves, and chooses that is evil."[136] All this means, according to Wesley, that the sin in an infant, or in a believer, is not that which makes one a sinner in the true sense of the word. It is his own personal turning to and choosing the sin as his own. A man does not sin because he has no grace, but because he does not use the grace that he has.[137] Genuine sinning is man's refusal of offered grace and willful continuance in inherited inclinations. It is this only that can bring condemnation, and it is this kind of sinning that is not in the believer.

Possibly it can be made clear now what Wesley meant when he said that the believer does not sin. He did not mean that the believer was free from a sinful nature, nor that he did not commit "sins" of ignorance. He simply meant that sin did not reign in the believer, and that one knowingly and willingly depends on grace and refuses the evil thing. There is no free acquiescence to the inner nature. The believer does not yield to the evil inclinations.

Wesley described how a believer can slip back into willful, condemning sin. "Whosoever is born of God doth not commit sin" (I John 3:9).

> So long as he thus believeth in God through Christ, and loves him, and is pouring out his heart before him, he cannot voluntarily transgress any command of God, either by speaking or acting what he knows God hath forbidden: So long that seed which remaineth in him, that loving, praying, thankful faith, compels him to refrain from whatsoever he knows to be an abomination in the sight of God.[138]

How then does a believer progress from grace to sin? Here are the steps:

> (1.) The divine seed of loving, conquering faith, remains in him that is born of God. "He keepeth himself," by the grace of God, and "cannot commit sin." (2.) A temptation arises;

51

whether from the world, the flesh, or the devil, it matters not. (3.) The Spirit of God gives him warning that sin is near, and bids him more abundantly watch unto prayer. (4.) He gives way, in some degree, to the temptation, which now begins to grow pleasing to him. (5.) The Holy Spirit is grieved; his faith is weakened; and his love of God grows cold. (6.) The Spirit reproves him more sharply, and saith, "This is the way, walk thou in it." (7.) He turns away from the painful voice of God, and listens to the pleasing voice of the tempter. (8.) Evil desire begins and spreads in his soul, till faith and love vanish away: he is then capable of committing outward sin, the power of the Lord being departed from him.[139]

For one who accepts the teaching of the possibility of losing faith after having believed, there is probably no better account as to how it happens than this one from Wesley. It is very clear that Wesley recognized the difficulty of the problem. He did not maintain that it is easy to know when sin has been committed. He saw a degree of yielding to inner sin while one is yet a believer. But the commission of a full-grown, willful sin cannot occur until faith and love have fled. This helps one to see that what Wesley called willful transgression can never be committed where there is saving faith. It is a religious rather than speculative concept and fits the Pauline and Johannine instructions that Christians do not sin. Wesley wanted to chisel this definition to a sharp point and concluded that the believer does not willingly sin, as does the unbeliever.

Wesley did not think through all the implications of his concept of voluntary sin. He realized that the line between the sin of an unbeliever and the partial yielding to sin by the believer is not a perfectly clear one. In his sermon on the "Spirit of Bondage and Adoption," he said that the unawakened child of the devil "sins willingly," the awakened one "sins unwillingly," and the child of God "sinneth not." These three are classed as the natural man, the man under law, and the one under grace. The man under law, as shown in Romans seven, fights against sin, but the sin conquers. This man sins unwillingly.[140] But Wesley had hope for him. He is not yet a believer but soon will be. Is his sin one of condemnation? Wesley was hesitant to say and later in life thought the legal state could be one with the faith of a servant, if not of a son.[141] So there seems to be a place between the sinning unbeliever and the unsinning

52

believer where "servants" may be committing sin unwillingly. But for Wesley this is not the experience of the believer who has victory over sin, for he does not sin in this sense at all.

Flew criticizes Wesley in his definition of voluntary sin on the basis that "our worst sins are often those of which we are unconscious."[142] Wesley might have agreed with Flew here if the discussion were entirely on the qualities of various inward sins, such as pride, selfishness, etc. But Wesley could not call these sins "worst" in the sense of guilt, provided a person is a believer, or is fighting against all sin. The only sin that can bring eternal death is a personal sin which involves rejection of grace. It is the willful sin that entails personal guilt and this alone can make one liable to eternal death. Surely this would be the "worst" sin for the individual.

Flew thinks that this "narrower sense" in the meaning of sin is not even desirable. But Wesley could never free himself from the fact that man is responsible before God. Wesley recognized there was unconscious sinning in the unbeliever as well as in the believer.[143] However, man's unconscious sinning as a result of his fallen nature could not by itself condemn a man before God. Only when light comes revealing sin is man awakened, and the rejection of that light seals man's destiny.[144] This specialized concept of sin did not mean for Wesley that the blind sinner who "sins willingly" and "walks in utter darkness" is justified before God even though he is yet unawakened.[145] Nor did Wesley justify the praying Pharisee who thought he was free from sin and trusted in his own righteousness.[146] What Wesley did insist on was that no one would be lost eternally except for sins he could avoid by grace. And this kind of sin no believer commits while he has faith.

These "unconscious" sins and sins of ignorance will be discussed more fully in Chapter VI. It is important here to see that Wesley did define voluntary sins as the most proper use of the word. He would not go along .with Tennant, who made this sense the only meaning of "sin," but he did feel it had significance, especially for the believer.[147] How can the sins of the unbeliever who rebels against God and trusts in himself be of the same kind as the

sins of the believer who loves and trusts his Christ? It is
at this point Wesley saw a real and definite change from
sinner to believer, and in this sense the believer does not
sin. This definition needs more clarity and should not be
ignored or set aside. The unbeliever does sin in some willful
way that should be absent from the Christian. But the
believer does have sin, as will now be seen.

F. Sin in Believers

Sufficient has already been said in this paper to show
that Wesley taught both the total corruption of man's nature
and the prevenient grace, which begins a partial cure. In
the next chapter it will be shown what actually occurs when
a person is justified and regenerated. In this section the
nature of the sin that remains in the justified will be discussed. It is vital to make clear what Wesley taught on this
topic because it is this kind of sin that he claimed is cleansed
in the experience of entire sanctification. Already it is
clear that this sin in believers is not willful sinning, which
is found only in the unbeliever or in the one who has lost
faith.

For some reason Sangster thinks that Wesley never attempted a definition of "sinfulness," but only of "a sin"
which was a voluntary transgression.[148] But later on he
says that Wesley thought of sin as a thing, like a cancer
or a rotten tooth, to be removed.[149] But Wesley did define
sinfulness. A short review of his sermon "Sin in Believers"
ought to dispel any doubt about this. Here he clearly asserted the sinful condition in man. But even sinfulness is
not a "thing" or "substance," for if it were it would be
material or soul substance, neither of which Wesley believed.
He defined this inward sin as follows:

> By sin, I here understand inward sin; any sinful temper,
> passion, or affection; such as pride, self will, love of the world,
> in any kind or degree; such as lust, anger, peevishness; any
> disposition contrary to the mind which was in Christ.

This condition is called the "flesh, evil nature," which
opposes the Spirit and is a "principle." So there are two
principles in the believer—the flesh and Spirit.[150]

When Wesley wrote "Sin in Believers," he was having

difficulty with the Moravians. They taught that one was justified and entirely sanctified all at once and that no sin remained in the believer. Wesley felt certain that he was in agreement with the general Church teaching on this subject. No one, except Zinzendorf, taught a complete sanctification at justification. All others held to a continuance of sin in believers.[151]

Wesley did call these remains of sin in the believer by the name of sin. To say Wesley held to but one definition of sin is misleading. He distinguished among the guilt, the power, and the being of sin. When one truly believes the guilt is gone, the power of sin is broken, but the *"being"* of sin remains. This "flesh has no dominion over us," but it still exists.[152]

Foster called it "a root on which sin has a tendency to grow," It is a condition that must be remedied.

> This depraved nature, we allow, is sinful in these two senses: first, that it tends to sin from the beginning—tends to courses of action which in a responsible being would be sins; second, when tolerated, accepted, and followed by a responsible being, it is sin or he becomes a sinner on account of it.[153]

Miley took a similar position in saying this condition may be called sin, but it has no demerit.[154]

Concerning Romans seven, Wesley could not believe that here is a picture of the believer who is born again.[155] The man depicted here according to Wesley is under the law, awakened to his sinful condition, but not yet come to justifying faith. This position is opposite to that of the reformers, who held that Romans 7 pictures the believers.[156] One's exegesis of this passage will depend on his theological bias, but Wesley's view shows where he differed from the reformers. One can say that the evil nature of man, for both the reformers and Wesley, is the corrupted nature inherited from Adam. But for Wesley this nature is not sin in the proper sense, while for the reformers it is still sin in the proper sense. A comparison of the Council of Trent and the Augsburg and Westminster Confessions helps locate Wesley:

> The council of Trent declared: (Tr. by Sugden) "There remains in the baptized concupiscence or the fuel (of sin). This concupiscene, which sometimes the Apostle calls sin, the Holy

Synod declares that the Catholic Church has never understood to be called sin because it is truly and properly sin in the regenerate, but because it arises from sin and inclines to sin."

The Westminster Confession (IV, 5), on the contrary, asserts: "This corruption of nature during this life doth remain in those that are regenerated; and although it be through Christ pardoned and mortified, yet both itself, and all the motions thereof, are truly and properly sin!" The Augsburg Confession says of the corruption of human nature: "Nor is it by any means abolished or done away by baptism, since sin always issues forth from this woeful source, as water from a fountain."[157]

From these it will appear that Wesley stood somewhere between. With the Council of Trent he held that this evil in believers is not properly sin, while with the Westminster divines he held that it is a corruption of nature.

Does this mean that Wesley saw a greater victory in regeneration than did the reformers? Very likely he did at the point of the breaking of the power of this corruption. Of the Reformation, Wesley wrote:

> And what is the condition of the Reformed Churches? It is certain that they were reformed in their opinions, as well as their modes of worship. But is not this all? Were either their tempers or lives reformed? Not at all. Indeed many of the Reformers themselves complained, that "the Reformation was not carried far enough." But what did they mean? . . . You ought vehemently to have insisted on an entire change of men's *tempers* and *lives;* on their showing they have the "mind that was in Christ," by "walking as he also walked."[158]

Wesley may have been partly mistaken on this charge, but many will agree with him that the reformers neglected the "Be ye holy."[159] Wesley feared that the gospel would be shorn of its strength if Romans 7 pictured the normal believer's life. He believed that this sin, or evil nature, remains in the believer but it does not reign.

Berkouwer quotes Barth as saying, "The subject Sinner is not annulled by the predicate Righteousness"; and Luther as having declared, "Flesh and spirit, sinner and righteous man, dead and freed from death, guilty and not guilty," and further, "and both to the hilt and both at the same time."[160] It is evident from these and other statements that Wesley's concept of the sin in the believer was different from that of both the reformers and contemporary theologians of the Reformed tradition. Wesley did not and could not believe that this root of sin in the believer was producing fruit. Its activity had ceased; it was in bonds; it no longer reigned.

What was the nature of this sin in the believer? "The flesh lusteth against the Spirit, and the Spirit against the flesh: and these are contrary the one to the other." This meant for Wesley that the flesh, the evil nature, opposes the Spirit, even in believers. He described the struggle as follows:

> These continually feel a heart bent to backsliding; a natural tendency to evil; a proneness to depart from God, and cleave to the things of the earth. They are daily sensible of sin remaining in their heart, pride, self-will, unbelief; and of sin cleaving to all they speak or do, even their best actions and holiest duties.[161]

Thus there is an activity of a kind, but a "bound" kind. One feels it, is aware of it, but keeps victory over it. He walks "not after the flesh, but after the Spirit." *"Having sin* does not forfeit the favour of God; *giving way to sin* does."[162] So the believer does not give way to this sinful nature.

Yet, after Wesley had said that this remaining sin in believers does not reign, and does not condemn, and does not have the consent of the will, he can describe it in strong terms. The believers have in them the "seeds of pride and vanity, of anger, lust, and evil desire, yea, sin of every kind." This is a "matter of daily experience" with them. The "babes in Christ" at Corinth were believers in a "low degree" because "much of sin remained in them, and the carnal mind, which is not subject to the law of God!" They "feel the flesh, the evil nature in them," but they "do not yield thereto," nor give place to the devil, but "maintain a continual war with all sin" so that "God is well-pleased with their sincere, though imperfect obedience." Then Wesley insisted further concerning the believer:

> Although they are continually convinced of sin cleaving to all they do; although they are conscious of not fulfilling the perfect law, either in their thoughts, or words, or works; although they know they do not love the Lord their God with all their heart, and mind, and soul, and strength; although they feel more or less of pride, or self will, stealing in and mixing with their best duties; although even in their more im-

mediate intercourse with God, . . . they are continually ashamed of their wandering thoughts, or of the deadness and dulness of their affections; yet there is no condemnation to them still, either from God or from their own heart.[163]

Wesley insisted that the hearts of the believers need to be unveiled. They should "be abased," "be humbled in the dust," see themselves as "nothing and vanity" while yet they trust their Christ.[164] Believers can be deceived, and imagine they are free from sin while evil is still there. So they need to be convinced of "pride," "self will," and other sins. Without the "clear light of God" one cannot possibly conceive "a propensity to pride, self will, anger, revenge, love of the world, yea, and all evil; a root of bitterness, which, if the restraint were taken off for a moment, would instantly spring up," and "such a depth of corruption" that dwells in the heart.[165] The believer can be deceived about it for a while but is soon awakened to his evil.[166] Here it is apparent Wesley did realize there could be "unconscious" sin; that is, a person could have pride and not realize it. Sangster is wrong when he says Wesley rejected the idea of "unconscious sin."[67] Certainly this kind of sin could not condemn the believer, but it certainly is present with him. One of Wesley's constant emphases was that one should be fully awakened to his sinfulness.

In reality the picture Wesley drew of the carnal heart in the believer is not too different from that drawn by Luther, Calvin, and others in the Reformed tradition. This may be surprising to those who know that Wesley taught that no believer sins willfully and that he can be cleansed from all sinfulness of heart in this life. To believe this, in the reformers' opinion, would necessitate a faulty conception of sin. Why is it then that Wesley saw sin in believers in the light he did and yet could teach complete deliverance now?

The question will be answered more fully later. But it is helpful in this context to venture a few reasons. Wesley's belief in the voluntariness of proper sin and his belief that this consenting to sin ceased at justification resulted in the concept that a more drastic change occurred at the beginning of the Christian life for the believer. The nature of sin receives a deadly blow in regeneration from which it cannot recover so long as the believer progresses in faith. The power of the sinfulness is gone though its corruption remains.

Then, further, Wesley did not associate sinfulness, or evil nature, either as a part of the body or as intrinsic to the human nature. This evil is that which is removable without destroying either the body or basic human nature. It is a disease the absence of which will make human existence richer. Luther associated sin so closely with the body that no deliverance is possible until the "body is turned to ashes and a new body is raised up."[168] Warfield taught that there is an "eradication" of the old nature which is completed in death.[169] This latter position is quite general in Reformed theology and leaves the impression that freedom from the old nature would mean freedom from the earthly existence. Wesley made no such association.

Another essential difference is that in Reformed thought all imperfections flowing from an imperfect body and mind are short of perfection and therefore sinful. All imperfections, since they fall short of perfect obedience, are consequently sins.[170] Wesley's definition of both voluntary sins and of sinfulness in the believer allows for imperfections flowing from a broken body and mind. Mistakes and infirmities are neither accountable sins nor are they fruit from a nature of sin. They flow from an innocent nature that has suffered in the fall of man. This fallen nature is sinful only in the sense of suffering the consequence of sin.

These are distinctions that many have considered to be valid. They are at least worthy of very careful consideration. And they must be made if one is to understand Wesley's concept of perfection. The understanding of another's terminology is often difficult, and the misunderstanding is occasion of much controversy. But whatever terms Wesley used, it is important to come to grips with the goal at which he aimed.

G. "Sola Fide"

Before one closes this chapter on "Sin and Grace" it is necessary to get some idea as to how Wesley viewed the conditions under which grace operated. Since grace is free and offered to all men, what do some men do that brings to them the works of grace that other men refuse? Did Wesley hold to the "by faith alone" and not of works, or was this concept modified by him? In this section Wesley's concept of faith will be considered.

Wesley inherited the doctrine of works-righteousness pretty much from his parents and the Church of England. His early idea of faith was largely one of assent to truth, and his concept of salvation was that works availed for his acceptance. From the years 1725 to 1738, Wesley set himself to the task of saving his own soul. His declared reason for going to Georgia in 1735 was "to save his own soul."[171] After being in Georgia for two years he wrote, "I went to America, to convert the Indians; but O! who shall convert me? who, what is he that will deliver me from this evil heart of unbelief?"[172]

Although he was a faithful son of the Church of England and knew its formularies, which had been greatly influenced by Reformation theology, Wesley still, before 1738, was essentially ignorant of the doctrine of justification by faith alone.[173] On his journey to and from America, and while in Georgia, Wesley became acquainted with the Moravians. On his return to England he met Peter Bohler, the Moravian who finally convinced Wesley that he had no faith. It was in a Moravian Society meeting where Wesley heard from Luther and was led to put his trust in Christ alone for forgiveness.[174] For the first time Wesley came to believe in this doctrine of justification by faith alone, since now he had experienced that faith. From neither the doctrine nor the experience did he ever depart.

Lee would be inclined to believe that Wesley's earlier experiences may not have been so dark as he depicted them,[175] but, however that may be, this *sola fide* was to him a new doctrine in 1738. He learned this "new doctrine" from Luther and through the Moravians. Wesley may have heard these or similar words on that memorable night in May, 1738:

> Faith, however, is a divine work in us. It changes us and makes us to be born anew of God; it kills the old Adam and makes altogether different men, in heart and spirit and mind and powers, and it brings with it the Holy Ghost . . . Faith is a living, daring confidence in God's grace, so sure and

certain that a man would stake his life on it a thousand times. This confidence in God's grace and knowledge of it makes men glad and bold and happy in dealing with God and with all his creatures; and this is the work of the Holy Ghost in faith. . . . Pray God to work faith in you; else you will remain without faith, whatever you think or do.[176]

Franz Hildebrandt holds that Wesley and Luther meet squarely in their proclamation of "The Lord Our Righteousness" as the *articulus stantis et cadentis ecclesiae*.[177] Some think that faith may be to Luther what love is to Wesley.[178] If this is true, there will be some variations in the *sola fide*, although Wesley believed he never deviated from the reformers on his justification by faith. On this doctrine they had spoken the truth.[179]

Faith for Wesley was a condition of salvation, by which he meant that it was "necessary in order to receive forgiveness or salvation." He did not mean it was a "procuring or meritorious cause."[180] Why did God make faith the only condition of justification? One answer, he said, is *"to hide pride from man."*

It was therefore an instance of wisdom worthy of God, to appoint such a condition of reconciliation for him and all his posterity as might effectually humble, might abase them to the dust. And such is faith. It is peculiarly fitted for this end: For he that cometh unto God by this faith, must fix his eye singly on his own wickedness, on his guilt and helplessness, without having the least regard to any supposed good in himself, to any virtue or righteousness whatsoever. He must come to God as a *mere sinner* . . . pleading nothing of his own but sin and misery. Thus it is, and thus alone, when his *mouth is stopped,* and he stands utterly *guilty before* God, that he can *look unto Jesus,* as the whole and sole *Propitiation for his sins.*[181]

Not only is faith a necessary condition for salvation but it is a gift of God. This fact may seem surprising inasmuch as Wesley saw man acting by believing, but he insisted often that faith is a gift. Speaking of faith Wesley wrote that "it is the gift, yea, and the free gift of God." One has need of patience as he waits for this faith.[182] A person can believe that God is able and willing to do His work in his heart, but true faith as a gift from God is beyond this and should be expected. Wesley exhorted people to keep believing and obeying, and God will give faith.[183] This

61

"holy faith is the gift of God; and he is never straitened for time. He can as easily give this faith in a moment as in a thousand years."[184] Whether this faith was the initial faith for forgiveness or the complete faith for sanctification, it was the free gift of God. It is clear here that this faith is not just a doctrine to be preached or accepted, but it is to be experienced.[185]

Wesley did define faith in general ways such as the faith of a materialist, of a deist, of a heathen, of a Jew, of Roman Catholics, of Protestants. But this faith cannot save.

> But what is the faith which is properly saving; which brings eternal salvation to all those that keep it to the end? It is such a divine conviction of God, and the things of God, as, even in an infant state, enables everyone that possesses it to "fear God and work righteousness." And whosoever, in every nation, believes thus far, the Apostle declares, is "accepted to him." He actually is, at that very moment, in a state of acceptance. But he is at present only a *servant* of God, not properly a *son*. Meantime, let it be well observed, that "the wrath of God" no longer "abideth on him."[186]

Here Wesley described the faith of a servant, which is the kind of faith he had before 1738, and which the man of Romans 7 had. This account was given 50 years after Aldersgate, and Wesley had revised some of his opinions. He now believed there is a beginning of faith prior to the assurance of acceptance. One can be an accepted servant, obeying God out of fear, and so has faith in an "infant state."[187]

Wesley struggled over this point for a long time. He seemed to expect a faith such as Bohler described that would be complete. He did feel faith on the night of May 24, 1738. But this faith wavered, was strong, then weak. At first he declared he was no Christian prior to 1738. Later he revised his judgment. He came to believe that one could have faith, even though weak and servantlike, which was yet faith that saved from wrath and guilt.[188]

In Wesley therefore there are not different kinds of saving faith, but various stages in it. There is a faith of a servant, then of the son. This faith is described as a "disposition," which God hath wrought in his heart; "a sure trust and confidence in God, that, through the merits of

62

Christ, his sins are forgiven, and he reconciled to the favour of God."[189]

> Christian faith is then, not only an assent to the whole gospel of Christ, but also a full reliance on the blood of Christ; a trust in the merits of his life, death, and resurrection; a recumbency upon him as our atonement and our life, *as given for us,* and *living in us;* and, in consequence hereof, a closing with him, and cleaving to him, as our "wisdom, righteousness, sanctification, and redemption," or, in one word, our salvation.[190]

But even the faith of a son is often weak and lacks completion, as Wesley learned. This faith is only a stage beyond that of servant and can become greater still.[191] There are "degrees in faith," and a weak faith can be a true faith.[192] Believers are exhorted to go from faith to faith, or they are in danger of backsliding. It is possible for the faith, once given, to be lost. Yet it can be regained.[193]

This faith given to sinful man, even in the beginning stages, bears fruit. It brings pardon, forgiveness, and the Holy Spirit. It brings peace, joy, love, and power over sin. It brings assurance of acceptance with God and all the fruit of the Spirit. In other words this faith brings salvation.[194] It is a "sense" by which we walk in the spiritual world and come to know spiritual things. And the stronger our faith, the more we can see and experience in life.[195]

This faith for Wesley was not an end in itself but a means to an end. The end to be attained is love, while faith is the means to that end.[196] For this reason Wesley did not make faith to comprise the whole of religion but it is the ordained way of God to the whole. The whole of religion for Wesley is love. When faith begins, even in the earliest stage, this love begins. As faith grows, so does love. When faith is perfected, then it is that pure love reigns. So it was possible for Wesley to speak of justifying faith and sanctifying faith. He was not thinking of two kinds, or even two acts, of faith so much as he was thinking of the beginning and the finishing of faith. When one first believes, he is justified; when one grows and reaches a point where he can, he believes for holiness and is sanctified wholly. Faith is the only condition for justification; it is the only condition for entire sanctification. But these are not two faiths but two stages in the same faith.[197] Yet in every stage this faith is a gift of God!

Has Wesley done an injustice to the *sola fide* doctrine? It is very evident that he made the whole of salvation dependent on faith alone as the immediate condition and that this faith is of God. Berkouwer's greatest fear in the discussion of sanctification is that it will do injustice to the *sola fide*.[198] He acknowledges that Wesley claimed to accept the doctrine of "by faith alone" but fears he did injustice to it. His reason is that Wesley had synergistic and nomistic tendencies. Wesley's synergistic tendencies have already been shown to be in a monergistic framework where all is of grace. So since faith comes from grace, and any believing on man's part is of grace, neither the *sola gratia* nor the *sola fide* is set aside. Whether Wesley had nomistic tendencies will be discussed in the next section. Berkouwer claims that for Wesley the "sola fide becomes a point of departure and breaks its connections with sanctification."[199] But it has just been shown that Wesley held to faith alone, and this not a different faith, as the condition for the whole of salvation. There is no broken connection. If *sola fide* means that man does nothing in believing and God believes for him, then Wesley could not hold the doctrine. But Berkouwer does not appear to mean such. If he means that justification and sanctification both are included in the *sola fide,* then Wesley is in agreement.

H. GOOD WORKS

One of the great problems faced by Protestants in their doctrines of *sola gratia* and *sola fide* is what to say about good works. If justification is by faith alone exclusive of works, then the danger of antinomianism is always present. Anyone who attempts to give any special emphasis to good works in relation to the Christian life is accused of nomism, legalism, or moralism. Is there a meeting place somewhere between antinomianism and nomism? Can one insist on good works without being a legalist, or on faith alone without being antinomian? The answer to this problem is not easy, but most theologians have attempted to answer.

Perfection, or sanctification, is closely related to this same problem. To be sanctified means to be freed from selfishness and pride with the result that the works performed become holy and righteous. The tremendous fear on the part of the Reformed writers is that such good works would be a basis for pride and self-esteem, and thus would destroy full trust in Christ. This part of the problem will be dealt with in Chapter IV. In this section the relation of good works to the general problem of sin and grace will be noted. Is it possible to speak of good works along with *sola fide* and *sola gratia*? Is there any way that good works are essential to faith, or a necessary part of faith? Are works in any sense a condition for either faith or salvtion?

That this problem of the relationship of good works to faith was not settled by the reformers and is not yet settled by heir successors is very evident when one reads an attempted discussion of sanctification, or perfection, or of the work of the Holy Spirit, by contemporary writers. Berkouwer discusses at length the battle at this point and says, "Modern theologians have been put upon their mettle afresh by these questions." The real question is on the *simul justus, simul peccator*, but it involves good works and sanctification. "The culprits are Kuyper and Bavinck, over against Kohlbrugge, Bohl and Barth." Brunner also enters into the debate.[200] A seeming "grim disavowel of sanctification" in Barth and a neglecting of the "bond between sanctification and Sola-fide" in others are seen by Berkouwer.[201]

Cherbonnier claims that Augustine insisted on good works, but that they do not fit his system. Also he claims that this matter is the greatest embarrassment of the Reformation. The logic of the reformers "cut the nerve of good works." Cherbonnier says that Luther insisted on good works, but that this insistence did not absolve him of the responsibility for the logical implication of his doctrines—which is that sinners are honest in that they act the part, and those who try to be good are hypocrites.

> It goes without saying that to flirt with such pagan notions was the farthest from Luther's intention. The point is that they represent the ultimate outcome of a chain of reasoning which had been set in motion by two of his fundamental doctrines, the cleavage between faith and works and the definition of original sin. Short of repudiating these, there is no consistent escape from antinomianism.[202]

Wesley faced this same logic in his dealing with the Moravians. They accused Wesley of rejection of *sola fide* because he insisted on the means of grace. Wesley saw in them a quietist form of mysticism that led directly to antinomianism.[203] At the same time, he read Luther's *Commentary on Galatians,* and came up with this response:

> I was utterly ashamed. How have I esteemed this book, only because I heard it so commended by others; or, at best, because I had read some excellent sentences occasionally quoted from it! But what shall I say, now I judge for myself? Now I see with my own eyes? Why, not only that the author makes nothing out, clears up not one considerable difficulty; that he is quite shallow in his remarks on many passages, and muddy and confused almost on all; but that he is deeply tinctured with Mysticism throughout, and hence often dangerously wrong. To instance, only in one or two points:—How does he . . . decry reason, right or wrong, as an irreconcilable enemy to the Gospel of Christ! . . . Again, how blasphemously does he speak of good works and of the Law of God; constantly coupling the Law with sin, death, hell, or the devil; and teaching that Christ delivers us from them all alike. . . . Here (I apprehend) is the real spring of the grand error of the Moravians. They follow Luther, for better or worse. Hence their "no works, no Law, no commandments."[204]

Wesley failed to see that Luther emphasized good works. He looked upon Luther as a man "highly favoured of God, and a blessed instrument," then he wrote, "But O! What a pity he had no faithful friend! None that would, at all hazards, rebuke him plainly and sharply, for his rough, untractable spirit, and bitter zeal for opinions, so greatly obstructive of the work of God."[205] Apparently Wesley would have liked to get Luther into one of his class meetings, and, applying St. James's admonition of "confess your faults one to another," picked out some of the "straw" in Luther's life! Although he saw Luther as an able exponent of justification by faith alone, he saw him as most ignorant and confused in his doctrine of sanctification.[206] Niebuhr sums up this conflict of Wesley with the Moravians as a "miniature of the whole controversy between the Renaissance and Reformation."

> The one rightly maintains the moral imperatives of the gospel and wrongly imagines that they can be completely realized; the other rightly understands the limits of historic

existence but is wrongly tempted to an antinomianism, which allows men "to continue in sin that grace may abound."[207]

Of course Luther opposed antinomianism, and in some of his tracts he "disposed of antinomians and mystical quietists in phrases more violent than had any place in John Wesley's genteel vocabulary."[208] But Luther taught good works only "in time and place, that is to say, when the question is concerning works, and toucheth not this article of justification."[209] Evidently he could not discuss good works in connection with the *sola fide,* and this separation is a dangerous one.[210] When Luther could get away from this "article" in his discussion, he spoke of good works almost in the terms of Wesley.[211]

In the Neo-Orthodox return to some of the principles of Reformation theology, there is a tendency again to devalue good works. Barth claims that to change from the recognition of what God has done for us in Christ, and in us through the Spirit, to the exhortation for us to do something places us in "great peril." A "chasm" opens up. I am still just as I am, "earthbound." To be other than I am would be the "end of the way," while we are only on the way.[212] Barth says further that there is an activity on our part, but it is not God's; it is ours. It is pleasing to God only because it testifies we have heard Him.[213] Actually it is no different from what it was before we heard. Brunner denies that there is any moral effort on man's part to make himself better than is acceptable to God.[214] This Neo-Orthodox negation of man's moral effort is criticized by Gerrit Berkouwer from the standpoint of Reformed theology. He maintains that Brunner, in order to avoid antinomianism, after he divorces the believer from the "Thou shalt," has to "spy around for a way back." The atmosphere "beyond the law" gets too rare for him, so he starts talking about "a law without legality." According to Berkouwer, Brunner's distinction between law and commandment, and between law and love, is untenable.[215]

As already suggested, Berkouwer fears that Wesley's view leads to nomism. He considers that Wesley wanted "to see sanctification in concrete forms," that "he was troubled by the problem of the necessity of good works and the distinction between merit and condition. In this connection he offered sharp opposition to the Reformed doctrines of election and irresistible grace and the perseverance of the saints."[216] Berkouwer can see here that the real difference with Wesley is at the point of election, grace, and perseverance. Again we must say that if *sola gratia* and *sola fide* are valid only in connection with unconditional election and irresistible grace, then they are "out" for Wesley. In the way the reformers meant these terms, it may be possible Wesley did "fail to do justice to it." But in Wesley's understanding of both grace and faith as he saw them in the Scriptures, which he supposed the reformers intended to follow at all costs, he did justice to the "by faith alone."

If nomism, legalism, and moralism mean that one is to keep the law, obey God, and that he endeavors to the limit of his ability to do so, then Wesley was guilty of the name. But if these terms mean that in keeping the law and obeying one depends on them for acceptance with God, then Wesley is not guilty. These terms are usually taken in the latter sense, and are understood to carry the idea of merit for the doer, and a natural ability to perform. All of this Wesley rejected completely, as has already been shown. To accuse Wesley of nomism is to misunderstand his doctrine of grace.

Did Wesley believe then in a salvation by works as well as faith? He certainly believed in works as essential to salvation. In answering the question whether repentance is necessary to justification Wesley answered:

> God does undoubtedly command us both to repent, and to bring forth fruits meet for repentance; which if we willing neglect, we cannot reasonably expect to be justified at all: therefore both repentance, and fruits meet for repentance, are, in some sense, necessary for justification. But they are not necessary in the *same sense* with faith, nor in the *same degree*. Not in the *same degree;* for those fruits are only necessary *conditionally;* if there be time and opportunity for them. Otherwise a man may be justified without them. as was the thief upon the cross; . . . but he cannot be justified without faith; this is impossible. Likewise, let a man have ever so much repentance, or ever so many of the fruits meet for repentance, yet all this does not at all avail; he is not justified till he believes. But the moment he believes, with or without those fruits, yea, with more or less repentance, he is justified.— Not in the *same sense;* for repentance and its fruits are only *remotely* necessary; necessary in order to faith; whereas faith

is *immediately* and *directly* necessary to justification. It remains, that faith is the only condition, which is *immediately* and *proximately* necessary to justification.[217]

In another context Wesley said that "repentance absolutely must go before faith," by which he meant "conviction of sin, producing real desires and sincere resolutions of amendment." But he did not term these as yet good works because they do not spring from faith.[218] These works of repentance, as has already been shown, are a result of prevenient grace, and so do flow from grace, not from any natural ability in man. Man's willingness to choose to follow grace leads him to repentance and faith. It is a cooperation with grace afforded man by grace itself. So these works before faith are of grace, and must precede faith. Yet these works are not enough, though necessary, to justify a man. The person must also be given faith as the "immediate" condition.

It is interesting to note that Wesley made faith, even though it is a gift of God, to be a *condition* of justification. A person must believe. If he does not believe, even though he has repented, he cannot be saved. This act of man, even though it is a gift of God, is a form of work. It is not a work of merit, but a work of God whereby a person does trust Christ. When Wesley first heard of justification by faith, and experienced it, he preached it all over England. Opposition arose to this preaching, but he and his friends carried on, expecting this persecution.

While they were so employed, a storm arose from a quarter not expected. Some of their familiar friends declared that they were preaching salvation by works. "This we could not in any wise understand; we wondered what they meant." Salvation by works they abhorred, and declared they did preach salvation by faith. But the opposition continued. Wesley considered the ones opposing them were too good a people to be acting out of ill will. He wrote, "The wonder therefore remained, how they could impute to us a doctrine which our soul abhorred, and which we were continually opposing, and confuting with all our might."

I was in perplexity when a thought shot across my mind, which solved the matter at once. "This is the key: those that hold, 'Everyone is absolutely predestinated either to salvation

> or damnation,' see no medium between salvation by works and
> salvation by absolute decrees." It follows, that whosoever denies
> salvation by absolute decrees, in so doing (according to their
> apprehension) asserts salvation by works.
>
> And herein I verily believe they are right. As averse as
> I once was to the thought, upon further consideration, I allow
> there is, there can be, no medium. Either salvation is by ab-
> solute decree, or it is (in a Scriptural sense) by works.[219]

Wesley went on to declare that neither can it be by faith,
for "unconditional decree excludes faith as well as works."
So he felt, and with good reason, that the *sola fide* stands,
because it is a faith that works by love.[220] Why did not
Wesley say, as did the Catholics, that it was salvation by
faith *and* works? He did not, for he held that *faith alone*
was the immediate and final condition, since salvation rested
wholly on the merits of Christ, and not on any of the
works. This kind of faith took away all boasting from the
believer except in Christ.

Wesley believed strongly in the means of grace. He
opposed the Moravian method of waiting quietly and doing
nothing until faith came. Wesley organized his bands, or
class meetings, for the purpose of pursuing after God. While
one waited for faith to come he should pray, read the
Scriptures, f a s t, take Holy Communion, and perform
various Christian duties. None of these were looked upon
as gaining any merit; they helped to prepare the way for
grace to operate. Wesley considered that Whitefield did a
great work in America, but the work was coming to nought
because there was no discipline and no societies.[221] The
work of grace could not progress in the lives of believers
without the use of every means of grace possible and obedience
to God's commandments.

In his teaching on sanctification Wesley declared that
faith was the only condition. One was not made perfect by
works.[222] However one could not hope to have this complete
sanctification without earnest obedience, disciplined life,
self-denial, and doing all he could. There was even a repentance for sanctification.[223] Wesley considered this holiness
necessary for final salvation in the sense of making one fit
for heaven.[224] "Without which [holiness] no man shall see
the Lord." Yet in all his appeal for a holy life, never did
Wesley look upon it as meritorious. Faith is in Christ alone

for the holiest person. Good works and holiness are always tied to the *sola fide*. In Wesley there was no separation of faith and works.

Actually the essential difference with the reformers that Wesley had on sin and grace was his rejection of unconditional election. Since this rejection leaves in man a work of grace that can be hindered or assisted by man's activity, which itself is of grace, the door is left wide open for faith to grow, for more grace to come, and for the believer to attain the highest in grace. In other words, the possibilities of grace are unlimited for the believer who aims for the highest. The power given to man to cooperate with this grace has no limit within God's promises. Wesley can be expected to explore these possibilities to the limit of human reach. But he does it as a man who knows he is nothing, except for the grace of God.

CHAPTER III

STAGES IN PERFECTION

To claim that the term perfection has only one meaning would be to reject not only Wesley, but also the Scriptures. Much of the opposition to Wesleyan perfection has been created by those who fixed a certain meaning for the term and then used the term with that specialized meaning against Wesley's views. Wesley had to tell his critics often that he did not mean by perfection the same as they did. He constantly challenged his opponents to show by Scripture wherein he was wrong.

> If, therefore, you will please to point out to me any passages in that sermon which are either contrary to the Scripture, or not supported by it, and to show that they are not, I shall be full as willing to oppose as ever I was to defend them. I search for truth, plain, Bible truth, without any regard to the praise or dispraise of men.[1]

Wesley had no particular fondness for the term perfection. He claimed that he seldom used it, but that his opponents thrust the term at him for explanation. He espoused it because he thought it was scriptural. He wrote, "I am always willing to receive more light. . . . Whoever, therefore, will give me more light with regard to Christian perfection, will do me a singular favour."[2] He was convinced it was the doctrine of Paul, James, Peter, and John. He disclaimed that the doctrine was exclusively his own. "For it is His doctrine, peculiarly, emphatically His; it is the doctrine of Jesus Christ." He felt that no Christian could speak against it when he understood its true, scriptural meaning.[3]

Again and again Wesley attempted a definition of Christian perfection. Using biblical terms, he wrote that it is "loving God with all our heart." It is "a heart and life all devoted to God"; it is "regaining the whole image of God." Perfection is "having all the mind that was in Christ" and "walking uniformly as Christ walked." He asked, "Do you object to this?" and, "Do you desire less?" "If anyone means anything more, or anything less by Perfection, I have no concern with it."[4] If perfection were set too high, it would drive men into needless fears; if it were set too low, it would drive them to hell.[5] Wesley worked hard to set the meaning of perfection as do the Scriptures.

Sangster's criticism of Wesley's terms may appeal to some but it hardly touches the real problem in Wesley's mind.

> The word "perfection" is an extraordinarily difficult term. Wesley and Fletcher found it so. That was why, in their day, they made such laboured distinctions between Paradisaical, Mediatorial, and Christian Perfection, and that is why subsequent writers, sympathetic to their teaching, have distinguished the terms relative and absolute perfection, the perfection of the stage and the perfection of the end. Oddly and sadly enough, the adjectival use of the word Christian with the word Perfection has not burnished the noun but tarnished it. This was inevitable. An illimitable term must shine in lone splendour. The misguided effort to furbish it is worse than gilding the lily and has the precisely opposite effect from the one desired. When Wesley linked the sublime name "Christian" with the sublime term "perfection," he produced a title which was not sublime. In the critical minds of those who followed him keenly, and in his own frank exposition too, Christian Perfection was set out as something less than perfection, and he was exposed to the sneer which we have noted already: it was possible to be a perfect Christian without being a perfect man.
>
> The term "perfection," for what Wesley had in mind, must be dropped. Indeed, it appears plain that he wanted to drop it himself. It is a mystery that he made such free use of a name he did not like and which was so fruitful of trouble and misunderstanding. He used it, no doubt, for the same reason that he used the name "Methodist:" because others used it and because it was the swiftest way to recognition.[6]

But, in answer to Sangster, it must be remembered that Wesley used the term perfection a long time before he encountered opposition to its use. Also Wesley claimed he used it because it was found in the Bible. To say he should have dropped it would be to say that Paul should have dropped it. He used the word "Christian" with it to distinguish it from other perfections which have little to do with the Christian, such as, divine, angelic, or Adamic perfection.

Flew, in describing Pauline perfection, is much nearer to what Wesley had in mind.

> 1. In the first place, he distinguished between absolute perfection, which was reserved for the future (I Cor. 13:10; Phil. 3:12-14), and a relative perfection which he regarded as

realizable by himself and his converts. Indeed, that relative perfection was the goal of apostolic work (Col. 1:28; 3:14; 4:12; I Cor. 2:6; Eph. 4:12-13).

2. The absolute perfection, the final destiny of believers, is described as the face-to-face vision of God. It is contrasted with the obscurer vision to which believers now attain (I Cor. 13:12). We may identify this final destiny with "the prize of the high calling of God in Christ Jesus," and the resurrection from the dead, to which St. Paul hoped to attain (Phil. 3:14 and 11).

Such a description of absolute perfection should preserve us from the error into which many scholars have fallen, of assuming that St. Paul's admission that he had not attained the final goal is equivalent to an admission that the whole course of the Christian life in this world must be marked by sin.

3. The relative perfection attainable in this life is a progress towards the goal of the final destiny. It is tempting to interpret St. Paul, as many do, as saying that the essence of this relative perfection is the striving after absolute perfection, and to leave it at that. But such a description would be inadequate. There is a positive gift of God to the believing soul. The Christian walks by the Spirit, and so can fulfil the law of Christ (Gal. 6:2).[7]

Since, for Wesley, perfection is attainable in this life, as he felt Paul taught, he conformed his definition to this concept. Christian perfection does not exempt from ignorance, mistakes, infirmities, or temptations.[8] Nor is it the perfection of angels, nor of Adam. It is the "love of God and man," "the mind which was in Christ," "the fruit of the Spirit," "the image of God." It is a universal holiness, an entire dedication of self to God, and a freedom from sin.[9]

Wesley identified perfection and holiness. To be perfect was to be holy. Religion was holiness and religion was salvation. Salvation was holiness of heart and life. Furthermore, to be sanctified is to be holy; so actually in Wesley's mind perfection, holiness, salvation, religion, and sanctification were all about the same thing. Wesley gave more of a religious content to these terms than theological. There are times when Wesley gave a more precise meaning to these terms, but, generally speaking, no distinctions were drawn between them.[10]

Wesley taught that there are several stages in the Christian life. Some Christians are babes, some are young men, and some are fathers. The only perfect Christians are the latter, although there is a sense of perfection at all stages.[11] He spoke of freedom from sin as perfection both in the sense of willful sin and of inward sin.[12] He wrote of the new birth, which is the beginning of holiness or perfection, as having both a higher and lower stage.[13] Wesley could speak of pardon as salvation begun, of holiness as salvation continued, and of heaven as salvation finished.[14]

For one who thinks of perfection only in an absolute sense Wesley's view of degrees in perfection may seem weak. Yet it is not hard to think of degrees in holiness. One may be holy and become more holy. Since for Wesley to be perfect was to be holy, "perfection certainly admits of degrees." He allowed a "perfection of kinds" and a "perfection of degrees." He knew of no ancient or modern writer who did not agree with such distinction.[15] He wrote to Miss Furly that she had experienced a taste of salvation when she was justified. Since justification, she had experienced salvation itself, only in a low degree. She was yet to look for an instantaneous as well as a gradual change.[16] All of these were degrees of salvation, so therefore degrees in perfection.

Even those who had attained that stage of perfection where sin is destroyed and the heart is made perfect in love were still short of a higher goal. The best and holiest of saints still fell short in many things. There was room to grow all through life and even in eternity. There was a perfection which the holiest had not yet attained.[17]

But Wesley could not allow this final perfection to be the only kind. He felt that his brother Charles at times set the goal so high that none could reach it. To do so discouraged seekers.[18] John wanted to place perfection within the reach of all, as he felt that the Scriptures did. But even within the reach of men was a perfection having stages. It began, continued, reached a climax called entire sanctification, or perfect love, and after the climax one could grow in perfection.

Wesley was a seeker for perfection from the year 1725. He was led to believe that when he was justified by faith he would arrive. In this he was disappointed in 1738.[19] So he continued his pursuit for Christian perfection. He urged others to pursue the same course with him. He later saw that faith came in degrees, that salvation was by stages,

75

and at no stage was perfection absolute. He did see two essential stages or levels of experience. One was the initial stage of justification and regeneration. A later stage could be reached which he called the experience of entire sanctification or Christian perfection. This second experience was not a final goal for the Christian. There was growth after the second crisis. The next chapter will deal specifically with this second crisis, or present perfection. In this chapter a further investigation will be made of these various stages in perfection.

A. JUSTIFICATION

Before 1738, Wesley was a seeker for holiness, salvation, and perfection. To say he had not found any part of these before the Aldersgate experience would be misleading and contrary to his own later corrections. He supposed, before 1738, that his efforts toward perfection, and his partial attainment of it, were grounds for his justification. He did not doubt of his acceptance with God until after his contact with the Moravians.[20] With these people he came to believe that one is justified by faith, and since he did not have a full faith, he doubted he was justified. He sought for this faith and claimed to receive it in May, 1738. However, it did not bring to him all that at first he had thought it would.[21] But he did receive something he had not known before.

There are those who have concluded that Wesley actually attained Christian perfection at the Aldersgate experience.[22] As already noted, Wesley did correct his journals by indicating that he had the faith of a servant before 1738. But was he justified according to his own principles? His own testimony was that he, before 1738, was "under the law." He felt the wrath of God upon him and often relapsed into sin. He did fight against sin but was often held in bondage by it. This struggle he could not avoid until he was justified by faith. His own mother did not enjoy this justification until after John had received it.[23] Yet she and John had lived righteous and godly lives many years before these renewal experiences.

It is not easy to give precise theological expression to all phases of religious experience. The faith Wesley professed on May 24, 1738, was a perfected faith for forgiveness, so therefore the faith of a son. With this faith came assurance of forgiveness and a break with willful sinning. This faith had begun sooner but was weak and uncertain. Did it justify? In some sense, yes, as was noted earlier in this paper. But Wesley is never free to call it by the classic name of justification by faith.

Did perfection actually begin before this justification by faith? Wesley was assured before 1738 that God heard him and he was given light and truth.[24] He knew what it was to have a degree of peace.[25] His lack was because of ignorance and would not have meant eternal death had he then died.[26] He was a seeker for salvation, but this salvation was perfect holiness, or perfection, which he disclaimed for himself. He was not saved while in Georgia, not because he was rejected by God, but because he was unfit for heaven—that is, he was not perfect. Yet this salvation had begun, for salvation begins "from the first dawning of grace in the soul." In speaking further of this salvation in the soul, Wesley wrote:

> If we take this in its utmost extent, it will include all that is wrought in the soul by what is frequently termed natural conscience, but more properly, preventing grace;—all the drawings of the Father; the desires after God, which, if we yield to them, increase more and more;—all that light wherewith the son of God "enlighteneth every one that cometh into the world," showing every man, "to do justly, to love mercy, and to walk humbly with his God;"—all the convictions which his Spirit, from time to time, works in every child of man. . . .[27]

From this statement it would appear that salvation begins with prevenient grace. There is a sense in which holiness or perfection begins with this early work of God in all men's hearts. It is not brought to fruition because some men stifle this grace.

This prevenient grace, when yielded to, becomes a "convincing grace." This conviction is the first real step on the way to salvation.[28] It leads to the repentance which, as has been shown, is a condition of justifying faith. Yet the grace, the repentance, and the conviction are a part of this first stage of salvation and necessary before true justification.

Justification for Wesley meant the present forgiveness, or pardon, of sins and acceptance with God. It is a remission for the sins that are past. One is justified when he has true faith but not before. This true faith is born out of the grace, conviction, and repentance which precede it.[29] The foundation for forgiveness is not any work man does but Christ Jesus our Lord. Christ's righteousness is imputed to believers only in the sense that for His sake alone they are forgiven. This justification is based entirely upon "what Christ has done and suffered for them."[30]

> The plain scriptural notion of justification is pardon, the forgiveness of sins. It is the act of God the Father, whereby, for the sake of the propitiation made by the blood of his Son, he "showeth forth his righteousness (or mercy) by the remission of sins that are past." . . . To him that is justified or forgiven, God "will not impute sin" to his condemnation. He will not condemn him on that account, either in this world or in that which is to come. His sins, all his past sins, in thought, word, and deed, are covered, are blotted out, shall not be remembered or mentioned against him, any more than if they had not been.[31]

The faith by which one is justified is a gift of God.[32] Because of its nature one cannot have this faith without knowing it.[33] Evidently this faith can be present before justification in a weak and servant-like form. But when it becomes true faith, the faith of a son, one is justified freely. Prevenient grace can take one so far, but at a certain point justifying faith must act before salvation proper can come.[34]

Actually for Wesley there was no justification without an inner change. This inner change really begins before justification in the sense already noted. But at the moment faith acts, one is not only justified, but a great inner change occurs. This inner change is not justification, nor is it a requisite for the justification, but it is a work of God accomplished concomitantly with justification. Justification and sanctification are not the same.

> What is *justification*? . . . And it is evident, from what has already been observed, that it is not the being made actually just and righteous. This is *sanctification;* which is, indeed, in some degree, the immediate fruit of justification, but, never-

theless, is a distinct gift of God, and of a totally different nature. The one implies what God does for us through his Son; the other, what he works in us by his Spirit.[35]

Yet though these two works are distinct, God does not justify any whom He does not sanctify. God is not deceived in those He declares to be righteous, for He does not account them to be otherwise than they are. The consequence is that God does not justify any except whom He sanctifies, at least initially, with the result that one who is declared righteous actually is made righteous at the same time, although the two acts of God are different works.[36]

One can conclude that Wesley made justification a gate or door to salvation, holiness, or perfection. Justification by faith is a first stage in the beginning of perfection. The preliminary acts of grace lead to repentance and faith. Justification opens the gate and true salvation begins. Justification marks the first great stage in the order of salvation, although it must be remembered there are the dawnings of light and salvation even before.

This justification by faith is retained by continual obedience and faith. It is retained so long as there is faith, but faith can be lost, as has been shown. Final justification, then, is dependent upon continued good works and obedience springing from holiness of heart.[37] In this sense holiness is essential to our acceptance in the last day.

Wesley believed he was in agreement with the reformers on justification, although he saw they were doctrinally weak as to the inner change.[38] However, it is clear that there was a vital difference. The reformers tended to make justification more comprehensive and include in it the concept of holiness or sanctification. Their conception "extends the bounds of justification until it comes to include almost the whole of the Christian life and makes it synonymous with final salvation itself."[39] Wesley made justification the gate to holiness, which is religion or salvation itself, and the final goal was the fully restored image of God. For him justification did not lose its significance but it did not comprise in itself full salvation or perfection. Berkouwer fears this concept does injustice to justification by faith alone.[40] However, it cannot do so unless one identifies *sola fide* with unconditional election, as was noted earlier.

Justification for Wesley was not holiness, or perfection, but it was a step necessary to such. He did make justification and sanctification to be the two parts of salvation by faith, but here salvation is used in a wider sense than holiness.[41] Actually there is no holiness or sanctification without justification nor any justification without sanctification. If one has the one, he has the other. But for Wesley they were not the same. True sanctification begins with justification, but it is capable of growth, while justification is complete when one believes. When a man believes, he has full forgiveness and acceptance by God, but he is not fully saved. He is on the road to perfection.

B. Regeneration

When one begins to draw lines of distinction between justification and regeneration on the one hand, and between regeneration and sanctification on the other hand, he immediately runs counter to considerable theology on these subjects. However, it is necessary to draw these lines if Wesley is to be understood. It was suggested above that Wesley's concept of justification was narrower than that of the reformers. In Luther justification included a "making righteous" as well as "declaring righteous." He taught that faith brings Christ truly to the heart. Christ's righteousness and life flow out into those who are partakers of them. The Spirit is infused and dwells in the believer. This entire inward transformation Luther included under the terms "justification, making righteous, righteousness." The primary conception is forgiveness, but there is also inward operation, called inward justification, by which the heart is made upright, believing, pious, and good.[42] Luther clearly identified regeneration and initial sanctification with justification.

Calvin also held that in justification "a man is righteous, not in himself, but because the righteousness of Christ is communicated to him by imputation." These justified men are "made righteous no otherwise than as they are purified by being cleansed from all their defilements by the remission of their sins."[43] Calvin identified repentance, conversion, and regeneration. These are effects of the believer's participation with Christ. Regeneration is the restoration of the divine image, is a continual process, and confirms the adoption of a child of God.[44] It would seem that in Calvin justification included a receiving of Christ's righteousness, at which time repentance began. This repentance, which is identical with conversion, regeneration, and sanctification, continues until death but is never complete in this life. Wesley differed with Calvin in that he made repentance to both precede and follow faith. Conversion for him was regeneration and was instantly complete; sanctification began at conversion but continued in growth. All of these—repentance, conversion, regeneration, and sanctification—were distinct from justification.[45]

Wesley did not hold that justification made a person righteous even in Christ. As already shown, imputed righteousness did not mean for him a "cloak of righteousness" for the sinner. Justification is the declaring of one righteous on the basis of his faith in Christ's righteousness alone. At the same time the sinner is justified he is also made anew, or made righteous. But this "making righteous" is not justification, but regeneration, or conversion. The sinner is changed from death to life, so that when God declares the sinner righteous, he actually becomes so. God is not deceived in His reckoning. What is this change that occurs at the same instant as justification?

> It is that great change which God works in the soul, when he brings it into life; when he raises it from the death of sin to the life of righteousness. It is the change wrought in the whole soul by the almighty Spirit of God, when it is "created anew in Christ Jesus;" when it is "renewed after the image of God in righteousness and true holiness;" when the love of the world is changed into the love of God; pride into humility; passion into meekness; hatred, envy, malice, into sincere, tender, disinterested love for all mankind.[46]

Wesley used the figure of a physical birth to illustrate the new birth. Before regeneration one cannot see, hear, or feel in spiritual things. But when he is born again there is a total change. His spiritual senses are awakened. He now "feels, is inwardly sensible of, the graces which the Spirit of God works in his heart." He is conscious of peace and joy and love. Spiritual life has begun in the soul. It is that very beginning that is regeneration. What came before was a preparation for birth, as in the natural birth. There are growth and maturity after birth, as with the baby. For the believer this growth is sanctification or perfection. But the actual birth into life is regeneration.[47]

Wesley was not willing to confuse regeneration and sanctification. Sanctification is by degrees and is inward and outward holiness. These begin when one is regenerated but are not to be identified with regeneration any more than the birth of a child is to be identified with its subsequent growth. "The same relation, therefore, which there is between our natural birth and our growth, there is also between our new birth and our sanctification." Regeneration, or the new birth, is a part of but not the whole of sanctification; "it is the gate to it, the entrance into it."[48] There were times, especially soon after Aldersgate, when Wesley used the term new birth in a broader sense. In February, 1739, he spoke of persons born again in the "full sense" and in a "lower sense." By this he meant the initial experience at justification—the remission of sins—as the lower sense, and the full sense was the "thorough, inward change" which he later called entire sanctification.[49] But usually Wesley did not make the new birth that broad.

In this "lower sense" the new birth is a real change of mind. There is given a new mind even though it is present in corruption. There is genuine righteousness present in the believer. In the reformers this righteousness was not reached until *after* Christian development and life. In Wesley the righteousness was first given, and the process of growth followed.[50] Wesley did not lower the first experience in order to make room for a second grace. Even though justification and regeneration are gates to holiness, it is also true that a real holy life has begun.[51] Righteousness is infused into the believer.[52] Man becomes righteous in himself but not from himself. He is holy in heart and life. This infused righteousess becomes inherent. If one is "really holy, then he is inwardly and inherently holy."[53]

Naturally this kind of talk startles thinkers in the Reformed tradition. How can one be holy until he is fully holy? One cannot be righteous in himself until he is perfectly righteous. In the Canons of Dort there is a question as to how much change is allowed for the believer. There is a fear of talk about any empirical change. The most that occurs is just a beginning.[54] Berkouwer feels that Wesley wanted the change in "concrete forms," and for "commonplace reality."[55] It is true that Wesley insisted on a real change in the believer, and that the justified is righteous and must be righteous to see God. It is at this point that Wesley diverges widely from the Reformed position.[56]

As noted above, Wesley used the term conversion as synonymous with regeneration. J. E. Rattenbury quotes Miss Evelyn Underhill as defining conversion or repentance as "the first step in the spiritual life," which "consists in change of direction." This is a "non-Methodist use" of the term, and it can be applied in part at least to the Reformed usage. Rattenbury writes that the "use of the word conversion in the Synoptic Gospels is undoubtedly nearer to that of Miss Evelyn Underhill than to that of Methodism." But it had come, in the time of Wesley, to be used in different manner. "Repentance brings," according to the Methodists, "a man to God, but conversion is what God does in a man when he comes to Him in penitent faith."[57] To be converted, then, is to be born again and this is an act of God in the heart.

This conversion, or regeneration, is the first stage of perfection. Wesley declared that babes in Christ are so far perfect as "not to commit sin."[58] The kind of sin that Wesley here referred to was discussed above in Chapter II. Cannon writes that "Wesley employs the word 'sin' in a double sense." Before conversion all man's deeds are evil, but at conversion man's nature has been sufficiently purified so that he has power over outward sin. This outward sin has the narrow meaning of willful violation of God's law.[59] This perfection Wesley taught, but it was an initial stage in the process of the perfecting grace. Only of the strong and mature can it be said that they are perfect so as to be free from inward sin.[60]

Wesley saw the new birth as bearing clear and unmistakable fruit in the believer's life. Where justification takes away the guilt of sin, regeneration takes away its power.[61] No longer has sin power in the believer's life. The believer has power over both outward and inward sins insomuch that there is no willful sinning. Even though sin remains in his heart, the believer has peace and hope and love. Clearly this is a part of that perfection toward which every Christian moves when he shall be "perfect," even as his Father "in heaven is perfect."[62]

Such a concept of regeneration as found in Wesley runs counter to Neo-Orthodox concepts. The new birth for Brunner is the "complete reversal of the direction of man's life." The fact that such a redirection takes place is the man's knowing that his life is a "gift from God, not a life straining after God."[63] Brunner repudiates the Pietist conception of the new birth, which is similar to Wesley's, and sees it as a real change in the relationship with God and in one's attitude toward himself. To him a psychological change would be magic and unscriptural.[64] For Wesley this concept could not be regeneration and only a mutilated form of justification. Even Luther's emphasis upon a transformed life has been rejected by both Brunner and Barth. Barth labels as heretical "a divine quality inhering in the soul" attributed to the Holy Spirit. These ideas cannot be squared with the Apostle Paul, nor with Wesley. "St. Paul does what Barth forbids: *he predicates* of the human subject of redemption what is, for Barth, exclusively to be predicated of the divine Subject in redemption." The theologian Barth has robbed man of "his proper subjectivity—his depth and his freedom."[65]

Wesley gave a corrective to this one-sidedness. God does a real work in the objects of redemption. There is a faint beginning before justifying faith in the prevenient grace that brings the first dawning of light and conviction for sin. Justifying faith brings acceptance with God and new life to the soul of the believer. Salvation proper has now begun, and the believer is on the way of holiness, or perfection. But there is much ahead.

C. INITIAL SANCTIFICATION

Before proceeding to a discussion of the progress in perfection which leads to Christian perfection, maturity, and final glorification, it is well to investigate more closely Wesley's concept of sanctification in its initial stage. It is true that Wesley sometimes used the term sanctification in the sense of entire sanctification; but when he was making clear distinctions, he stated that there was a difference. The difference was not in kind but in degree. Sanctification began at regeneration, continued by gradual growth, reached a new level in the experience of entire sanctification, and then continued progressively afterwards. What is this very beginning stage?

In Wesley there was no clear distinction made between regeneration and initial sanctification as there was between them on one hand and justification on the other. As already suggested, sanctification comes in degrees, but justification is completed instantly. In this sense one can speak of a perfect justification. What about regeneration? Is it perfect as a work of God, or is it incomplete as is sanctification? As already seen, regeneration is the gate into sanctification and is the beginning of it but not the whole of it. Consequently they cannot be identical. Nor should one say that regeneration is only an incomplete form of sanctification. There is a sense in which it is a perfect work in itself, and it should never be called incomplete. This has been done, but such does not correctly portray Wesley's view.[66]

It is true that when Wesley defined regeneration he included ideas which are clearly initial sanctification. The marks of the new birth for Wesley included perfect love, continual obedience, holiness, and perfection.[67] Yet for Wesley the perfecting of love, the making one holy or perfect, was God's sanctifying gift. He also called sanctification the inward renewal by God's power which expels "the love of the world, the love of pleasure, of ease, of honour, of money; together with pride, anger, self will, and every other evil temper."[68] Though Wesley said that regeneration and sanctification were not the same,[69] yet he failed to draw the line between them as clearly as one could wish. In defining perfection Wesley wrote:

> It is not only a deliverance from doubts and fears, but from sin; and from all inward, as well as outward sin; from evil desires, and evil tempers, as well as from evil words and works. Yea, and it is not only a negative blessing, a deliverance from all evil dispositions, implied in that expression, "I will circumcise thy heart;" but a positive one likewise; even the planting all good dispositions in their place; clearly implied in that other expression; "To love the Lord your God with all your heart, and with all your soul."[70]

Clearly in this account are elements of regeneration—"planting all good dispositions," and of sanctification—"deliverance from all evil dispositions."

It is clear that for Wesley, when a person truly believed, he was justified, regenerated, and initially sanctified. Justification is the forgiveness of his sins and his acceptance with God. It is a work done *for* the believer. At the same instant he is born again, renewed, changed from death to life. This regeneration is a "real change" and is a work done *in* the believer. At the same moment there is a deliverance from sinning, a breaking of the power of sin, and a beginning of holiness or perfection. This last can be properly classified as initial sanctification. That regeneration and sanctification are distinct was made clear by Jesse Peck:

> There is a broad and necessary distinction between the existence of a thing and the state of the thing existing, between the fact of life and the mode of life, between a soul spiritually alive and the moral condition of the living spirit. . . .
>
> Regeneration appropriately designates the former, sanctification the latter. . . .
>
> The word sanctification just as appropriately denotes certain treatment of the soul, which God has brought to life, as regeneration does the fact of bringing it to life . . .
>
> Now here are two things totally distinct from each other, as much so as a fact and a quality of a fact, a thing and an accident of a thing can be; and here are two terms, of entirely different import, completely adapted to represent these two things respectively—regeneration, the production of spiritual life; sanctification, the treatment of the soul spiritually alive—neither of which can, without violence to the laws of language, perform the office of the other.[71]

The work of regeneration, as is justification, is a perfect work when given this clear meaning. The dead soul of the sinner is brought to life; the graces or qualities of this new life are all planted in the believer. This new life is in infancy, as a newborn babe, and is capable of growth. This new creation is perfect in its kind but capable of growth. At the same time that the new life is planted in the soul, God begins the cleansing of sin. The power of sin is broken. Man is made holy, pure, clean, but not entirely so. This cleansing work is the beginning of sanctification. It is holiness begun. It can be called initial because it is just a beginning. This new life exists where some evil is still present.

> He was humble, but not entirely; his humility was mixed with pride: he was meek; but his meekness was frequently interrupted by anger, or some uneasy or turbulent passion. His love of God was frequently damped, by the love of some creature; the love of his neighbour, by evil surmising, or some thought, if not temper, contrary to love. His will was not wholly melted down into the will of God. . . ."[72]

In these words Wesley pictured the believer who was re-generated and initially sanctified, but before he was entirely sanctified.

Initial sanctification then is that point of beginning in the Christian life when sin is given a deadening blow by the Spirit of God but is not entirely destroyed. Although justification and regeneration are complete and perfect works instantly given, the initial act of sanctification is incomplete and awaits a later instant for perfection. However, it is perfection begun because the believer is able to live without committing sin. This initial work makes a person so far perfect as not to commit sin. It is the initial perfection. "There is a perfection that is initial, a perfection that is progressive, and a perfection that is final."[73] This initial stage is "holiness in embryo and infancy."[74] Since in Wesley's view holiness and perfection were terms for the same thing, then holiness started was also the beginning of perfection.

Obviously this initial holiness or perfection is not just a perfection in Christ that has not yet come down to the believer. As already seen, it is not an imputed perfection which actually belongs only to Christ. One is made holy because Christ is holy, but he is not reckoned holy in view of the fact that Christ is holy. The believer is reckoned holy because he *is* holy. He shares in Christ's holiness in a way that makes him personally holy.

> Scripture holiness is the image of God; the mind which was in Christ; the love of God and man; lowliness, gentleness, temperance, patience, chastity. And do you coolly affirm, that this is only imputed to a believer, and that he has none at all of this holiness in him? Is temperance imputed only to him that is a drunkard still; or chastity, to her that goes on in whoredom? Nay, but a believer is really chaste and temperate. And if so, he is thus holy in himself."[75]

Of course this holiness is not *from* himself, but it is truly *in* the believer who is made holy. He truly has love and patience and other graces of the Spirit. These are to grow, and evil dispositions which are still present need cleansing. Insofar as he has love he is clean and thus has a degree of perfection, although much yet lies ahead for the Christian.

That holiness begins at justification is acknowledged by many theologians outside the Wesleyan tradition. Kuyper recognized the beginning of sanctification when the believer is justified. Apart from the fact of a perfect sanctification in Christ, he taught that one is perfect in parts though imperfect in degrees.[76] For him one must be perfect to enter heaven, although this final perfection cannot be reached before death.[77] Warfield and Berkouwer agree with Kuyper and Wesley as to this beginning of holiness in the believer at justification, although there are variations in expressions.[78]

Wesley made some distinctions that many Protestants do not make, but in general his concept of initial sanctification and its progress is not too different from the general Protestant view. He deviated from the Reformed view most at the point of entire sanctification or present perfection for the believer.[79] Wesley believed that, when a person was justified, he was also sanctified initially and that he was to push forward to completion of this beginning.

D. GRADUAL SANCTIFICATION

That Wesley taught both gradual and instantaneous sanctification is admitted by careful students of Wesley. Many have followed Wesley's teaching on gradual sanctification to the neglect of his doctrine of entire sanctification. Others have emphasized the instantaneous experience but often with a neglect of the gradual aspect. Wesley, as well as Fletcher, clearly taught both gradual and instantaneous sanctification and was able to hold the two aspects in proper balance. However, the tendency to overemphasize one aspect to the neglect of the other can be seen in early Methodism. John Peters notes that Adam Clarke emphasized the instantaneous cleansing aspect while Richard Watson taught the gradual.[80] Both men's works became standard reading for American Methodists.[81] According to Peters this marked deviation between Clarke and Watson found fruition in the distinction later seen between Methodism on the one hand and the holiness movement on the other.[82]

It would be possible to make out that the two ideas of gradual and instantaneous sanctification are incompatible.

> It has been felt also that there is inconsistency in Wesley's oscillations between perfection given in an instant and perfection as a growth. But Wesley faced this objection in his own day and believed that he had answered it. His analogy of human birth carries the substance of his reply: there is growth in the womb before birth and a long, long growth after, but the birth itself is a matter of moments and can be timed upon a clock. He would have said, concerning the life of holiness, that you do not grow into it: you are born *into* it, and grow *in* it. It is true that, if one takes isolated phrases from his writings, first about the instantaneous character of the birth and then the slow maturing of the growth, it is not hard to sharpen the contrast into a series of antithetic phrases and produce the appearance of plain inconsistency. But that is to do despite to his meaning.[83]

Evidently the concept of holiness conveys two ideas. One is the growth and development of something alive. The other is the removal of a disease that hinders the growth. When these two ideas are confused, an instantaneous holiness sounds like an instant maturity of growth, which is impossible, or it sounds as if it takes *time* for God to cleanse the heart. There must be a distinction between cleansing from defilement and growth of Christian graces. Does Wesley make the distinction?

It cannot be doubted that Wesley often expressed gradual sanctification in terms that mean both cleansing and growth. "From the time of our being born again the gradual work of sanctification takes place." He also wrote that "as we are more and more dead to sin, we are more and more alive unto God."[84] This statement could be taken to mean that when one is completely dead to sin, he then is completely alive unto God with no further growth possible. But Wesley did not mean such even though he wrote that the whole work of sanctification is not at once. Christians are to gradually grow up, and they will have "many storms, before they come to the full stature of Christ."[85]

> Christian perfection, therefore, does not imply (as some men seem to have imagined) an exemption either from ignorance, or mistake, or infirmities, or temptations. Indeed, it is only

another term for holiness. They are two names for the same thing. Thus, every one that is holy is, in the Scripture sense, perfect. Yet we may, Lastly, observe, that neither in this respect is there any absolute perfection on earth. There is no *perfection of degrees,* as it is termed; none which does not admit of a continual increase. So that how much soever any man has attained, or in how high a degree soever he is perfect, he hath still need .to "grow in grace," and daily to advance in the knowledge and love of God his Saviour.[86]

Clearly Wesley had an idea of Christian perfection or holiness which was not growth only, but it came as a stage in that growth.

The manner in which Wesley taught the gradual work of God's grace in the heart of man has already been suggested. This work begins with prevenient grace and continues until final glorification.

Salvation begins with what is usually termed (and very properly) *preventing grace:* including the first wish to please God, the first dawn of light concerning his will, and the first transient conviction of having sinned against him. All these imply some tendency towards life; some degree of salvation; the beginning of a deliverance from a blind, unfeeling heart, quite insensible of God and the things of God. Salvation carries on by *convincing grace,* usually in Scripture termed *repentance;* which brings a larger measure of self knowledge, and a farther deliverance from the heart of stone. Afterwards we experience the proper Christian salvation; whereby, "through grace," we "are saved by faith;" consisting of those two grand branches, justification and sanctification. By justification we are saved from the guilt of sin, and restored to the favour of God; by sanctification we are saved from the power and root of sin, and restored to the image of God. All experience as well as Scripture, show this salvation to be both instantaneous and gradual. It begins the moment we are justified, in the holy, humble, gentle, patient love of God and man. It gradually increases from that moment, as "a grain of mustard seed, which, at first, is the least of all seeds," but afterwards puts forth large branches, and becomes a great tree; till, in another instant, the heart is cleansed from all sin, and filled with pure love to God and man. But even that love increases more and more, till we "grow up in all things into Him that is our Head;" till we attain "the measure of the stature of the fulness of Christ."[87]

Several facts should be noted from this important paragraph from Wesley's pen. First, salvation is gradual from the earliest dawn of grace to its consummation in glory.

Since for Wesley salvation was holiness and holiness was perfection, the attainment of full holiness or complete perfection was identical with the coming of full salvation. Second, in this process, "proper Christian salvation" comes after repentance and when one believes. Third, it begins "the moment we are justified," and gradually increases. Fourth, another instant comes when the heart is fully cleansed and filled. Fifth, after this cleansing and filling, there is still increase of love.

Evidently Wesley's idea of sanctification or salvation contained two aspects—a negative and a positive. The negative aspect dealt with sin, or the "heart of stone." From this sin one must be delivered, but this deliverance is gradual with instantaneous stages, like the rocket that puts the satellite moon into orbit. Justification frees from the guilt of sin although one gradually approaches this moment. Sanctification frees from the "power" of sin at the same moment as justification, and from the "root" of sin at a later instant. This later instant is gradually approached by a "dying to sin." But the moment comes when one is dead to sin, when his heart is pure, and when only pure love fills the heart.

The other aspect of salvation is the positive one. It is light coming to the sinner. There begin new and good desires. When he is justified he is also born again. New life is placed into him. The love of God is shed abroad in the heart. This new life with all its graces increases more and more. There is more love, more joy, more peace, more of God. The negative sanctification removes hindrances so the growth can be more rapid. Entire sanctification gives a great boost to this positive aspect of salvation, but there is much still ahead. While the negative aspect of sanctification finds a completion or perfecting at the instant of entire sancitfication, the positive work is never finished, either now or in eternity.[88]

As already seen, Wesley taught that man must cooperate with God's grace if that grace is to be effective in his life. Man must work for the gift of God to increase in the soul. In fact failure to work can mean loss of grace and even of justification. Wesley did not thunder hell and damnation to those who enjoyed the beginning of salvation but failed to press on to perfection. He felt they were in a good way and would find mercy at last, but there would be a great loss if they failed to go on. To work the "more excellent way" the Christian should rise early for prayer in the morning, should make his prayers fervent, should go about his business for the glory of God. He ought to practice self-denial, order aright his conversation, refrain from needless diversions, and use properly his money.[89] This active response on the part of the believers makes it possible for God to increase His grace to them and to accomplish His work within them.

Wesley did not identify good works and sanctification, but works were made a condition for holiness. Faith is the immediate condition for entire sanctification, but good works are necessary while one waits.[90] Rattenbury made the interesting observation that Wesley taught sanctification by faith, by rising at four o'clock in the morning, and by fasting.[91] Faith can come only by such practices.

> There is a particular frame and temper of soul, a sobriety of mind, without which the Spirit of God will not concur in the purifying of our hearts. It is in our power, through his preventing and assisting grace, to prepare this in ourselves; and he expects we should, this being the foundation of all his after-works. Now, this consists in preserving our minds in a cool and serious disposition, in regulating and calming our affections, and calling in and checking the inordinate pursuits of our passions after the vanities and pleasures of this world. . . . There is nothing more certain than that the Holy Spirit will not purify our nature, unless we carefully attend to his motions, which are lost upon us . . . while we squander away our thoughts upon unnecessary things, and leave our spiritual improvement, the one thing needful, quite unthought of and neglected.[92]

Wesley was not a moralist in the sense of making good works necessary to gain merit for salvation. Nor was he one in the sense of insistence upon an outward conformity to a set rule. For Wesley true religion was always inward.[93] However, inward holiness cannot be separated from outward holiness.[94] Any who make sanctification a form of legalism fail to follow Wesley in the full meaning of his thought. One is made holy at heart and he endeavors to the limit of his ability to conform the outward life accordingly. There is a gradual destruction of inward sin until the moment that it is gone from the heart. Before this instant, and ever after, the true Christian seeks to let the inner light shine in his outward life. The one goal, inward cleansing, can be attained by faith and in life; the second is a lifelong job which cannot be perfected in the present life, as will be seen later in this study.

J. A. Wood, a Methodist writer of the last half of the nineteenth century, made careful distinction between purity and maturity. For him purity was holiness and was attained in the experience of entire sanctification. This purity would be the negative aspect of holiness as noted above. Maturity was the growing of the graces planted in regeneration. As long as one's heart is impure, growth is hindered. But when sin is destroyed in the believer, then growth is freer and much more rapid.[95]

Wood quoted Dr. Hibbard as denying that there is a "gradual growing out of sin." There is a growth in grace, but such growth is not in itself the removal of sin. One can grow in grace, do good works, and reach a degree of maturity without being pure at heart. Purity is the result of an act of God in the heart of the believer.[96] Purity is attained, not gradually, but instantly by faith.[97] Maturity comes to one after many years of growth and culture. Wesley did not make the same kind of distinction, although his teaching becomes clearer when such a distinction is made. However, where Wood emphasized the instantaneous character of cleansing as in a moment, Wesley was more insistent on a gradual cleansing from the beginning of sanctification at regeneration to its completion in entire sanctification. Wesley saw an increase in purity, as well as in maturity, between the two works of grace. There is a gradual death to sin.[98] The perfecting grace is negative as well as positive.[99]

Although Wesley differed with the reformers on the doctrine of regeneration by making it a more drastic inner change than they, his concept of gradual sanctification was not too different. Luther taught that the believer has "grace" and "gift." Grace makes the believer wholly gracious, and "all his sins are fully remitted." But the believer is not fully healed. The "gift" is the sanctifying gift.[100] Of course Luther did not see a perfecting of this healing in the present life, as did Wesley.

Interestingly enough Warfield, a Calvinist, who opposed perfectionism so strongly, taught an incomplete eradication of the sin principle in this life. He claimed that the Scriptures did provide for the "eradication" of sin, not just a "counteraction" of it. To cleanse the stream is to cleanse the fountain. But he saw no complete cleansing in this life, only a continual act which is completed "hereafter."[101] Calvin taught that sin is destroyed in the believer by a continual process, but such cleansing is not complete before death.[102]

On gradual sanctification Wesley appeared to follow the Reformed teaching. On this subject he had little controversy with his opponents. Real disagreement arose over his teaching of entire sanctification, or Christian perfection, as attainable here and now. Many were ready to agree with the teaching of a perfecting grace that was progressively working, but few would agree to a completing of that process in this life. It is in this idea that one encounters Wesley's major emphasis in his doctrine of perfection.

E. Entire Sanctification

Many who will go with Wesley on his earlier stages of perfection refuse to grant the possibility of entire sanctification in this life. For them it is a "hereafter blessing" reserved for the heavenly existence. Christians may have the beginnings of it now, but that perfection can be only for the saints in heaven.

But Wesley was insistent that this advanced stage of Christian perfection was for the Christian in this world. As early as 1726 he saw that "simplicity of intention, and purity of affection" along with "one design in all that we speak or do, and one desire ruling all the tempers" were the prerequisites for ascending to God. This perfection, he taught in 1733, "is that habitual disposition of soul which, in the sacred writings, is termed holiness; and which directly implies, the being cleansed from sin . . . and the being endued with those virtues which were in Jesus Christ. . . ."[103] Wesley claimed to have this same view in 1777.[104]

As already suggested, Wesley believed in two instantaneous experiences: justification, which was also concomitant with regeneration; and initial sanctification as given in a moment in response to saving faith. It is preceded by a gradual work of God leading to repentance and faith.

After this first experience there is a gradual sanctification including both dying to sin and growing in grace. At another point along this pathway God speaks the second time and the believer is sanctified wholly. From this moment of second blessing growth in grace continued toward the final triumph of the saint.

In this section it will be pointed out what importance Wesley attached to this special experience. Since this stage is called Christian perfection and was the distinct message of Wesley, the entire next chapter will be devoted to this "Present Perfection." This experience of entire sanctification was instantanous and came by faith. For Wesley it was scriptural and could be proved by experience. This special blessing could be lost and later restored. It was a higher way for the Christian but enabled him to live a more complete life with much yet ahead. Basically, entire sanctification was a freedom from all sinfulness of heart.

At first Wesley was not certain whether this entire sanctification was obtained gradually or instantaneously. The question was not whether it could be attained or not—he believed it could be. But the "how" of attainment was disputed. Wesley declared that "the Scriptures are silent on the subject . . . the point is not determined, at least in express terms, in any part of the oracles of God." Because of this silence Wesley felt a certain degree of liberty should be allowed on the point. Yet he urged that, whether instantaneous or gradual, one should not rest until the work was wrought in the soul if he desired to dwell in glory with God.[105]

Why then was Wesley so insistent on the instantaneous teaching? He observed closely over a period of 45 years the lives of many who professed the blessing. In all that time he did not find one who claimed to be sanctified wholly in a gradual manner. The change was always wrought in a moment. Wesley could have accepted a testimony to a gradual change, but none was to be found. So he was forced to conclude on the basis of experience that entire sanctification was commonly, if not always, an instantaneous work.[106] Wesley was more sure of the doctrine of the instantaneous change after 1760 and declared it more emphatically.[107] Without doubt it was the main doctrine of his ministry.[108]

In fact Wesley believed that the teaching of the instantaneous sanctification was an essential prerequisite for gradual sanctification.

> You are all agreed, we may be saved from all sin before death. The substance then is settled; but, as to the circumstance, is the change gradual or instantaneous? It is both the one and the other. From the moment we are justified, there may be a gradual sanctification, a growing in grace, a daily advance in the knowledge and love of God. And if sin cease before death, there must, in the nature of the thing, be an instantaneous change; there must be a last moment wherein it does exist, and a first moment wherein it does not. . . . Certainly we must insist on the gradual change; and that earnestly and continually. And are there not reasons why we should insist on the instantaneous also? If there be such a blessed change before death, should we not encourage all believers to expect it? and the rather, because constant experience shows, the more earnestly they expect this, the more swiftly and steadily does the gradual work of God go on in their soul; the more watchful they are against all sin, the more careful to grow in grace, the more zealous of good works, and the more punctual in their attendance on all the ordinances of God. Whereas, just the contrary effects are observed whenever this expectation ceases. . . . Therefore whoever would advance the gradual change in believers should strongly insist on the instantaneous.[109]

Obviously Wesley saw no inconsistency or overlapping in his acceptance of both gradual and instantaneous sanctification.

Entire sanctification came by faith. This experience was, in Wesley's mind, similar to justification as to the conditions by which it came. Works are essential to the faith and are a remote condition for sanctification, but the immediate condition is faith. "Believe, and be saved." This sanctification is "received by plain, simple faith."[110] This idea of Wesley's is found in the Catholic tradition, although Catholics do not teach instantaneous sanctification.[111]

Wesley always insisted that the goal of entire sanctification be placed at the proper level—that is, not too high. It was a perfection consistent with man's present existence and must be kept within biblical bounds. Those who opposed his teachings always placed the state too high. A contemporary writer opposes Christian perfection because of a different definition:

> It is the uniform experience of all who have come to Christ for saving mercy that *in Christ* they are *sinlessly per-*

fect, while in themselves they remain unclean. Since the
heart of a Christian has been regenerated, he enjoys holy
affections. Yet, a defect in his will remains, for though he
cordially assents to the mind of Christ, he finds that it is
not possible to match that decision with perfection in act.
And since absolute perfection is a good will coupled with good
actions, it follows that saving goodness resides in Christ, not
in the Christian.[112]

This definition by E. J. Carnell makes perfection to be what
neither Wesley, Catholics, nor Paul intended it to be! According to Wesley between the "absolute perfection" and
"regeneration" suggested above there is a Christian perfection
attainable by faith.

Even though Wesley placed this perfection within the
reach of all, he believed only a few attained it.[113] Many
who attained this experience later lost it, but it could be
regained.[114] It was the privilege for all, and all Christians
should strive for it. However, Wesley did not teach that
attainment was a necessity for salvation. He wrote, "Let it
be well remembered, I do not affirm that all who do not
walk in this way are in the high road to hell." If Christians
walked the lower way, they would find "mercy in the close
of life, through the blood of the covenant."[115] But Christian
perfection, the higher way, is within the reach of every
Christian.[116]

Nor did Wesley set Christian perfection as the final goal
for the Christian life. There is much ahead for the entirely
sanctified.[117] With the Apostle Paul the entirely sanctifed
could disclaim the perfection which will come with the prize
(Phil. 3:12) while he was among the perfect, the "strong in
faith," who are running the race (Phil. 3:15). In his comment
on this passage Wesley observed that there is a difference
between the perfect and the perfected. "The one is fitted
for the race, ver. 15, the other, ready to receive the prize."[118]

However, Wesley did insist that this stage of perfection—
this Christian perfection—is a freedom from willful sinning—
this comes with regeneration; it is more than power over
inbred sin—this victory also is for all Christians. It clearly
is freedom from all inward sin that remains in the believer.
"It is not only a deliverance from doubts and fears, but
from sin; from all inward as well as outward sin; from evil
desires, and evil tempers, as well as from evil words and

works."[119] This phase of holiness will be dealt with more minutely in the next chapter, but it is at this point that Wesley encountered his greatest opposition.

It was this kind of perfection—freedom from all sin in this life—that found no place with the reformers or with men in the Reformed tradition. "Neither Calvin nor Luther had any conception of a life lived on earth so full of love that it would be free from sin."[120] A. Kuyper, a nineteenth-century Reformed theologian, saw the body as so corrupted that there was no freedom from sin apart from freedom from the body. Yet for him such perfection was necessary for heaven.[121] Luther wrote that the believer "should not presume that 'by-and-by' he will be changed thoroughly into a new man. He will keep some of his old vices cleaving to him, however good and perfect a Christian he is." The reason is that we still live in the flesh that lusteth.[122] Calvin did not see any deliverance from the "relics" of sin that remain. This sinfulness is to humble the Christian and cause him to depend on the saving Christ.[123]

Is this stage of perfection in Wesley's thought a valid one? He believed so and held that without it the whole cause for holiness was lost. If an attainable goal were not held out before the believer, he would become discouraged and fail to grow. People can hardly be blamed for not being what they are taught they cannot become. David Roberts in his book, *Psychotherapy and a Christian View of Man,* makes an interesting observation:

> Divine love (*agape*) is taken as the norm for human life; insofar as a man falls short of it, he is sinful; insofar as it is being fulfilled in him, he is redeemed and tending toward salvation. Yet because Christ is regarded as the only man who ever has or ever could perfectly embody *agape,* this norm is put beyond the reach of the rest of the race. From such a perspective it is always possible to condemn men for failing to follow Christ; but if they are told that Christ alone could fulfill such perfection anyway, they are hardly to be blamed for thinking that the condemnation is unreasonable. This doctrine scolds them for not being replicas of Christ, and then scolds them if they believe that they could be . . . If there is nothing in the individual akin to Christ, then Christ, as a norm for his life is simply alien—and powerless.[124]

Wesley believed that the Christian was "akin to Christ," that Christ was the "norm for his life," and that what was expected of the Christian by God could be fulfilled. A transformation was needed—a deeper one than at justification—and this one came to the believer and lifted him to a plane where he could live holy. On this plane of perfect holiness one could "live" and "grow" and experience the pure love (*agape*) of God in the heart. He now possessed the fully restored image of God that was lost in the fall of man. This realizable goal is a necessity for Christianity.

> We reach, then, this broad conclusion, that the seeking of an ideal that is realizable in this world is essential to Christianity. It is essential to the corporate life of the Church that this principle should be enshrined at the heart of its doctrines, its hymns, its confessions of faith, its institutions. It is essential for the individual Christian that the goal set before him should be not merely conversion, nor merely a life of service, but perfection. Or if the term is disliked, let it be Wesley's phrase—"perfect love," or "sanctity," or "holiness." "If we have no hunger and thirst after that righteousness which is Christ, we are not Christians . . . at all." Christianity is not Christianity unless it is aiming at Perfection.[125]

F. GLORIFICATION

This final stage of perfection, if it can be called final, is attained in the resurrection. It could be called resurrection perfection. It was possible for Wesley to see three main stages in salvation—justification, sanctification, and glorification. This final stage was heaven, or what came after death.[126] A clear analysis of Wesley's thought reveals that he saw in glorification another great change in man. It would be misleading to ascribe to Wesley the teaching that Christian perfection affected a glorification.

Although Wesley allowed certain degrees of perfection to be attainable in this life, he always held that final perfection came after death. One did wrong to think he could possess a perfection now that belongs only to angels. Even Adam had a perfection in Eden which no man could attain before death.[127] There was a perfection of knowledge, and a freedom from mistakes, infirmities, and temptation that could come only in the next life.[128] Wesley constantly opposed setting Christian perfection too high by including in it ingredients of the resurrection.[129]

Wesley never hesitated to deny certain ideas of perfection as being possessed by Methodists. He headed his treatise

The Character of a Methodist with the caption, "Not as though I had already attained, either were already perfect." He wanted to be excused from the claim of being perfect, and of sinning "not in thought, word or deed." He wrote, "I have told all the world I am not perfect. . . . I tell you flat, I have not attained the character I draw."[130] Wesley did not in this denial disclaim Christian perfection so much as he was denying the absoluteness of perfection in the Christian's life. He knew there was much yet to gain before death and afterwards, as will be seen in Chapter V.

As already suggested, Wesley did not teach that the person who was not yet entirely sanctified was under condemnation.

> By "perfection," I mean "perfect love," or the loving God with all our heart, so as to rejoice evermore, to pray without ceasing, and in everything to give thanks. I am convinced every believer may attain this; yet I do not say, he is in a state of damnation, or under the curse of God, till he does attain. No, he is in a state of grace, and in favour with God, as long as he believes. Neither would I say, "If you die without it, you will perish;" but rather, till you are saved from unholy tempers, you are not ripe for glory. There will therefore more promises be fulfilled in your soul, before God takes you to himself.[131]

Yet Wesley held that one must be ripe for glory before death if he were to be saved eternally. This can only mean that the believer who is living in faith but who has not yet experienced the change of entire sanctification would sovereignly be made thus perfect if death overtook him.[132]

There is a significant distinction made by Wesley between the sins of the heart, or inward sinfulness, and the weaknesses and infirmities of the body. He believed that all sin, outward and inward, must be gone before death came. Death did not separate us from sin. Such separation came by a supernatural work of God in the heart, or spirit of man, and was a change wrought in this life.[133] But this deliverance from sin did not mean a freedom from the body, or from finite existence. The body of man is corrupted, but is not sinful.

> *A sinful body?* I pray observe, how deeply ambiguous, how equivocal, this expression is! But there is no authority for it in Scripture: the word *sinful body* is never found there. And as it is totally unscriptural, so it is palpably absurd. For no

100

body, or matter of any kind, can be *sinful*: Spirits alone are capable of sin. Pray in what part of the body should sin lodge? . . . Only the soul can be the seat of sin.[134]

Wesley held that Paul's use of the world "flesh" did not refer to the body in most cases, but to man's condition as a natural man apart from God and in unbelief. For him it was just as possible to sanctify a man while in the body as out of it. In fact it was God's purpose to purify the soul while it was resident in the earthly body.

Though the body could not keep the soul from being pure and holy, it could be a "clog" to it as the life of holiness was being lived. "In this state, our bodies are no better than clogs and fetters, which confine and restrain the freedom of the soul. . . . Our dull, sluggish, inactive bodies are often unable, or backward, to obey the commands of the soul."[135] This limitation upon man's present perfection will be discussed in Chapter V. The point to make here is that Wesley taught a perfection attainable while in a corruptible body. The stage of final perfection could be only when this body shall be changed. In this glorification the consequences of sin will be done away.

> And, indeed, this is the principal difference between a mortal and a glorified body. This flesh is the most dangerous enemy we have: we therefore deny and renounce it in our baptism. It constantly tempts us to evil. Every sense is a snare to us. : . . . The best of men are forced to keep it under. . . . How soon does it jade our minds when employed on holy things! How easily by its enchanting pleasures, does it divert them from those noble exercises! But when we have obtained the resurrection unto life, our bodies will be spiritualized, purified and refined from our earthly grossness; then they will be fit instruments for the soul in all its divine and heavenly employment; we shall not be weary of singing praises to God through infinite ages.[136]

The only connection Wesley saw between a fallen, corruptible, weak, and erring humanity, and sinfulness was that the depraved body was occasion for sinning, and could keep the soul from any perfect expression of its pure desires. But in no sense could the natural body itself be sinful or keep the soul from purity.

In this concept Wesley was different from the Reformed position. Whether the reformers placed sin in the physical nature of man may be questioned, but the relation to the body was so close that separation seemed to them impossible. Luther wrote that the "Christian man hath a body, in whose members . . . sin dwelleth and warreth." This sin is the root and the tree, rooted "in the baptized flesh of every Christian" and holds it captive. It forces him mightily to do wrong.[137] He further wrote that "all apostles and saints confess that sin and the sinful passions remain in us till the body is turned into ashes, and a new body is raised up which is free from passion and sin."[138] Glorification for Luther also meant entire sanctification.

For Barth being a man in the temporal state is the same as being sinful. To expect any change now would be to want time to run its course and to stand at our destination. In this life we are still prisoners of evil and of the devil.[139] This view, which Barth later modified, identifies sin and human existence and makes any freedom from sin impossible for now. Niebuhr considers sin to be inevitable in human existence.[140] For Wesley the only inevitable sins were the "sins" growing out of fallen human existence, but these were not sins in the proper scriptural sense. The line between these "sins" and the willful sins or sins of the heart could be drawn, and Wesley attempted to do so. But Niebuhr feels the command to love one's neighbor is impossible in this life. This love commandment is an "impossible possibility." The faith that thinks it possible is rooted in a faulty analysis of human nature and fails to see man as a creature of finiteness.[141]

If Niebuhr be right, then, in Wesley's view, the faulty analysis of human nature is in the Bible, not only in the "faith." The Bible teaches a present deliverance from sin, but this freedom is not from finiteness. Temporal human existence ceases when man is glorified and the natural body is made perfect. It then becomes a perfect instrument for the soul. Wesley clearly distinguished between the present perfection of soul attainable in this life and the future perfection of human nature attainable in the next life. The first frees the believer from sinfulness of heart; the second will free him from all the evil consequences of sin.

CHAPTER IV

PRESENT PERFECTION

That Wesley taught a perfection that is attainable in the present life by believers none will deny who know his writings. It was this teaching that was the point of issue in his own day and is still the point of controversy when the battle line is drawn between the teaching of perfection and imperfection. Neither group has won in this controversy, and neither can win. It is only when it is resolved into a sympathetic understanding of definitions that any peace can be found.

There are several categories into which the opposing schools on perfection can be placed according to Henry Brockett.

> The first taught a radical cleansing or freeing from indwelling sin by the blood of Christ, and the baptism with the Holy Spirit and fire as a definite second work of grace. . . . The second class taught the need of the filling of the Spirit for power in service, but they were not clear and definite as to what Christ did with indwelling sin in the heart. They seemed to teach a cleansing of a sort, but it still left indwelling sin in the heart. In the third category were those who were horrified at the very idea of an actual cleansing of the heart from indwelling sin in this life. They resolutely opposed this teaching and contended strongly for the necessary continuance of indwelling sin in the heart of every Christian so long as we are in this world.[1]

This classification by Brockett is a modern one. It points out the association of cleansing with the baptism of the Holy Spirit by the first group. Also it indicates that the real contention is at the point of what happens to sin in the heart.

Warfield was a consistent opponent of any perfectionism. For him "perfection is a superlative notion and admits no growth beyond it."[2] With this definition no kind of perfection could be attainable here and now. To think so is a great evil:

> One of the gravest evils of the perfectionist teaching is that it tempts us to be satisfied with earthly attainments, and to forget the heavenly glory. It is an old remark that the

more saint-like a man is, the less saint-like he feels: the less evil there is to see in him the more evil the evil that remains is seen to be.[3]

Obviously Warfield had little conception of what Wesley was trying to teach in his doctrine of Christian perfection. In fact in his two-volume work Warfield makes no analysis of Wesley's own writings, which he claimed were the source of most perfectionist teaching. It is only right that, whether one agrees with Wesley's terms or not, he should endeavor to discover what it was Wesley was trying to convey with these terms.

McConnell criticized Wesley for using the word perfection as an attainable goal now. It should be a goal but only a goal. Wesley, he said, was sound in urging men to push toward the goal but unsound in thinking one could claim attainments. He thought that Wesley tried to adjust to facts but that he created confusion. "There is not much spiritual edification to be found in most Methodist exposition of perfection."[4] Whether or not there is spiritual edification in the exposition of perfection, the truth Wesley taught should not be lost for want of a better term.

In this chapter Wesley's concept of Christian perfection as a present reality will be investigated. What was this experience that the believer could attain in this life? Is there a level in the process of Christian growth where one is made perfect in love? Can this new level be called entire sanctification, or freedom from sin? Is this properly called a second work of grace, and if so, is it possible for all believers? What is actually done in the believer in this act of God, and what is not done? Wesley's answers may drive away some of the confusion.

A. IT IS ATTAINABLE

Martin Foss defines perfection as the "conformity of a reality to its concept. Wherever a thing is found adequate to the idea which we have of it that thing is perfect." And again "purpose, end is the essence of perfection."

We may speak of a perfect butler, a perfect cook, a perfect physician. In society where men are usually objectified, classified according to their purposes, or according to their usefulness, the concept of perfection plays a great role. Society

> simplifies and abbreviates its members to executors of their
> social purposes, their social professions. This far and only this
> far they are evaluated, and if they are adequate to their purpose
> in the social scheme, they are called perfect. So we have
> perfect typists, perfect lawyers, perfect accountants.[5]

Certainly if the term perfection can be used in this relative fashion to denote various spheres of life, it would not be invalid to speak of a stage of perfection in the Christian life that would be short of an absolute perfection. When a certain end or purpose is formulated as a goal, then its attainment can be classed as perfect. This is exactly what Wesley has done as he attempted to follow Christ and Paul. There is a goal attainable in this life for the believer, and when that goal is reached, in this sense one is perfect.[6]

Clearly, such use of the term perfection does necessitate definition, and Wesley was adept at such. Because he defined, and occasionally varied his definitions, some have accused him of change of view. "He did not modify his teaching on the subject of perfection in the direction of less *insistence* upon it; if anything, he urged it even more strongly."[7]

> Usually Wesley adhered tenaciously to what he considered
> the essential thing while he made modifications in minor
> matters. Thus all along he emphasized the doctrine of Christian
> perfection and strongly presented the duty of Scriptural sanc-
> tification. These words were prominently mentioned in the
> Bible and involve important Christian and Biblical doctrines.
> Wesley never abandoned them, nor their teaching, but he was
> not always insistent as to certain subordinate questions or
> minor details connected with them.[8]

In his definitions Wesley was insistent that the goal of perfection be kept at an attainable point. He felt that setting the goal too high was wrong, as well as setting it too low. Whether Wesley succeeded in making this goal a scriptural one and within the reach of all will be noted in the next two sections. It is here suggested that Wesley had a right and obligation to set an attainable goal for the Christian believer. Who will strive for a goal he is told he cannot attain? The surest way to defeat is to be told you can never arrive. Wesley firmly believed that there was an experience for every believer somewhere between justification and final glory and that he was called to help people attain that blessing. He held out hope that all could attain it.[9]

Failure to insist upon an attainable goal in Christian life results in a weak Christianity. Sangster believes that holiness is the deep privation of the Church. Too many, he thinks, want to leave holiness to the cranks after reading a couple volumes like Warfield's *Perfectionism*. He says that "no man has a right to put a limit to what the grace of God can do." He concludes that, whether preachers like the word perfection or not, they are hirelings if they fail to preach holiness.[10] Sangster sees that modern scholars such as Dr. Flew and Dr. Vincent Taylor agree with Wesley in the conclusion that "the New Testament plainly teaches that the Christian need not sin."[11]

Whether or not God's grace perfects the heart of the believer to the point that some claim, it does bring him to some point, and that point needs defining.

> How far the sanctifying of the heart can go is open to question. There is sharp genuine difference of opinion among the various theological traditions regarding the possibility of achieving holiness during earthly life. A thoroughgoing treatment of this question is clearly impossible here. But lest the quest for perfection be too summarily dismissed, let it be said that the problems entailed in affirming the possibility of achieving it in this life are no greater than the dangers of comfortable satisfaction with imperfection when the possibility is denied.

> Jesus' words, "Blessed are the pure in heart: for they shall see God," show the necessity for the entire consecration of the inner life . . . Purity of heart is essential to continuance in the way of salvation.[12] (Copyright 1950 by Pierce and Smith.)

However, any definition of the attainable experience will have its limitations. Many people experience something which it is impossible to clearly formulate in a theory.

> In spite of extravagances and misinterpretations, the experience was too widespread to be denied and too fundamental to be destroyed by ridicule or contempt. He would be a strange critic who could read the intimate confessions of so many obviously sincere people, and conclude that they were empty vapourings. It would be more reasonable to say that in them are movements of the Spirit, too great to be confined within the limits of a theory and too varied to be brought down to a common denominator. In attempting to reduce such experience to a formula there is always the danger of imprisoning the soul.[13]

Wesley did not imprison the soul, but left the door open for great spiritual heights. Many successors to Wesley may have developed stereotyped concepts of God's work, but not John Wesley. He constantly sought for better ways to inspire the soul to holiness.[14]

Roberts claims that the central question in salvation has to do with the effectiveness of ideal standards. There are two conflicting answers—static and dynamic. "The static view assumes that ethical and religious progress is most effectively promoted, and the perils of indifference and irresponsibility are best avoided, by holding before the eyes of men a vision of perfection which will keep them perpetually ashamed of themselves." This ideal is actualized in Christ, and this actualization is accessible to the race by divine grace. Man could not achieve it for himself, but Christ did achieve it. Yet it imposed an obligatory pattern without regard to the needs of a changing individual, on which pattern one is approved or condemned. "Such a view keeps belief and conduct at odds with each other; it anticipates and asserts that man must always fall short of what he believes." This believer is to repent continually. His salvation is outside and apart from himself and his need. "Indeed, if he believes that he can make any positive contribution toward it, his failure to acknowledge complete dependence upon God is a sign of pride, and additional indication that he is enslaved to sin." It is static because salvation is thought of, not as discovery and dynamic change in man, but as an alteration of status before God. Such leads to hypocrisy, self-righteousness, and despair.[15]

On the other hand, the dynamic view of salvation is preferable. It resolves the conflict and brings organic harmony. "It cures the guilt, not by putting forward ideas which assure men willy-nilly that they are 'all right,' but by releasing a power which removes the causes of guilt." The stock objection to this is that men would accept themselves at a low level. "But clinical data of psychotherapy point to an opposite conclusion. Most emotional disorders and behavior problems reveal a pattern where the individual has *not* reached self-acceptance. . . ." Salvation then needs a realizable ideal, and should be thought of in terms of a "dynamic transformation" of the man. In this change the "creative and redemptive power of God" brings a condition of wholeness and freedom.[16]

This dymanic view of salvation by Roberts expresses very well the Wesleyan concept. Many of Wesley's contemporaries who were Calvinistic asserted that complete cleansing came at death by a stroke of divine power. Wesley held that this victory could be antedated by five, 10, or 20 years. What could come at death could come now, he reasoned.[17] Niebuhr is incorrect when he says that Wesley "declared that there was no moment in life for which real perfection could be claimed except the moment just before death."[18] Even a casual reading of Wesley reveals that he did teach a perfection attainable before death and he constantly urged believers to aim for it. This was a "real" perfection although it was not "final" or "absolute." Speaking of instantaneous sanctification Wesley wrote:

> *Thou* therefore look for it every moment! Look for it in the way above described; in all those *good works* whereunto thou art "created anew in Christ Jesus." There is then no danger; you can be no worse, if you are no better, for that expectation. For were you to be disappointed of your hope, still you lose nothing. But you shall not be disappointed of your hope: It will come, and will not tarry. Look for it then every day, every hour, every moment! Why not this hour, this moment? Certainly you may look for it *now,* if you believe it is by faith. . . . Expect *it by faith,* expect it *as you are,* and expect it *now!*[19]

Whatever this reality is for which Wesley was aiming and which he urged upon others, it is clear that it was attainable in life. Wesley was convinced of this. And it appears reasonable that Wesley should have had an attainable goal. The next question is, Did he include in this goal elements that are beyond man's earthly reach? Did he go beyond Scripture and valid experience?

B. It Is Scriptural

Reinhold Niebuhr thinks that Wesley's conception of perfection contained the largest biblical element as compared to other perfectionist teachings. The deliverance that Wesley taught was from sin, not from finiteness, and the process was in existential and not in contemplative terms.[20] Wesley considered himself to be scriptural in his doctrines and would have discarded any theory which he found to be contrary to the Bible. Many of Wesley's critics would agree that he was scriptural in his general view of salvation but oppose his view that the believer can be entirely sanctified in this life. It is this idea of present perfection that ran into difficulty with others.

Sangster quotes the Reverend Mr. Webb-Peploe at the Keswick Convention in 1895 as saying:

> "When I read such words as dear John Wesley's, 'The evil root, the carnal mind, is destroyed in me; sin subsists no longer,' I can only marvel that any human being, with the teaching of the Holy Ghost upon the Word of God, can thus deceive himself, or attempt to deceive others. It is, I think, a miracle of blindness that we can study God's word, and imagine that any man can be free from sin experimentally while here in the mortal body."[21]

Very likely Wesley would have wondered at Webb-Peploe's "blindness" in not seeing the scriptural freedom from sin! Again it must be emphasized that the definition of sin could make the difference of understanding. If the following is an example of the exegesis of those who desire to allow for sinfulness, its soundness might be questioned.

> And the present tense in the declaration, "No one that is begotten of God sins," appears to open the way to understanding it of the general life-manifestation, rather than of a particular act. What John means in that case is not that he who has been begotten of God never commits a sin, but that not sinning is the characteristic of his life. We may say, if we choose, that ideally, in principle, he that has been begotten of God does not sin. It is probably best to say simply that this is what it is to be one who has been begotten of God—not to sin; and Christians who have been begotten of God are therefore in process of becoming sinless. That they are not yet sinless does not prove that they have not been begotten of God, but they have not yet reached their goal.[22]

Would it not be better to let the Apostle John mean what he says, and let the sin he is talking about be according to his own definition—meaning "lawlessness" (I John 3:4)? Wesley was right when he said that the regenerated sinner is finished with this kind of sin, as St. John declared.[23]

What about the person who is cleansed from the root of sin? Does Wesley have scripture for this teaching?

We cannot say, on the ground of grammar, that Scripture teaches that perfection is unattainable on earth. It is not a just inference from the grammatical form to suggest that it is "only an ideal" in the New Testament: that the exalted standard is set before us without either expectation of possibility of our achievement, and that we have dealt seriously with the solemn admonitions of Scripture if we put them in the same category as the proverbial impossibility of "hitching your wagon to a star."

To suggest that God lays commands on mortals which are utterly incapable of fulfillment is to make nonsense of the moral passion of the New Testament and to reflect adversely on the holy character of God. How else can God—or man—lay a charge on others except in the imperative mood? Nor need it be inferred, because the future tense is used, that it must necessarily be the distant future long after death.[24]

Reference has been made in this paper to Turner's investigation of the scriptural basis for the Wesleyan message. Concerning the Old Testament he concludes as follows:

1. The exhortation to moral integrity, wholeness, soundness, sincerity, or perfection is very prominent in the Old Testament, especially in the prophetic literature.

2. Of the some two hundred and thirty occurrences of synonyms for perfection about seventy-two refer to man's character.

3. A "perfect" man is one characterized by moral integrity, sincerity, and loyalty to Jehovah.

4. Such perfection is commanded and expected of all the people of God.

5. This concept of perfection emphasizes the possibility of man's becoming like Jehovah in character.

6. Such a divine-human fellowship is based on the ideas of holiness, such as separation unto God and cleansing from all defilement whether ceremonial or moral.[25]

Concerning the results of the New Testament study Turner writes:

On the whole the New Testament ideal of perfection, while more implicit than explicit, envisions the complete redemption of man from sin. It emerges from the following beliefs: (1) sin is not only an act but a principle; (2) this remains in believers; (3) believers have the alternative of either (a) maintaining the "status quo," or (b) going on to perfection—purification and maturity in love and grace; (4) God is holy and heaven is a holy place, hence sin must be dealt with either in the next life, at death, or in this life; (5) it is during this life that God promises to "save his people from their sins" and to perfect them in love. Unlike Gnosticism it is not the emancipation of man from matter, unlike philosophy it is not deliverance from ignorance; it is rather deliverance from sin and this assurance is voiced without qualifying reservations.[26]

Many will agree with Turner that God does demand holiness of His people, and that He promises to make them perfect, and that this work of perfecting has begun and will continue in life. But when the claim is made that this work of making holy can have a terminal point before death, a great number will object. Can one be certain and was Wesley sure that the Bible taught this victory could come before death?

Wesley did deal with this problem specifically many times. He allowed that the Calvinists were right in claiming that many who have died were not sanctified until a little before death. He agreed that people who were justified are sanctified, though not entirely. He granted that the inspired writers seldom wrote to the entirely sanctified, but mainly addressed the justified believers. He saw that the point of division with his opponents was that the believer could be sanctified wholly, or saved from all sin, before the article of death. Then he asked, "Is there any clear Scripture promise of this; that God will save us from *all* sin?"

> There is: "He shall redeem Israel from *all* his sins," (Psalm CXXX, 8.) This is more largely expressed in the prophecy of Ezekiel: "Then will I sprinkle clean water upon you, and ye shall be clean; from *all* your filthiness, and from *all* your idols, will I cleanse you. I will also save you from *all* your uncleanness," (XXXVI, 25, 29.) No promise can be more clear. And to this the Apostle plainly refers in that exhortation: "Having these promises, let us cleanse ourselves from all filthiness of flesh and spirit, perfecting holiness in the fear of God," (2 Cor. VII, 1.) Equally clear and express is that ancient promise: "The Lord thy God will circumcise thine heart, and the heart of thy seed, to love the Lord thy God with all thy heart and with all thy soul," (Deut. XXX, 6.)[27]

Wesley then went ahead to list promises, prayers, and commands concerning perfection and holiness found in the New Testament. Then he asked, "How does it appear that this is to be done before the article of death?" His answer was, "From the very nature of a command, which is not given to the dead, but to the living." The command to "love"

111

is to love now while we live. Then he quoted Titus 2:11-14, which declares that "we should live soberly, righteously, and godly, in this present world" and that we are to be purified a "peculiar people, zealous of good works." Also in Luke 1:69-75, we are to be delivered from our enemies so we can serve God in holiness and righteousness "all the days of our life."[18] Wesley saw in these scriptures an experience for the believer which was for this life, not after death. This holiness or perfection was needed now while in the present world. It need not and should not be postponed until death.

There is a "Scriptural perfection" according to Wesley. No one in conscience can object to it unless he "would send the Holy Ghost to school, and teach Him who made the tongue." One who loves God and his neighbor is scripturally perfect and can become so if he is not yet there, because "the scripture cannot be broken." Wesley never contended for absolute or infallible perfection. He did not see any sinless perfection in the Bible. No perfection that demanded a keeping of the whole law was found in the Word, so Wesley protested against any such perfection. He desired to keep the concept of perfection with its scriptural meaning.[29]

Wesley knew his Bible. He claimed to be a man of one Book.[30] He knew the original languages of the Bible. He sought the guidance and help of the Holy Spirit. To him it was not a new doctrine as justification by faith was. He taught and believed it over a period of 60 or more years and felt he had not basically changed his concept.[31] To him it was the reason for his calling and the basis for the revival. This doctrine was Wesley's great contribution to the Christian Church.

> The first thing that will strike a careful student of Wesley's doctrine is the essential sobriety of it. Here is no theological subtlety or devotional extravagance. It is the plain teaching of Scripture, and the actual experience of believers, that is the standard throughout. Wesley would never have dealt with this matter of Christian Perfection at all if it had not been an actual element in the experience of believers, both as reflected in the New Testament and as discovered afresh in the lives of his own followers.[32]

Whether or not one agrees that Wesley's doctrine of Christian perfection is founded on the Scriptures will depend largely on his point of view and religious bias. It is difficult to discard Wesley's central doctrine without discounting his effective role in the history of Protestantism. It may be that the neglect of his central doctrine may mean the loss of a central message of the Bible!

C. It Is an Experience

The term "experience" can be given a very broad meaning. When it is "particular acquaintance with any matter by personal observation or trial of it," it is made the equivalent of personal knowledge of external facts and of all internal states of feeling. It is better to look upon the objective facts as "experiment" and upon the subjective as experience. "Experience more specifically relates to the internal states and feelings, existing as present, or recalled as past, consciousnesses, through which one has passed or is passing."[33] A Christian experience, then, is the "subjective life implanted in the soul" of which one becomes conscious. It is a direct act of God upon the human soul by which he is made a Christian soul. These experiences are varied with individuals, and do have successive stages, but are wrought by the one Holy Spirit.[34]

With Wesley salvation was to be experienced. It was not something wrought by God in the past and *made known* to man in the declaration of the gospel. This objective fact was the great act of God in Christ in behalf of man, while salvation was the work of God through the Spirit in the hearts and lives of men. With the very dawn of consciousness grace begins to work in men. As they yield to that grace they experience more and more of its power. It leads through successive stages of experience from the early conviction for sin to the final glorification after death. For Wesley this could be one long, grand experience ever increasing in glory throughout time and in eternity.

However, it must be remembered that Wesley saw Christian experience not only as a continual work of grace but also as an instantaneous crisis. He actually taught two major crises in the work of salvation. The first he called justification, although it included regeneration, initial sanctification, and adoption. These all occurred at the same moment. There was the gradual approach to this crisis experience, but there

113

came the instant when the gift was given, and the work of grace was accomplished. This instantaneous act of God was a perfect one in the sense that the sinner was perfectly forgiven and was given a new life and truly adopted into God's family. The initial sanctification was real in that the power of sin was broken, but there remained yet a finishing of this work of sanctification.

It was in the fact of an incomplete sanctification of the believer in the first crisis experience that Wesley saw a need for a second work of grace. This second experience would be preceded by a gradual sanctification and followed by continual growth. But there could come an instant in the life of the believer when he might experience this deeper act of God in the entire sanctification of his heart. It is this deeper, or second, experience with which this section on present perfection is concerned.

Is Wesley correct in looking upon religion as an experience? It is important to understand the place Wesley had in the formulation of the theology of experience.

> The investigator who turns from the literature of religion in the sixteenth century to examine the works of John Wesley will be struck with the appearance of a new term in theology: Experience. If the investigator comes to his subject with adequate discipline in the history of Christian thought, he will receive a similar but stronger impression. Before John Wesley the word "experience" does not occupy the conspicuous position in the preaching, teaching, writing of any master of doctrinal and practical Christianity. The reference to experience does occupy for the first time in the history of the Christian thought the conspicuous position in the Wesleyan understanding of the Gospel. In fact the appeal to experience is so pervasive and powerful as to determine its historical individuality. It is a theology of experience. It rests, to be sure, on two pillars: Scripture and experience. These are, however, taken and accepted not as alien and antagonistic, but cognate and congenial principles. The early Reformers, Luther and Calvin, introduced the principle of private judgment into Biblical theology and assumed the active mind to be essential to the practical religious use of the Scriptures. But owing to well-known circumstances the free activity of the mind on the subject matter of the Scriptures was in the sixteenth century hemmed and hedged within the narrowest limits. Two centuries later the reference to experience in theology, implicit in Protestantism, emerged in the midst of a great age of scientific discovery into power in the Wesleyan understanding of the Gospel.[35]

114

It is possible to push this matter of Christian experience too far as an objective authority:

> First of all, then, Wesley and the early Methodists grounded religion and theology in the fact of experience. This was a revolution in theological practice, for it was the revolutionary application to theology of what is really scientific method. At the Reformation, Catholicism took its final stand on the authority of the church, and Protestantism took its first stand on the authority of the Bible. Methodism, without altogether realizing what it was doing, shifted the ultimate authority in religion to the last place and the right—religious experience.[36]

Bett claimed further that "there is no mistaking the fact, that, with Wesley, experience is always the final test, though he probably did not always realize that it was so."[37] In this claim Bett cannot be entirely accurate, for Wesley never made experience valid unless it was based on the Scriptures. But the Scriptures are made authentic by "the sure testimony of experience."[38] Cell here correctly makes Scripture plus experience the final authority for Wesley.

This teaching on experience by Wesley placed him in the tradition of mysticism, although many mystics did not emphasize the authority of the Word.

> Mysticism and Methodism both build upon the foundation, not of argument or observation, but of conscious spiritual experience. The doctrine of assurance is not far removed from a belief in the 'inner light.' Hence Mystics and Methodists are one in their claim for spiritual certainty, though the claim is stated by the Mystic in more unguarded language than by the Methodist.[39]

It is true that Wesley spoke harshly of the mystics but apparently he meant the quietists.[40] They taught that moral striving and the means of grace were not essential. Wesley could not lay aside the Scriptures, reason, or the means of grace in his search for deeper experience. Wesley opposed an "enthusiasm" which rested entirely on feelings and which failed to recognize any other authority.[41]

In order really to know divine things Wesley believed one's "spiritual senses" must be opened. "It is necessary that you have the hearing ear, and the seeing eye, emphatically so called." These are found in a new class of senses opened to the soul different from organs of flesh and blood. They are "avenues to the invisible world" and they "discern spiritual objects." Until one has these "internal senses" he has no idea at all of divine things. One cannot cross the chasm to this knowledge until "the Almighty come in to your succour, and give you that faith you have hitherto despised."[42] Actually no one can understand the love of God until he has felt the "inward workings of the Spirit of God."[43] In other words no one can really understand forgiveness, new life, or sanctification until these are experienced in the soul. "For most people what is needed most is not a definition, but an experience, and then a sufficient working definition is found."[44]

In Reformed theology there is less emphasis on the transformation in the believer and more on the change in relationship with God. The real experience of the believer is the gift of faith whereby he sees himself as a sinner and helpless and yet at the same time wholly relies on Christ for forgiveness. There is little or no emphasis upon the inner change wrought in the heart of the Christian. It is more what God through Christ does *for* us, less on what He does *in* us. Obviously this fact leads to less significance for experience. Certainly Luther knew of a Christian experience and recognized a work of God *in* the believer. Hildebrandt believes that Luther was as much a mystic or enthusiast as was Wesley. Yet it is very evident that Wesley made much more of experience than did Luther. Primarily for Luther the holiness of the believer was outside himself—a heavenly holiness. There was a beginning of sanctification, but one could never experience a total cleansing.[45]

According to Henry Thiessen a believer is holy in Christ, so that he has a positional sanctification which is perfect. What he now has in Christ he is to work out in his life. The process of sanctification is carried out by the acts of man, not by an act of God. It is the believer who sets himself apart, not God.[46] Warfield saw this continuing work of sanctification as a work of God, but there was no "at once" experience of full cleansing.[47] John Murray sees sanctification as specifically the work of the indwelling Holy Spirit. But the work is gradual in experience and will not be complete in this life.[48] None of these writers in the Calvinist tradition allow for an experience of complete sanctification in this life.

Nonetheless there must be some explanation for that experience that comes to some people before death which is variously described by them. It is one thing to be dubious of the doctrine of a fuller or deeper experience in Christian grace; it is quite another thing to limit God's power to work a great transformation in the believer or to deny that He has done so. Many witnesses rise up to declare that God has wrought an experience within them subsequently to the first experience at justification, that this experience was instantaneous and produced a complete victory over sin. That the person who experienced this "second blessing" may be faulty in his definition can be allowed, but that one who has not so experienced could produce a better definition is questionable.

Cecil Northcott in discussing enthusiasm as "religion of the heart" sees religious experience as coming both personally and through the church ministration. He agrees with Ronald Knox in his book *Enthusiasm* that there were valid experiences in the Waldensians, Hussites, Catharists, Lollards, and in Wesley. This enthusiasm often created fresh division, but it also provided fresh life and the impetus of a new drive in religion. Northcott claims that on each side of the "Great Divide" between personal experience and tradition there is an enthusiasm that is "equally valid and vital." He feels that there has been a separation between the experiences derived through traditional church means and those which have come personally to individuals. Why not merge the two, he asks? While we wait in the religious experiences derived through traditional Christian worship, let us look for a revival of vital and authentic personal experience![49] This view corresponds quite closely to that of Wesley, who insisted on both the gradual and the instantaneous experiences.

One cannot set aside easily the great experiences of the mystics of all ages. In the Gospel of John, in Paul, Augustine, Bernard, Bonaventura, Thomas, Eckert, Tauler, Groote, Catherine of Siena, John of the Gross, Fox, Pascal, and in many others there is a common testimony. Though varied, their claim is single "that in this life they have known at first hand the living God; that he has invaded their souls and begun the transformation of their ground of being into harmonization with his own." This change is not just a faith, or hope, or aspiration, or promise, but "a fact that has happened to them." These mystics have seen this as a special grace given by God and have never claimed that if a person had it not he was not a child of God. This experience is universal in its drawing power and not closed to any. These mystics have gone ahead into the promised land before death and have reported back its bliss. This deeper level of transformation can be prepared for by fasting and prayer and mortification of the body, but these do not bring the experience; they only express the hunger. Always with them grace is uppermost.[50] Wesley had no doubt but that this experience of the mystics was possible for all. What the mystics and Methodists claimed as theirs he tried to define as the experience of a present perfection.

How can a believer enter into this second crisis experience? With the mystics Wesley believed that works prepare the way for this gift of God. One does not sanctify himself by fasting, prayer, and mortification, but these prepare the way for faith by which one is sanctified. Faith is the immediate and only condition for the experience, although good works are "remotely necessary." In other words, no one can expect God to give the faith essential to this experience if he is not striving toward it with every possible means. One is to look for the "blessing" every moment, but he is to look for it while he carries out the "good works" whereunto he is "created anew in Christ Jesus." Yet one must not feel that certain things *must* be done first; he is to expect this instantaneous experience *as he is* and *now*.[51]

Wesley was convinced that many of his people entered into this experience of Christian perfection. After recording the details of two such testimonies Wesley wrote in 1760:

> I observe the spirit and experience of these two run exactly parallel. Constant communion with God the Father and the Son fills their hearts with humble love. Now this is what I always did, and do now, mean by perfection. And this I believe many have attained, on the same evidence that I believe many are justified. May God increase their number a thousand fold![52]

Nor did Wesley consciously allow himself to be deceived. His examinations were painstaking on March 12, 1760:

> Having desired that as many as could of the neighbouring towns, who believed they were saved from sin, would meet me, I spent the greatest part of this day in examining them one

by one. The testimony of some I could not receive; but concerning the far greatest part, it is plain, (unless they could be supposed to tell willful and deliberate lies,) 1. That they feel no inward sin; and to the best of their knowledge commit no outward sin: 2. That they see and love God every moment, and pray, rejoice, give thanks evermore: 3. That they have constantly as clear a witness from God of sanctification as they have of justification. Now in this I do rejoice, and will rejoice, call it what you please; and I would to God thousands had experienced this much: let them afterward experience as much more as God pleases.[53]

Wesley did not hesitate to claim that he had seen "very many persons changed in a moment . . . from sinful desires, till then reigning over them, to a pure desire of doing the will of God." These, he said, were facts to which he was almost daily a witness. He wrote this letter as early as April, 1738.[54] As time went on, Wesley was slow to accept testimonies to the second experience. In 1747 he admonished that "we ought not hastily to believe, but to suspend our judgment, till we have full and strong proof" that persons have attained perfection.[55] A survey of the questions he would ask those who claimed the experience reveals how exacting his tests were.[56] Of all those he examined none received the experience gradually but instantaneously by faith. This kind of proof was final for Wesley.[57]

Obviously these people in Wesley's day, and many before that day and since, have entered into some sort of personal experience after they became Christians and before death. What is this that they experience? Does this attainment in grace correspond to the New Testament ideal of holiness and perfection? Many think so, as did Wesley. Various explanations are given by others. Whatever these people experience in their lives, there is a common denominator. They are more conscious of God; they have an inner victory over sin; a greater and purer love is theirs. Special emphasis is given to the work of the Holy Spirit. Whatever it is that happens to these people, Wesley called it Christian perfection and saw it as the second blessing.

Wesley taught that it was possible to enter this experience and then fail to maintain it, with the result that the new level reached is lost. In fact some of them backslide so far as to lose also the first experience of justification.

This could happen to the strongest of them when they failed to continue in this grace. However, though they lost the experience of holiness or the first experience of justification, they could be restored. "They have received the blessing they had before, with abundant increase." Even those who had lost all, even regeneration, "have, at once, recovered both a consciousness of his favour and the experience of the pure love of God."[58] Experience was, for Wesley, not something "once gotten, forever retained," but an inner work of God that must be maintained if retained.

Wesley's emphasis on experience may help to explain both his understanding of faith and the act of God in man. Those in the Calvinist tradition are disturbed by any suggestion that a believer could lose spiritual life or forgiveness. To them this gift of faith is a gift of life. Since it is God's work it stands secure; no one can lose it.[59] It is evident that these who so believe see the work of Christ more as something done *for* man rather than *in* him. The believer is secure because the work done in Christ cannot be altered. Wesley went further than this. He taught that what Christ had done *for* us was to be worked *in* us. Faith in Christ alone brings forgiveness, but it also produces a change in the believer. This change is experienced. Since the change is experienced—a subjective change—it needs to be maintained or it will be lost. If lost, it can be regained. When Wesley talked about the gaining, the losing, and the regaining of stages in Christian experience, he was not talking about the objective act of God in Jesus Christ. He was talking about the subjective work of the Spirit in the life of the believer.

D. It Is Purity

It should be clear by now that Wesley had no intention of confusing present perfection with a final perfection. He believed that the Bible taught a present perfection which he called Scripture or Christian perfection, and he did not feel that he was lowering the ideal to describe a perfection possible for the present life. An essential meaning that he put into this concept of the perfect was purity. To be perfect was to be pure. A clean heart was a perfect heart.[60] It was perfect in holiness.

Now be thou pure in heart; purified by faith from every unholy affection; "cleansing thyself from all filthiness of flesh and spirit, and perfecting holiness in the fear of God." Being, through the power of his grace, purified from pride, by deep poverty of spirit; from anger, from every unkind or turbulent passion, by meekness and mercifulness; from every desire but to please and enjoy God, by hunger and thirst after righteousness; now love the Lord thy God with all thy heart, and with all thy strength![61]

Evidently for Wesley the purifying of the heart from evil desire, tempers, and pride was the same as perfecting the heart in holiness. From the moment a person experiences the great change when there are no more "pride, anger, self will, and unbelief," he has in the same moment "all faith and love." From that moment he has continual fellowship with God, "always rejoicing, praying, and giving thanks."[62] It is in the absence of opposites to love and praise that perfection is found.

J. A. Wood defined Christian purity as "that state of heart, in which all the virtues composing a real Christian, exist in this simple and unmixed state." The sense in which the entirely sanctified are made perfect or complete is in purity. "The fruits of the Spirit are perfect when they exist in the soul in exclusion of every *opposing principle,* every *contrary temper*—perfect in *quality.*" In this sense faith is perfect when there is no unbelief; love is perfect when there are no opposites to it; patience is perfect when impatience is excluded.[63] This is not the same as saying that love has reached maturity, that faith cannot grow, that patience cannot become greater. They are pure as to quality but can increase in quantity. It is in this narrower sense that Wesley understood Christian, or present, perfection.

On this same subject Jessop quotes from Thomas Cook, in his book, *New Testament Holiness:*

"There are various degrees of impurity, but, strictly speaking, there are no degrees of purity. According to Webster, the word 'pure' means 'entire separation from all heterogeneous and extraneous matter, clear, free from mixture; as pure water, pure air, pure silver or gold.' "

"The word in the New Testament which is most frequently translated 'pure' occurs in some of its forms nearly seventy times. . . . The idea is that that which is pure consists of one thing; it is uncompounded, without mixture or adulteration; it has all that belongs to it and nothing else. Gold that is free from alloy, unmixed with any baser metal, we call pure gold; milk that contains all that belongs to milk, and nothing else, is pure milk; honey that is without wax is pure honey. In like manner, a pure heart contains nothing adverse to God. Where there is a mixture there cannot be purity. By purity of heart we mean that which is undefiled, untainted, free from evil stains, without earthly alloy. . . . Purity is the removal of whatever God could not admit into His immediate presence, and fellowship with Himself; in other words, the abolition of sin itself.

"By mtaurity we mean all this, and much more. The error of confusing purity of heart with maturity of Christian character lies at the base of nearly all the objections made to instantaneous and entire sanctification. . . .

"The Scriptures always discriminate between purity of heart and ripeness and fulness of Christian virtues. The one is the work wrought within us in a moment by the omnipotent power of the sanctifying Spirit, and the other a natural process involving culture and discipline. Purity has reference to kind or quality, but maturity has respect to degree or quantity. . . . Holiness is both a gift and a process, and as such is both instantaneous and gradual."[64]

In this quotation clear and explicit expression is rightly given to a truth which is implicit in Wesley's teaching on holiness. Growth does occur from the time of regeneration even though impurity is still present in the believer. The purifying act of God's grace frees from the hindrances to growth and makes possible a more rapid maturing of the Christian graces.

Without question Wesley taught a perfection that is freedom from sin. As already shown, this cessation of sin is not only the end of overt acts or willful transgressions but is the destruction of evil desires and tempers. Wesley's comment on the scripture in I John 1:9, "If we confess our sins, he is faithful and just to forgive us our sins, and to cleanse us from all unrighteousness," was that this deliverance is wrought in this world; it is for the living Christians. Also it is a deliverance from *all* unrighteousness, for if any remained the verse loses its meaning. Nor can the meaning be a cleansing from the guilt of the sin, because that is done in the forgiveness in the preceding clause. "It remains then, that Christians are saved in this world from all sin, from all unrighteousness; that they are now in such a sense perfect, as not to commit sin, and to be freed from evil thoughts and evil tempers."[65]

Nor could Wesley conceive that this perfection or purity or holiness was only in Christ and not in the believer. To teach that Christ alone is pure and righteous while man remains impure and unrighteous is a "blow at the root" of all holiness. This teaching, he thought, stabbed Christ in the house of His friends.

> Here is Wisdom! though not the wisdom of saints, but wisdom from beneath. Here is the masterpiece of Satan: Farther than this he cannot go. Men are holy, without a grain of holiness in them! holy in Christ, however unholy in themselves; they are in Christ, without one jot of the mind of Christ in themselves; in Christ, though their nature is whole in them. They are "complete in him," though they are, in themselves, as proud, as vain, as covetous, as passionate as ever. It is enough: They may be unrighteous still, seeing Christ has "fulfilled all righteousness."[66]

Obviously Wesley had no confidence in a doctrine that made no change in the Christian. And that change was from sin to holiness. To be perfect in holiness meant to be free from sin. This freedom was to be experienced now!

Perfect love and Christian liberty were the same for Wesley. These two expressions are scriptural and mean the same as holiness. To have this Christian liberty means that sin is destroyed. The love for God and one's neighbor is a good temper. When this love reigns in the soul, the opposite tempers—"worldly mindedness, malice, cruelty, revengefulness"—are destroyed. "I use the word *destroyed,* because St. Paul does: *suspended* I cannot find in my Bible." This purity is derived from Christ, but it is within the heart of the entirely sanctified.[67]

This freedom from sin is also expressed in terms of death to sin. Actually this death to sin is a death to self and occurs in such a way as to result in "poverty of spirit, mourning, meekness, hunger and thirst after righteousness, the love of our neighbour, and purity of heart."

> Be thou poor in spirit; little, and base, and mean, and vile in thy own eyes; amazed and humbled to the dust at the love of God which is in Christ Jesus thy Lord! Be serious: let the whole stream of thy thoughts, words, and works be such as flows from the deepest conviction that thou

standest on the edge of the great gulf. . . . Be meek: Let thy soul be filled with mildness, gentleness, patience, long-suffering toward all men; at the same time that all which is in thee is athirst for God.[68]

From the moment of justification there is a gradual mortification of inbred sin until the moment one "experiences a total death to sin." This dying process may be for a long time, yet one is not dead to sin "till sin is separated from the soul." In that instant of total death, or freedom from sin, the soul "lives the full life of love."[69]

Did Wesley teach that sin was eradicated? He was not too concerned about terms used to express the truth as he was that the truth be preserved. When pressed for a definition, Wesley used strong terms to express this purifying. He declared that no one by the grace he has "can expel pride, self will, or inbred sin." He can "mortify the deeds of the body," he can *"weaken"* his enemies, but he cannot *"drive them out."* He cannot *"extirpate"* them. There is no way that a Christian can "wholly cleanse" himself. "Most sure we cannot, till it shall please our Lord to speak . . . the second time, 'Be clean:' and then only the leprosy is cleansed. Then only the evil root, the carnal mind, is destroyed; and inbred sin subsists no more."[70] If to eradicate means the same as to "expel," to "drive out," to "extirpate," to "wholly cleanse," then it is a valid description of Wesley's concept.

Pope has no hesitancy to use the words "entirely extinguish" to describe this cleansing from all sin.[71] The term "eradication" has its disadvantages, as do most terms used to describe spiritual things, but it also has a completeness and decisiveness about it.[72] Certainly it is no stronger than the words Wesley used. Warfield described this cleansing as an eradication.

> It surely would be better to be freed from the "principle of sin" in us than merely from its effects in our actions. And this is in fact what the Scriptures provide for. What they teach indeed is just "eradication." They propose to free us from sinning by freeing us from the "principle of sin" . . . Counteraction there is; and suppression there is; but most fundamentally of all there is eradication.

This eradication is going on, and continues, but is not completed until "hereafter."[73] Warfield and Wesley have agreed on the nature of the cleansing but have differed as to when completion occurred. Wesley's definition of sin allowed him to do this.

Sangster feels that the terms "eradication," "extinction," "suspension," or "suppression" are all wrong and misleading. Since sin is not a "thing," these terms do not apply.[74] but when one so argues as Sangster, he also dismisses such scriptural terms as "cleanse" and "destroy." Wesley and his successors must be considered scriptural in terms whether one agrees with them or not. Whatever the terms are made to mean, something does happen to sin.

> To believe that the human heart can be cleansed from sin is a bold, big thing to believe, and we have protested against any easy assumption that it has been done because this is fraught with dreadful dangers, not the least of which is a subtle discouragement against being honest with oneself. But the opposite conviction, so it seems to the writer, is not less terrible. To hold the fixed conviction that it simply *cannot* be done and that one must always mentally provide for sin in one's life suggests all kinds of rationalization to our sinful minds. How easy to ignore Paul's injunction, "Make not provision for the flesh, to fulfill the lusts thereof." How eagerly this desiring heart fixes on "inevitability" as an everready excuse. Can any man confidently and unswervingly press on to the utterly unattainable?[75]

Possibly there would be less objection to these terms describing what happens to sin in the cleansing act if agreement were possible on a precise definition of the sin that is cleansed. Wesley's concept of sin has already been discussed. When one does not confuse the idea of sinfulness as an inward temper with all infirmities and mistakes, it is easier to see a present cleansing that can be complete. If sin is so closely identified with humanity, or made to consist of flaws resulting from sin, then no full cleansing in this life is possible. To "eradicate" these flaws and limitations would be to remove us from human existence. Wesley never saw sin in this manner—at least the sin that needed purging —so it is wrong to accuse him of such.

Both Sangster and Flew criticize Wesley's definition of sin. Flew thinks the "stress on the consciousness and deliberate intention of the agent is the most formidable defect in Wesley's doctrine of the ideal."[76] Both Flew and Sangster think Wesley thought of sin as a "thing."[77] It is not so much that Wesley thought of sin as a thing as that he thought of sin in scriptural terms which may convey such a meaning. A careful study of Wesley reveals that for him sin was no "thing." It was not attached to the human body or any part of it. Sin had no existence in material essence any more than love did. How could "consciousness and deliberate intention" be "things"? Clearly they are notions related to spirit, not body.

Cell is aware that Wesley's concept of sin is identical with that of historic Christianity from St. Paul to Calvin. "It could not be blacker."[78] The fact that in the process of salvation the believer could reach a point of perfection derived from a clean heart did not mean for Wesley that sinfulness had to be minimized. The blacker the sin, the greater the grace by which it is cleansed. When Wesley declared that the heart of man was "deceitful and desperately wicked," he meant it. But he also declared that the atoning Christ could destroy that deceit and wickedness in the heart. Still more, he believed that the marks of sinfulness would remain in human nature that was free from the sin. This distinction in Wesley's thought will be investigated in the next two chapters.

"When Wesley is allowed to define his terms, and state his qualifications, the Biblical basis for this part of his doctrine is likely to be conceded."[79] Wesley did teach that sin could be "unconscious" and that only the Holy Spirit could awaken one to his deep need. Flew failed to grasp the deepest meaning in Wesley's concept if he thought Wesley excused "good people" who were "unconscious of their own selfishness," or the "revengeful man" who believed "that he is animated only by a proper self-respect."[80] A careful study of Wesley's sermon on the "Repentance of Believers" reveals that Wesley did not excuse self-will, love of the world, pride, revenge, or any evil in the believer's heart. The believer must be *convicted* of these sins before any full cleansing could occur. These sins are uncovered by the Spirit, so that one is made conscious of them.[81]

When the deep sin of his heart is made known by the Spirit, then by faith the believer can be entirely cleansed. That which is revealed to him can be removed. "He is able to save you from all the sin that remains in your heart."

The same Spirit that convicts of the sin and cleanses the sin abides continually to keep the heart "moment by moment." As long as faith is retained, the victory over sin is maintained.[82] In view of these facts Flew's statement that Wesley's concept of sin requires that the degree of sanctification attained by any agent "will depend on his previous moral development, on his own insight into motive, and on his knowledge of himself" loses its relevance.[83] Flew does not allow for the awakening and enlightening power of the Spirit and the deep operation of the Spirit. If the believer were left to his own insight to see himself and to cleanse himself, he would be endangered by a deceptive nature. But in Wesley's view he has not been left alone!

The sin to be cleansed in this life, then, is not that which is easily seen and set aside. It is a disease whose germ has infected the whole nature of man. The symptoms destroyed will not end the disease. It is necessary to get at the heart of the matter. The disease itself must be cured. Perfection means death to the sin, not necessarily an end to the marks that sin has made.[84] By the supernatural power of God sin may "subsist no more" while the broken body and human nature will continue in a weakened condition until death. Only as sin is seen in this manner can a present cure be acceptable.

Sin, therefore, is not located in the body as such. To think so weakens any concept of sin. The body's condition can influence the soul in its struggle, but to make it the basis or determining factor in man's moral struggle cannot stand.[85] Sin is "in the flesh" (Rom. 8:3), but flesh here should be understood to be human nature apart from divine grace. As such sin is "a hateful intruder" within and must be expelled from the heart.[86] This foreign element in man's nature should be seen as the opposite to love. When love is seen, as John Wesley saw it, as a gift bestowed by the Holy Spirit, then its opposite, sin, is that which can be expelled. Love cannot reign supreme until the opponent is destroyed. "Love has entire possession of" the entirely sanctified.[87]

What are some of the marks of this pure heart? Wesley expressed this inward purity in a number of ways. It is a "will steadily and uniformly devoted to God" or "a heart and life entirely devoted to God."[88] He that is "dead to the world is alive to God." The whole heart is given to God and there is no delight except "what tends to him."[89] In this pure heart there is no sin. The perfect "feel nothing but love." They feel no temper "contrary to pure love."[90] Wesley did not believe one could be deceived in this kind of love since such a person had truly repented of his sinfulness, and had fully trusted in the merits of Christ, and was continuing to do so. This inward purity is not outward holiness, but it prepares for such and results in it.[91] One could hardly be pure at heart and not show some outward evidences of it. But one must not assume that perfection is in the outward evidences. Perfection is in the heart.

Furthermore perfection is a purity of intention. Outward works are consecrated to God "by a pure and holy intention."[92] Outward works, no matter how good they appear, cannot be pleasing to God apart from pure, inward tempers. Without this inward, holy intention all outward works, however singularly good, are only pharisaical. We need the righteousness of the Pharisees all right, but it should "exceed theirs in the purity and spirituality of it." McConnell criticized Wesley's idea of pure intention with the suggestion that all men intend right and do not want to be suspected of intentional wrongdoing.[93] But this kind of criticism does not get to the core of Wesley's idea. Wesley spoke of something "deeper down and farther back." This perfection is "simplicity of intention, and purity of affection." It is "one design in all we speak or do, and one desire ruling all our tempers." It is a "habitual disposition of soul." It is a "pure intention of heart, a steadfast regard to his glory in all your actions."[94] This is something quite different from "a full intention to do right" which lacks proper exertion in determining what is right.[95]

There are two problems encountered by those who fail to see Wesley's doctrine of freedom from sin. One problem is created by thinking of the attainment as a naturalistic effort of man, who is blind to his own inner self. Certainly "the sin problem" cannot be solved alone by man, and the problem of sin will remain. The other problem is created by making sin to include all the infirmity consequent to sinfulness. If perfection as freedom from sin entails freedom from infirmity, then the sin problem is beyond solution in this life. Wesley did not create these two problems in his thinking. For him sin was a deepseated disease not natural to man and which could be cured. Its cure does not mean the removal of the weaknesses it has caused in the human nature. Furthermore this cure is effected, not by a human toil or natural growth, but by the cleansing power of the atoning Saviour. Perfection, for him, was a supernatural gift. This gift is given in a moment, even though a period of gradual growth and preparation precedes it. It is followed by continual growth and increasing blessing.

E. It Is a Work of the Spirit

Only a casual glance at the theological literature dealing with the Holy Spirit or sanctification reveals the general agreement that sanctification is a special work of the Holy Spirit. Reformed writers teach that sanctification is the work of the Spirit. Luther taught that the Spirit was given "to invest the treasure." The Spirit gives Christ into the heart and performs all the necessary good works. These works are not complete because sin and ignorance remain. Yet the Holy Spirit does dwell in the believer and makes him feel a love toward God. He liberates from sin and terror, but the work is not complete.[96] Here in Luther the beginning of a real sanctification was the work of the Spirit. Kuyper wrote that "to lead the creature to its destiny, to cause it to develop according to its nature, to make it perfect, is the proper work of the Holy Spirit."[97] Similarly Berkouwer sees sanctification as a work in man by the Holy Spirit:

> Any reflection on sanctification will have to concentrate on the nature of the "new beginning." This renewal of human life in gratitude and love has always been considered the work of the Holy Spirit. The Spirit alone could perform the miracles of making man walk in the road of sanctity without sense of his own worth.[98]

Murray holds that regeneration is wrought by the Holy Spirit and by this act of God the believer becomes indwelt by the Holy Spirit. "Sanctification is a work of God *in us*" and it is "specifically the work of this indwelling and directing

Holy Spirit."[99] This position clearly holds that the Spirit is given in regeneration, and the process of sanctification is carried out by the indwelling Spirit. It should be noted that these views do not see sanctification as a special gift of the Spirit subsequent to regeneration.

Nels Ferre claims that Wesley practically equated saving grace with the presence of the Holy Spirit. The Spirit is given when one is forgiven and turned to God. But holiness is also a gift of God's grace, so therefore a work of the Spirit. This gift is given only to those who repent of their self-righteousness. This gift of grace makes a people clean.[100] According to Wesley one was not yet a Christian if he had not received the Holy Spirit. A Christian is one who is "anointed with the Holy Ghost, and with power."[101] Before 1738, Wesley taught that the Holy Spirit as a gift "looks full to the resurrection; for then is the life of God completed in us." It is then that He shall be fully bestowed on the redeemed.[102] In 1744 he believed that no one has salvation until he receives the Holy Ghost.[103]

> For instance, I assert that "till a man 'receives the Holy Ghost,' he is without God in the world; that he cannot know the things of God, unless God reveal them unto him by the Spirit; no, nor have even one holy or heavenly temper, without the inspiration of the Holy One."[104]

Wesley believed that any change wrought within the heart of a person was by the inspiration of the Holy Spirit, and that until this holy love was "shed abroad in the heart" no one could enter heaven.[105] This teaching of Wesley may appear strange to some who insist that the Holy Spirit is given subsequent to regeneration at the time of a "second blessing," but in this concept Wesley is at one with most Reformed teaching.[106]

It has been a quite general teaching among holiness advocates that Pentecost, or the baptism of the Holy Spirit, is identical with the gift given at entire sanctification. C. E. Brown understands the coming of the Holy Spirit upon the Church in New Testament times as an experience only for the believer. He explains a number of scriptural accounts in that manner. All who received the Holy Ghost were already initially "saved" persons. In a second crisis of salvation, the believer is baptized with the Holy Spirit, at which time the heart is purified by faith (Acts 15:9).[107] Most of the writers in the modern holiness movement who follow the Wesleyan tradition are in substantial agreement with this position.[108] In all this investigation no one has been found in this tradition who objects to this identification, although all do not give it equal emphasis.

This teaching is that Christian perfection or entire sanctification is the baptism of the Holy Spirit such as the disciples received on the Day of Pentecost. At this time the disciples, who were already believers, were filled with the Spirit and thereby purified at heart. Is this teaching which has become explicit with the advocates of Wesleyan holiness also held by Wesley? There is no question that he saw holiness and perfection as a work of the Spirit *in us*, but was the crisis experience which he called instantaneous equivalent to the Pentecostal experience in Acts, often called the baptism with the Holy Spirit?

Wesley considered that the more excellent purpose of the giving of the Holy Spirit on the Day of Pentecost was not to give the gifts, but to give those present (what none can deny to be essential to all Christians in all ages) the mind which was in Christ, those holy fruits of the Spirit, which whosoever hath not, is none of His; to fill them with

"love, joy, peace, longsuffering, gentleness, goodness," (Gal. v. 22-24;) to endue them with faith, . . . with meekness and temperance; . . . and, in consequence of that inward change, to fulfill all outward righteousness, to "walk as Christ walked."[109]

Of course Wesley saw the beginning of this holiness in regeneration and initial sanctification. These are works of the Spirit wrought in the heart when the repentant sinner believes. Since that work of holiness is not then perfected, does the believer await a greater infusion of the Spirit when he is entirely sanctified? In 1738, when Wesley was in Germany, he heard that the full renewal of the believer did not occur until he received "the gift of the Holy Ghost." These Moravians in Germany taught that there was an "intermediate state" between the bondage of Romans 7 and the "full glorious liberty of the children of God." By them this "glorious liberty" came with the "descent of the Holy

Ghost at the day of Pentecost."[110] Obviously this concept
remained with Wesley, for in 1762 he wrote:

> Many years ago my brother frequently said, "Your day of
> Pentecost is not fully come; but I doubt not it will; and
> you will then hear of persons sanctified, as frequently as you
> do now of persons justified." Any unprejudiced reader may
> observe, that it was now fully come. And accordingly we did
> hear of persons sanctified . . . as frequently as of persons
> justified; although instances of the latter were far more
> frequent than they had been for twenty years before. That
> many of these did not retain the gift of God, is no proof that
> it was not given them. That many do retain it to this day,
> is matter of praise and thanksgiving.[111]

Clearly Wesley associated in his mind Pentecost and sanctification, and here he means entire sanctification. Also he
calls it the "gift of God," meaning the gift of the Holy
Spirit.

However, in 1770, Wesley hesitated to call this second
experience the "receiving of the Holy Ghost." Others may
do so, if they wish, he said, but the phrase "is not Scriptural,
and not quite proper; for they all 'received the Holy Ghost,'
when they were justified."[112] Apparently Wesley feared
that using the term "receiving the Holy Ghost" exclusively
for the second experience would lessen its meaning for regeneration. Never did Wesley want to lower the content of
regeneration to make room for entire sanctification. However
this may be, it remains true that Wesley looked upon the
"second blessing" as an instantaneous gift from God and
the completion of the cleansing process. Since sanctification
was a work of the Spirit, this second and higher act was
great and could be seen as a special work of the Spirit.
Certainly the idea is implicit in Wesley.

What was implicit in Wesley was much more explicit in
his associates. John Fletcher clearly taught that the "promise
of the Father" was fulfilled in Christian perfection. The
disciples were carried on to perfection in the outpouring
of the Holy Spirit. This "promise" is for believers in the
gospel of Christ who may receive a "peculiar power of the
Spirit" which enables them by faith to "embrace the promise
of full sanctification." "How many baptisms are needed to
wholly cleanse the heart?" Fletcher asked. If one does it,
so much the better. If two or more are necessary, the promise
is still good.

I may, however, venture to say, in general, that before we can rank among perfect Christians, we must receive so much of the truth and Spirit of Christ by faith, as to have the pure love of God and man shed abroad in our hearts by the Holy Ghost given unto us, and to be filled with the meek and lowly mind which was in Christ. And if one out-pouring of the Spirit, one bright manifestation of the sanctifying truth, so empties us of self, as to fill us with the mind of Christ, and with pure love, we are undoubtedly Christians in the full sense of the word.[113]

To this position Wesley had no objection.

Adam Clarke, a contemporary of Wesley, emphasized the work of entire sanctification as a "greater effusion of the Holy Ghost."[114] Without question he associated the work of purifying from all sin with the Pentecostal outpouring of the Holy Spirit.[115] Following in the footsteps of Fletcher and Clarke, and not doubting their adherence to Wesley, American Methodists of the nineteenth century associated entire sanctification with the filling of the Spirit. This did not mean that the Spirit's work in regeneration was set aside. It did mean that this special and instantaneous work of the Spirit was given special emphasis, especially by those Methodists who emphasized instantaneous holiness.[116]

More evident in Wesley's writings is his emphasis on the witness of the Spirit to Christian perfection. He taught that the believer could know that the work of full salvation was accomplished within himself. The Holy Spirit witnesses to the first work of God when one first believes. One should not "rest in any supposed fruit of the Spirit" but seek until the Spirit cries in the heart, "Abba, Father."[117] Further-more, this same Spirit will also bear witness to the work of entire sanctification. One can be just as certain of the "second blessing" as of justification. This second witness may not always be clear at first, but it can be both as clear and as steady as the first witness. It is a direct testimony from the Holy Spirit that one is sanctified wholly.[118]

He saw faith and the witness of the Spirit as being necessarily together. Faith necessarily implies an "assurance" or "evidence," and he who has true faith has the "witness in himself." This evidence is the witness of the Spirit.[119]

"But what is that faith whereby we are sanctified?—saved from sin and perfected in love?" It is a divine evidence and conviction, First, that God hath promised it in the Holy Scripture. . . .

It is a divine evidence and conviction, Secondly, that what God hath promised he is able to perform. . . .

It is, Thirdly, a divine evidence and conviction that he is able and willing to do it now. . . .

To this confidence, that God is both able and willing to sanctify us now, there needs be added one thing more,—a divine evidence and conviction, that he doeth it. In that hour it is done: God says to the inmost soul, "According to thy faith be it unto thee!" Then the soul is pure from every spot of sin; it is clean "from all unrighteousness."[120]

This "divine evidence and conviction" is the witness of the Holy Spirit to the believer's heart.[121]

Wesley had many followers who testified to this inner assurance of entire sanctification.[122] They had earnestly sought this "blessing." There came a time when they believed to the saving of their souls. At that moment the Holy Spirit wrought a great work in their hearts. The very work and the faith carried its own assurance; they knew it was done. The Spirit inspired the faith; He did the cleansing; He bore witness to the work that was done. This present perfection for them was a work of the Spirit.

F. Assurance and Testimony

It is clear that Wesley taught that one could know that he was made perfect in love and that he had experienced this greater work of the Spirit—entire sanctification. Did he believe that one who was so assured should bear testimony to the attainment? He was cautious at this point but he held that, once one had attained to this, he could "scarce be able to refrain, the fire would be so hot within him." After a time, however, he should refrain from speaking about it to those who "know not God." Nor should he speak to anyone about it "without some good end in view." Even then he should speak without appearance of boasting and in all humility and reverence. There are times when he ought to speak, let his light shine, and thus encourage "others to follow after the same blessing." He may be misunderstood, but there are times when he should speak.[123]

Wesley has been criticized most severely at this point of testimony to the attainment of the ideal by some of his most sympathetic students. Flew declares that the word "assurance" is a defect in Wesley's doctrine of perfection. He thinks that Wesley, though he never explicitly claimed the experience, "spoke and wrote about the experience as though he fully appreciated, as if from the inside, the gift." Wesley started with the principle that in salvation "perfect faith is attended by its interior evidence.[124]

> The word assurance carries with it one of the marks of the Christian life. The New Testament offers to those who repent and believe an awareness of God, a conscious communion. The consciousness is of the very essence of the new relationship. Just as every child was meant to know its father, so every man was meant to know God. But if our criticism of Wesley's doctrine of sin is valid, the word "assurance" is inapplicable to the uprooting of all indwelling sin. A man may bear testimony to his awareness of a God who is willing and able to 'destroy the last remains of sin.' He cannot know himself well enough to claim that God has already done it. He can be aware that he is in the hands of One whose presence floods his heart with the spirit of supernatural love. But he cannot without pride believe that he is now no longer on a permanently lower level, but on a permanently higher level. The first kind of assurance is a conviction about God. The second kind of assurance is a conviction about himself. The emphasis in such a trust will be upon a particular deliverance in the past rather than on the experienced Deliverer in the present.[125]

There is weight in this argument, but one must be cautioned against too ready repudiation of Wesley's concept of assurance. In the first place, Flew's criticism of Wesley's concept of sin is not entirely valid, as has been shown. "Indwelling sin" is not a "thing," nor does Wesley include in this "sin" all that Flew implies that he did. This will become clearer in the chapter on "'Sins' of the Sanctified." Secondly, Flew claims that one does not know himself well enough to claim God has already done a work in him. One can be assured of God's willingness and ability but not of His accomplishment. If Flew is correct in this statement, then a believer could not be certain of any change. Wesley saw this when he wrote concerning the witness of the Spirit to holiness:

> "Q. 17. But what need is there of it, seeing sanctification is a real change, not a relative only, like justification?
> "A. But is the new birth a relative change only? Is not this a real change? . . .

"Q. 18. But does not sanctification shine by its own light?

"A. And does not the new birth too? Sometimes it does; and so does sanctification; at others it does not. In the hour of temptation Satan clouds the work of God, and injects various doubts and reasonings, especially in those who have either very weak or very strong understandings. At such times there is absolute need of that witness, without which the work of sanctification not only could not be discerned, but could no longer subsist. Were it not for this, the soul could not then abide in the love of God; much less could it rejoice evermore, and in everything give thanks. In these circumstances, therefore, a direct witness that we are sanctified is necessary in the highest degree."[126]

Two things should be noticed in these words of Wesley. Justification, which includes the new birth, is more than a relationship to God; it is a real change. Also, the believer cannot always know the state of his heart by observation of himself—God must tell him! According to Wesley man does not need to "know himself well enough to claim that God has already done it"; He supremely needs to know the voice of God. This "conviction about himself" is based on a higher source of knowing that the "know thyself."[127]

A third defect in Flew's criticism of Wesley on this point is the use of the word "permanently" for the lower and higher levels of grace, and in the suggestion that the emphasis is upon a past deliverance, not "present Deliverer." These terms disregard Wesley's emphasis upon the "moment by moment" life.[128] If close attention is given to Wesley's definition to the sin that is cleansed in entire sanctification, and to his teaching on how to attain and maintain the perfect love, much of this criticism loses its weight. It is readily admitted that many with lesser insight than Wesley failed to safeguard his teaching at this point, but Wesley saw the dangers and tried to avoid them.[129].

Wesley was not blind to the dangers inherent in any claim to a perfect heart. Sangster believes the dangers are greater when the emphasis is upon the negative idea, "freedom from sin."

If a man is convinced that he is free from all sin: if, moreover, by some freak of faith he is convinced also that to doubt his freedom from sin is dishonouring to God and tantamount to disbelieving the Bible, he will necessarily be less likely to recognize the presence of sin when it rises in his soul. With his own hands he has built a wall between himself

136

and self-knowledge. He puts a bandage around his own eyes whenever he looks inwards, though when he looks outwards on others if often appears that his eyes are not only unbandaged but sharp with censoriousness.[130]

It must be observed immediately, as Sangster would admit, that Wesley left no such "trap" in his teaching. Every real thing has its counterfeit, and a person who can do what is described above has neither faith nor cleansing. Such counterfeits are no more an argument against "freedom from sin" as a doctrine than the evil priests and monks of the Middle Ages are arguments against the Christian Church, or hypocritical communicants at the Lord's table are arguments against the sacraments of the Church! *Sola fide* and *sola gratia* may have their antinomians, but these doctrines also are treasures of many saints.

The reason the person Sangster describes is in danger is that such a person has not followed Wesley nor the Scriptures. Wesley never taught that a perosn is to look within himself for his assurance of "freedom from sin." Such was the fatal flaw in the Pharisee who prayed in the Temple. He looked to himself and not to God's mercy. Anyone who looks within himself for evidence of freedom from sin endangers himself and his friends. That many have missed Wesley's teaching at this point, and need the corrective Sangster gives, is readily admitted. Also the emphasis upon the idea of "freedom from sin" rather than upon the presence of perfect love leads to dangerous delusion. It is only in the "moment by moment" life of trust, which will be discussed later, that this danger can be avoided.

Wesley did not believe that one could infallibly know when another was entirely "free from sin." In fact one could not infallibly judge concerning another's justification. But no one, he thought, ought to oppose a plain testimony when it was accompanied with reasonable evidence.[131] Of course presumption was a possibility, but Wesley was quick to uncover such:

> And, first, how is this testimony to be distinguished from the presumption of a natural mind? It is certain, one who was never convinced of sin, is always ready to flatter himself, and to think of himself, especially in spiritual things, more highly than he ought to think. And, hence, it is in no wise strange, if one who is vainly puffed up by his fleshly

mind, when he hears of this privilege of true Christians, among whom he undoubtedly ranks himself, should soon work himself up into a persuasion that he is already possessed thereof. . . . How then may the real testimony of the Spirit with our spirit, be distinguished from this damning presumption?[132]

Wesley's answer to this question on distinguishing the real from the presumption is found in the Scriptures. They describe in a plain manner the circumstances that go before, with, and after the genuine testimony, so that none need be deceived. "Whoever carefully weighs and attends these will not need to put darkness for light."[133] William Townsend believed that Wesley safeguarded the doctrine of assurance.

> Wesley's doctrine of holiness, of 'perfect love,' is really a corollary of his appeal to experience. For if a son is conscious of his relation to his father there must be the possibility that that consciousness shall be complete, 'without a cloud between,' and as such the source of exquisite joy and untroubled confidence![134]

Furthermore, as is well-known, Wesley overcame certain dangers by his appeal to "a social court." The class meetings, or bands, guarded against certain deceptions in people's claims. This was no sheer individualism.[135] Some have been disturbed because they cannot find in Wesley's writings any claim that he had attained Christian perfection. Some think Wesley never made the claim at all.[136] Cell is not so sure Wesley gave no testimony to his Christian experience. One goes astray, he argues, if he infers from "Wesley's consistent objectivity in his public preaching and writing that he did not at any time unbosom his Christian experience in the intimate circle of his class meetings." Wesley could hardly have stood outside this "experience-sharing" of the Methodist revival, but actually was its principal source.[137] Very pointed questions were asked in these meetings. Wesley could hardly have gotten by without opening up his heart to these earnest people.

With all the safeguards that one could place against any dangers present in the teaching of entire sanctification, the dangers are still there if sin is not given a proper definition. If the sin from which one thinks he is free includes ignorance, infirmity, and mistake, then one must be blind to profess such freedom. Or if this freedom means no more temptation or possibility of sinning again, its dangers are very evident. If this claim should mean no more need for heart searching, humility before God, confession, and constant dependence on Christ, it would be pagan. Or if freedom from sin means freedom from outward flaws and failures so that one lives a perfectly ethical life in all outward conduct, then such claim is downright hypocrisy. Wesley's freedom from sin was freedom from the opponents of pure love in the heart. Since God gave this purity, His work was a perfect one, and the heart so cleansed could cling to God without a rival within. But to make that pure love apparent in one's daily conduct is no easy task, for in doing this one encounters all the limitations of an earthly and corrupted existence. The person with a pure love for God and man can courageously attack his hostile environment, but his success is not the measure of his love. Love can be perfect in the presence of many imperfections.

G. Obedience to the Law of Love

Perfection in terms of the law has various meanings because law is variously defined. One could define law as being identical with God, and only He could perfectly observe that law. Or one might lightly make himself his own law, and set a standard which he perfectly keeps. Christian theologians have endeavored to define law in scriptural concepts, but even here variations occur. Some consider that law is the unchanging, immutable standard God has set for moral creatures, and there is no perfect keeping of it by fallen men. Others hold that God requires only the possible, and erring man can by grace reach His standard. What was Wesley's opinion on this theme?

Wesley, in commenting on Rom. 7:12, "Wherefore the law is holy, and the commandment holy, and just, and good," declared this law is the moral law. It was before the Mosaic, or Jewish, or ceremonial law. This moral law had its origin "beyond the foundation of the world." It is a law designed for moral, intelligent, and free creatures. It is the same law for angels and men, and was written in the heart "by the finger of God." Had there been no fall, this law would have been easily understood and clear at all times. In his rebellion man "well nigh effaced" this law "out of his heart."

But God "reinscribed" it on the sinner's heart "through the Son of his love." A clearer knowledge of this law was given to Israel, but it is written on the hearts of the believers so they can comprehend its meaning by the Spirit.[138]

According to Wesley it is correct to call the Mosaic dispensation "the law," but this law is "imperfect and shadowy." This is not the law which God writes on the heart. But the moral law is "an incorruptible picture of the high and holy One." "It is the face of God unveiled; God manifested to his creatures as t h e y are able to bear it. . . . It is the heart of God disclosed to man." In another way one can say that this moral law is "supreme, unchangeable reason; it is unalterable rectitude, it is the everlasting fitness of all things that are or ever were created." This law of God is a "copy of the eternal mind, a transcript of the divine nature."[139]

This law has several uses. Its first use is "to slay the sinner" by convincing him of his sin. The second use is to drive the sinner to Christ; "it acts the part of a severe schoolmaster." Another use of the law is "to keep us alive." This law does not come to an end. The Mosaic or Jewish ceremonial law is taken out of the way. There is a sense in which we are "done with the moral law"; it is not a means of procuring our justification. But, after justification, it is of use "in convincing us of the sin that yet remains," so we will seek cleansing, and "in confirming our hope of whatsoever it commands and we have not yet attained."[140] Wesley considered that the law was still in effect, in this sense, and was not abolished in Christ. The law leads us to Christ; the love of Christ causes us to love the law.[141]

Is perfection then perfect obedience to this law of God that leads to Christ? This law was given to Adam in Paradise and it required obedience in all parts as the condition to live. It was a perfect inward and outward holiness; there was no allowance for any falling short of God's glory. This perfect obedience "should be perfectly uninterrupted" and should "continue without any intermission" if man were to live eternally.

"Thou, O man of God, stand fast in love, in the image of God wherein thou art made. If thou wilt remain in life, keep the commandments, which are now written in thine heart.

Love the Lord thy God with all thy heart. Love, as thyself, every soul that he has made. Desire nothing but God. Aim at God in every thought, in every word and work. Swerve not, in one motion of body or soul, from him, thy mark, and the prize of thy high calling. And let all that is in thee praise his holy name, every power and faculty of thy soul, in every kind, in every degree, and at every moment of thy existence."[142]

Perfection for Adam would have been perfect obedience to this perfect moral law. This perfect obedience was perfection in both heart and work. No deviation was allowed. This was God's first covenant with man.

But Adam fell, so God provided a new or second covenant. Wesley taught that this new covenant does not require "unsinning obedience," for if it did none could be saved. "It does not require any impossibility to be done. . . . Indeed, strictly speaking, the covenant of *grace* doth not require us to *do* any thing at all, as absolutely and indispensably necessary, in order to our justification." Faith stands in the place of perfect obedience for our acceptance with God.[143] The covenant of works required Adam to pay the price himself; "in the covenant of grace, seeing we have nothing to pay, God 'frankly forgives us all.'"[144]

All the sons of Adam are under the covenant of grace, even the Jews in the Mosaic dispensation. This faith that is substituted for perfect obedience works by love and produces all obedience and holiness. The law is not superseded by faith, but faith produces love which fulfills the law. All the works that for a perfect man were required antecedent to faith are now as necessary as ever. However, for the believer these works are consequent to faith. No degree of obedience is set aside by the covenant of grace. Believers are required to be holy after justification.[145]

In this new relationship Wesley believed that the Christian is "under the law to Christ." "Under grace" he "now performs (which while under the law he could not do) a willing and universal obedience." This obedience is not from slavish fear but from grace which causes "all his works to be wrought in love." This "nobler principle" is evangelical and is no less powerful than the legal. One is not "less obedient to God from filial love" than he would be from "servile fear." From this kind of platform Wesley fired his fiery condemnations of antinomianism.[146] Grace in no wise destroys the law as the standard for obedience; it enables one to give a loving obedience to the whole moral law.

This inward, spiritual meaning of the law of God was hidden to the Jews and heathen. Nor was it observable where Roman Catholicism had spread, according to Wesley. Furthermore, even the greater part of the "Reformed Christians are utter strangers at this day to the law of Christ, in the purity and spirituality of it."[147] Love is the end of all the commandments. Faith is not to supersede but to produce holiness, or love.[148] Obviously Wesley's concept of faith differed from that of the reformers. "Faith is only the means, the end is love."[149]

> In the original state, we are told, love had no rival in the heart of man. Thus love existed before faith. Faith did not come until love had been lost through sin, and the intention is that it shall not survive the attainment of its purpose: the restoration of man to the love from which he has fallen. It follows that man's fellowship with God in sanctification is seen primarily as a fellowship not of faith but of love. . . . In the eternal life the perfect fellowship with God will be one of the love alone.[150]

In what way is this new law, the law of Christ, or the law of love, different from the old covenant? Adam was expected to render a perfect accomplishment in his obedience because he was able to give such. This meant that he not only was prompted by perfect love but must perform the acts of obedience with no flaw. Fallen man on the other hand could never perform a perfect, flawless obedience to the absolute law, although it continues as a goal before him. But he can keep the law of Christ which requires a pure love. One can render a loving obedience even though the performance is imperfect. The obedience is prompted by a perfect love, even though the carrying out of the law is hindered by conditions that pure love cannot remove. John Fletcher illustrated this truth thus:

> We do not doubt but, as a reasonable, loving father never requires of his child, who is only ten years old, the work of one who is thirty years of age; so our heavenly Father never expects of us, in our debilitated state, the obedience of immortal Adam in paradise, or the uninterrupted worship of sleepless angels in heaven. We are persuaded, therefore, that, for Christ's sake, he is pleased with an humble obedience to our present

light; and a loving exertion of our present powers; accepting our Gospel services "according to what we have, and not according to what we have not."[151]

Fletcher called this law "adapted to our present state and circumstances" a milder law, "the law of Christ." Under this law one, when he obeys, does not sin, although he still sins if considered under the Adamic law.[152]

Wesley was willing to rest his whole concept of Christian perfection on the principle of perfect love. There are many who prefer the term "perfect love" to "Christian perfection."[153] The word love limits the concept of perfection to a certain area and avoids application of it to the whole man. One could have perfect love and not be a perfect man in many other things. A perfect love need not be a love incapable of further development. It is a love that is free from any ill temper.

Wesley defined what it is to love God. It is "to delight in him, to rejoice in his will, to desire continually to please him, to seek and find our happiness in him, and to thirst day and night for a fuller enjoyment of him." This kind of love for God does not forbid other delights. One is to love his neighbor as himself, and to love God's other creatures. These other loves prepare us for the enjoyment of God.[154] Such a perfect love for God enables one to "rejoice evermore, to pray without ceasing, and in everything to give thanks."[155] The fruit of this kind of love is clearly revealed in I Corinthians 13.[156] Gentle, patient love is the "one thing needful" for all true Christians.[157]

This love for God is not developed out of any natural endowment of man. It clearly is a gift of God given by the Holy Spirit. The "natural man is entirely without Christian love." Love must come from above and man's "love must be born of God's love."[158] *Agape* is first God's love for man, but it begets a divine love in man for God. This love is perfected when all opposing loves are gone.

Perfect love enables one to keep the law of love. Wesley distinguished between a pure love and its ability to perfectly reveal itself:

> The plain fact is this: I know many who love God with all their heart, mind, soul, and strength. He is their one desire, their one delight, and they are continually happy in him. They love their neighbour as themselves. They feel as sincere,

fervent, constant a desire for the happiness of every man, good or bad, friend or enemy, as for their own. . . .

But these souls dwell in a shattered, corruptible body, and are so pressed down thereby, that they cannot exert their love as they would, by always thinking, speaking, and acting precisely right. For want of better bodily organs, they sometimes inevitably think, speak, or act wrong. Yet I think they need the advocacy of Christ, even for these involuntary defects; although they do not imply a defect of love, but of understanding. However that be, I cannot doubt the fact. They are all love; yet they cannot walk as they desire.[159]

Wesley admitted that perfect love was not the keeping of a perfect law. The perfect law was that given to Adam. It implied "thinking, speaking and acting right in every instance, which he was then able, and therefore obliged, to do." Since none of his descendants can do this kind of obedience, "love is the fulfilling of their law."[160]

Several observations can now be made as regards Wesley's views. One is that Wesley saw love or holiness, not as an act, but as an inward quality. God makes a man holy before he can do holy acts. Holiness is the "right state of our powers." It is the "right disposition of our soul, the right temper of our mind."[161] If a person were not holy at heart, or did not have perfect love, his life or acts would not be holy no matter how good or perfect they appeared. Furthermore, one could be pure in love, or holy at heart, and yet fall far short of any perfect performance because of faulty mind and body. Love means a holy heart with holy intents and purposes, created so by the Spirit, and this can be perfect while its expressions in life are imperfect. Christian perfection is not a perfect living of life, but a perfect fountain from which the life flows. The impediments to this outflowing of life will be discussed in the next two chapters. Here it is insisted that obedience to the law of love is concerned first with the *ab quo* of love, and secondly, with its *ad quem*.

But Wesley cannot be accused of teaching a holiness that is a treasure within a person without concern for the outward life. Actually it is the contrary. "He who verily loves God will try his best to do His will on earth as it is done in Heaven." He is happy in doing this will. Lindstrom contends that Wesley reconciled the idea of the law with an evangelical approach. The "law and the gospel are simply two different points of view." If a command is regarded as an order, it is v i e w e d as law; if it is seen as a promise, it is a part of the gospel. "Thus every commandment in the Scriptures is a veiled promise."[162] What God asks a man to do, he can do by the grace given. Love prompts him to do this asking, and his effort is gladly put forth.

Wesley had great optimism for this perfect love:

> "This love we believe to be the medicine of life, the neverfailing remedy for all the evils of a disordered world, for all the miseries and vices of men. Wherever this is, there are virtue and happiness going hand in hand. . . .
>
> "This religion we long to see established in the world, a religion of love, and joy, and peace; having its seat in the heart, in the inmost soul, but ever showing itself by its fruits; continually springing forth, not only in all innocence, (for love worketh no ill to his neighbour,) but likewise in every kind of beneficence, spreading virtue and happiness all around it."[163]

From the fountain of perfect love will spring forth conformity to the law of love. This loving obedience will bear fruit in every avenue of life. In this present life one can be so far perfect as to render loving obedience to this law of Christ.

In summary it can be said that Wesley did teach a present perfection. He wanted this perfection to be what was taught in the Scriptures and what was attainable during the present life. This perfection was a freedom from sin, but only when sin was defined as a flaw in the love. The attainment of perfect love came as an experience in which one knew the gift was given. This work was wrought by the Holy Spirit. The perfect love attained enabled one to keep the law of Christ, a law suited to man's present state. This present perfection was not a perfect and flawless performance of the perfect law, but it was a performance initiated and motivated by a pure heart of love.

CHAPTER V

THE HUMAN LIMITS

Wesley was as aware as anyone could be that there were human limits beyond which God's grace could not take a Christian in this life. The continuous criticism of his doctrine of perfection required him often to define his teaching in terms of human needs. Some have seen these definitions as limitations on the idea of perfection and thus a teaching of perfection that is not perfection.[1] It is readily admitted that Wesley defined perfection differently from many in his day, but in doing so he maintained a scriptural usage. Furthermore, no other word has ever been found that will express the truth he taught better than "perfect love." When the words "perfect love" are made to mean "perfect performance," or "perfect skill," or "perfect human nature," the fault will not be Wesley's. Certainly it is possible for a person to be pure in intent, purpose, and in the will to obey, while he may fail in the power or skill to carry out that intent or purpose.

Although the fountain of the stream of life has been cleansed, and the source of the stream of life's actions has been made pure, yet the life itself is still lived in a broken and fallen world. These human limits are not flaws in the perfect love but are restrictions upon the expressions and performances of this perfect love. These limits are not only found in the surrounding environment of the sanctified person, but they are also found within himself. A human person is a human soul or spirit, and he is also flesh and bones. He is limited not only by his finiteness and human existence, but he is also limited by a human situation that has been marred by the corruptions present in a fallen and sinful race of beings.

A. Finite Existence

Wesley's questions were not, "Can the human race be perfected?" or, "Does God's grace perfect the powers and skills of humanity?" or, "Can we create a perfect environment in which to live?" Rather he asked, "Will God so fill an individual with His love that he can love God perfectly, and his neighbor as himself?" His emphasis is upon what the individual can be in the midst of a hostile and adverse world. And even with the individual the emphasis is not upon his ability as a perfect lover but upon his perfect love. The perfect love is the pure desire to show love to others, to change men, to bring righteousness on earth. It is not the endowment of a special power to accomplish such an end.[2]

Some of the limits placed upon the Christian are found in his finiteness. Man is not God nor can he attain the state of the infinite. He is now and always will be dependent upon the Infinite and restricted by finite existence. There are limits beyond which he cannot go. It has not been easy for theologians to keep separate the two ideas of human finiteness and sin. Often opponents to perfection teaching confuse perfection and infinitude, or at least make perfection impossible to present human existence. To them the perfect Christian ideal is unattainable until earthly existence has ceased. Either they must believe that finite existence and holiness are incompatible or else that sin has so drastically changed present existence that a basic change in the mode of existence is essential before attainment of personal holiness. In either case, sin and finitude are closely associated.

> This confusion between finitude or creatureliness and sin is responsible for much confusion of the pathological element in religious experience. It would deepen religious experience and strengthen moral responsibility if this confusion could be eliminated.[3]

Graham Ikin further writes that the "modern psychological approach tends to endorse the distinction between creatureliness as such and actual sin."[4] This concept is quite different from that of McConnell, who claimed that the "body may not be strong enough to furnish the basis for anything like a normal moral experience." Or the body may be "too strong," or "too wild," or "too riotous for a moral career at all ideal."[5] Wesley might agree with McConnell that the body in its weaknesses or limitations fails to provide any quality of perfect love in the heart. The danger in McConnell's view is that ceaturely differences become a basis for judging moral experience. One must distinguish between natural instincts and desires on the one hand and moral quality on the other.

Wesley had no trouble understanding sin as apart from creatureliness. For him Adam was created holy, yet he was finite. In this original state Adam walked with God and kept the perfect law. At the same time he was a creature wholly dependent upon God. Adam did not sin because he was finite but because he was capable of choice and could be tempted. Sin for Adam was not inevitable, but it was possible. Adam could have remained finite and have refused to sin. Holiness was not hindered by finitude, but it was perfectly consistent with it. The reason man could sin was not that he was finite, or a creature, but that he was made like God, a free, intelligent being. Since he was like God in this respect, he could choose evil, and he did.[6]

As was pointed out earlier in this paper, Wesley taught that Adam had a twofold likeness to God. He resembled God in the constitution of his being as a spirit by possessing intellect, feelings, and will. This was called the natural image of God in man. He also resembled God in his moral quality. He was holy. He had the right use of his powers— a moral inclination to the right. This was the moral image of God in him.

When man sinned, the moral likeness was completely lost. The natural likeness was greatly marred, but it is retained as a salvable point by prevenient grace. These rational powers in man make up his human nature and are closely identified with his bodily powers. Both body and mind have suffered in the Fall and continue to bear the consequences of both racial and personal sin. Thus man in his present existence is not only human and finite, but he is marred in both rational and bodily powers. When one speaks of finite existence now, he has to mean fallen, or marred, finite existence. The two can no longer be separated except abstractly.[7]

Whether human powers are perfect as it is supposed they were in Adam, or marred and faulty as they are known to be in all men, they should not be confused with the use or direction a person gives to those powers. The loss of holiness is not the loss of the powers, or even their marring, but it is the loss of moral likeness to God. Where in holiness one's intent, purpose, and desire are inclined only to the right, in sinfulness they are disposed to the evil. In regeneration, when one is born from above, the moral likeness to God is restored. However, this restoration is not complete until all sinfulness of heart is cleansed, and perfect love alone reigns. In the experience of entire sanctification all that Adam lost in his moral likeness to God is recovered, so that fallen man can love God with as pure a love as Adam possessed. The lost holiness, or perfection, is recovered in Christ.[8]

Although Wesley taught that the moral likeness to God was fully restored to the entirely sanctified, he was also clear in his teaching that the natural image of God in man was not recovered in this life. Man's rational powers and his body were greatly affected by the Fall and continue through life limited and faulty. The Christian can be perfect in love, but he has this treasure in an "earthen vessel." The heart may be pure and the love perfect, but the body and mind are imperfect and deprived.[9]

B. THE CORRUPTIBLE BODY

The "heavenly treasure" of "all righteousness and true holiness" is "in earthly, mortal, corruptible bodies." Wesley spared no term to describe this body of the flesh. It is "brittle" like earthenware; its organs are "debased and depraved." The brain is "disordered" and will lead to "innumerable mistakes." There are "death," "sickness, weakness, and pain, and a thousand infirmities." Wesley saw this broken body as suffering the consequences of the Fall and without much hope of recovery until death comes. He knew the close identification of soul and body when he wrote that "the corruptible body presses down the soul."[10] The human body was an obstacle in the way for any perfect expression of pure love. However, rather than hindering holiness, such a broken state makes for gain to man and greater glory to God.[11]

In discussing the state of the entirely sanctified, Wesley made this obvious observation:

> "But even these souls dwell in a shattered body, and are so pressed down thereby, that they cannot always exert themselves as they would, by thinking, speaking, and acting precisely right. For want of better bodily organs, they must at times think, speak, or act wrong; not indeed through a defect of love, but through a defect of knowledge. And while this

149

is the case, notwithstanding that defect, and its consequences, they fulfill the law of love."[12]

This much is certain: they that love God with all their heart, and all men as themselves, are scripturally perfect. And surely such there are; otherwise the promise of God would be a mere mockery of human weakness. Hold fast this: but then remember, on the other hand, you have this treasure in an earthen vessel; you dwell in a poor, shattered house of clay, which presses down the immortal spirit. Hence all your thoughts, words, and actions are so imperfect; so far from coming up to the standard. . . .[13]

Wesley was teaching a perfection here that is not outward. The entirely sanctified are unable to perform as well as they feel at heart. The "shattered" body fails in responding to the inner pure love. Like a musician who has perfect skill would fail with a faulty instrument, so the pure in heart do often falter with their broken earthen vessels. But the "sour notes" on the broken instrument do not disprove the perfection of the prompting love!

Later "holiness" writers have recognized this physical corruption. H. A. Baldwin called it a physical depravity, as did John R. Brooks:

While we live in this world we will never be wholly free from physical desires and appetites. In themselves these desires and appetites are legitimate and are not a sign of depravity, but when men fell, their natural appetites became depraved, and will never, in this life, reach such a state that their possessors will not be forced to deny themselves daily—to keep their bodies under. In other words, while, in the article of holiness, moral depravity is removed, yet physical depravity remains, and a man must deny his inordinate appetites, tastes, desires and preferences. . . .[14]

Baldwin urged caution in the use of the words "depravity" and "inordinate." These are not "sinful" in the sense of moral depravity, but these terms are used for want of better expressions. They reveal the lack of perfection in the natural desires, which can be too strong and need denying. These natural desires "may be warped in the direction of one's own individual besetment." Such a condition is not "actual sin," but is proof of "physical depravity."[15]

By physical depravity is meant the impairment of the substance of the mind or body, resulting from the fall. This may be called the weakness of disease of our nature from which proceed many errors of judgment and consequent blunders in

150

the outer life, neither of which involves a bias toward evil—
a bent toward selfishness and sinfulness—the inclination to what
is inconsistent with love to God and man.[16]

Wesley, as was seen above, had no hesitancy in describing
the body as "debased," "depraved," "shattered," and "broken."
He did not see this "physical depravity" as a condition that
deprived a person of pure love. Even with this mortal, corruptible body, one could have spiritual victory and actually
attain a higher degree of holiness. It is very apparent that
this holiness is not outward performance but inward, pure
intention. This physical condition does affect the soul, because the soul is connected with it, and the body becomes a
means to temptation. Nonetheless, the soul can wholly rely
on God and be filled with *pure* love.[17]

In criticizing E. Stanley Jones, Sangster questions the
use of such phrases as "unconverted instincts," "instincts polluted by the streams of racial tendencies," and "the poison
of old instincts."

> Are the instincts polluted? Can they, in any accurate sense
> be poisoned? Is it devout—or even sensible—to pray that the
> grace of God will deliver us from the instinct of flight, re-
> pulsion, curiosity, pugnacity, self-abasement, self-assertion, sex,
> gregariousness . . . or any other innate psycho-physical disposi-
> tion which has been classified as an instinct? All these may
> be motives to sin, . . . but no one would argue that these
> instincts could be "eradicated" from human nature and leave
> the personality unimpaired. To be human is to have life on
> these terms and in these forms.[18]

Obviously natural desires and instincts are not and could
not be "eradicated" and humanity be preserved. That these
human desires and instincts have been, or at least are,
deprived of ideal qualities because of sin cannot be denied.
They are "warped" in most people. According to Wesley the
body, even of the entirely sanctified, is "liable to" many
"evils" every hour. Weakness and "disorders of a thousand
kinds" are its "natural attendants."[19] According to Brooks,
quoted above, one could have an impairment in his human
nature without retaining a "bent toward selfishness and sinfulness." In other words a person may have a "warp" in his
love. Whatever Wesley may have meant by his doctrine
of "perfect love," he did not mean perfect natural desires or
instincts, perfect bodies or perfect minds. Definitely, instincts

are not "eradicated" nor are they free from impairment. This aspect of human limits will be discussed further in the next section.

Wesley was aware of the need of discipline. Even an ideally perfect Adam needed more discipline than he used. How much more do his fallen sons need discipline for their weakened bodies! Many become spiritual failures because they do not keep their bodies under discipline. Certain perfectionist movements in nineteenth-century America bear witness to failures in utopian ventures because of wrong ideas of human weakness. Wesley advised proper care and discipline of the body.[20] His study of medicine grew out of a desire to help people spiritually by ministering to physical ailments.[21]

Wesley did not believe a perfect body was essential for Christian perfection or perfect holiness. A pure love in the innermost being producing pure affections and tempers may be experienced even while outward manifestations of that love are marred and distorted. For him this glorious treasure in this "earthen vessel" greatly exalts the grace of God. The broken body contributes greatly to personal humility.

C. THE FAULTY MIND

Already it has been suggested that the mind, as well as the body, suffered in the fall of man into sin. In fact it is difficult to distinguish between spirit and body since rational faculties are expressed through physical avenues. One can hardly discuss physical weaknesses without dealing with mental flaws and one cannot treat mental weaknesses without consideration of the body organs. So one need not be surprised at the confusion of terms in dealing with the topic of this section and the topic of the preceding one.

Wesley was quite free to speak of the body and soul as separate entities. He felt that the ego was not the body. The ego was centered in the soul and was "self-moving," a "thinking principle," possessing "passions and affections." This soul can exist apart from the body after death. Yet, Wesley admitted, in the present state the ego seems to consist of both soul and body. "In my present state of existence,

I undoubtedly consist of both soul and body: and so I shall again, after the resurrection, to all eternity."[22]

In this concept of dichotomy did Wesley teach a perfection of the soul in this life while the body was imperfect? There are some statements that appear to imply so. For instance he spoke of the soul being in a shattered body, which presses down the soul.[23] "He also spoke of the body as a 'clog' to the soul."[24] Does Wesley mean that a pure heart is a pure soul restored to an Adamic perfection in every sense except being in a physical body? Wesley did not say this. In fact he indicated otherwise. He taught, as was already observed, that man's likeness to God consisted in his rational powers. These were marred by the Fall, and recovery can be only in the resurrection. The rational faculties are thinking, judging, reasoning, imagining, and remembering. The soul is capable of "love, hatred, joy, sorrow, desire, fear, hope" and other inward emotions.[25] Wesley spoke of the redeemed in this manner:

> Yet still how weak is their understanding! How limited its extent! How confused, how inaccurate are our apprehensions, of even the things that are around about us! How liable are the wisest of men to mistake!—to form false judgments;—to take falsehood for truth, and truth for falsehood;—evil for good, and good for evil. What starts, what wanderings of imagination, are we continually subject to! And how many are the temptations which we have to expect, even from these innocent infirmities![26]

One might still argue that these "confused" apprehensions, "false judgments," "wanderings of the imagination" are directly caused by the broken body. But he could not wisely say that the soul is perfected in its powers, for these powers are still faulty, even after entire sanctification. Speaking further of these saints, Wesley wrote:

> "They are not perfect in knowledge. They are not free from ignorance, no, nor from mistake. We are no more to expect any living man to be infallible, than to be omniscient. They are not free from infirmities, such as weakness or slowness of understanding, irregular quickness or heaviness or imagination."[27]

Even wandering thoughts, the involuntary association of ideas, occur in the sanctified.[28] These flaws in the mind are consequences of sin, and they will remain with man throughout this life.

Consistent also with the entirely sanctified is heaviness of spirit. This heaviness may be so deep as to "overshadow the whole soul; to give a colour, as it were, to all the affections; such as will appear in the whole behaviour." In such a case as this "the soul rather presses down the body, and weakens it more and more."[29] Here in this case Wesley recognized a soul condition created, not by the body, but directly in the spirit. This sorrow or heaviness is caused by temptation. Bodily disorders or disease may lead to such. Calamity, or death of loved ones, may cause such a trial.[30] Whatever the cause, here is an experience that reveals the limitations of one's natural understanding.

Daniel Steele taught that "sin has impaired the powers of universal humanity." He wrote that infirmities "have their ground in our physical nature and they are aggravated by intellectual deficiencies." They "are without remedy so long as we are in this body."[31] Brockett quotes H. C. Morrison as saying:

> We do not profess to be angels when we receive the great blessing, but just common men and women, woefully weak, still under the curse of the fall as to mental and physical powers, but pure and holy in the heart, and filled with His perfect love.[32]
> Today his faithful people can have the sin problem completely solved, and come into his presence with a pure heart, but all these days we must carry with us the defects of our fallen and imperfect bodies, and the weaknesses and imperfections of our blighted mentality.[33]

Two things are especially clear by now in the teaching of perfection. There is no perfection of either the body as an instrument of the soul, or the soul in its rational powers or natural instincts. Human nature as such has suffered a disease and the scars remain. The disease can be cured and the fever may go, but scars abide in the affected parts. They are the natural consequences of a sinful race and of a sinning person. The removal of the scars must await the final perfection.

These scars of human nature are found in impaired natural powers. Yet these powers belong to the ego and make up the person. It cannot be rightly said that, after entire sanctification, all conflict is transferred to the outside and that there is no inner conflict. "Any battle in life that is a battle to *me* is on the inside."[34] The question to ask in this battle is whether it is with natural desires and instincts that clamor for satisfaction or with a moral desire or inclination which divides the loyalty of the will. Obviously there is a difference.

Paul Abel denies that human nature as such is impaired by sin. He rightly claims that "the essential constituents in human nature within each individual are neither moral nor immoral; they are morally neutral." Depravity, for Abel, is the "particular state in which human nature may be, but does not refer to human nature itself."

> Again, depravity does not necessarily mean that man's nature is foul or corrupted; rather, it means "that everything in human life is affected by the fundamental wrong relationship to God which lies at the root of man's being." In a word, it is the demerit which resulted from Adam's Primal Sin, by which human nature lost its organizing principle of fellowship with God. It is the *condition* of the essential human traits which inevitably gives direction toward evil, but is not the traits themselves. Thus, depravity is not in itself a defect in the primal elements of human nature; it is a defect in the organization of human nature.[35]

Abel uses the word "depravity" here only in the moral sense. Actually he would deny a "physical depravity," as used above by Baldwin and Brooks, when he says that "man's faculties are not impaired by sin." His correct emphasis upon the fact that humanity is not moral depravity has led him to conclude wrongly that human nature, as such, did not suffer loss in the Fall.[36]

This kind of mistake is easy to make and leads directly to the conclusion that when the depravity is removed in sanctification man is then restored to the Adamic perfection. For why would not the person who by grace is "reorganized, integrated, and made complete" be as Adam was? If this "depravity is removed" in entire sanctification, and "full integration takes place," and if "humanity finds its originally intended norm," there ought to be a perfect performance without mistake. To admit that there are mistakes made "through physical frailty and misunderstanding" is to recognize an impairment to human nature.[37] Human faculties since the Fall are not as easily directed and controlled as one could wish. It is in the full surrender to the "integrating Spirit" and in the being "unified about the principle of Perfect Love" that one finds the way to bring into captivity the broken human nature.

Paul Rees recognizes the possibility of conflict arising within a person's nature after the "invasion and control of Perfect Love."

> Receiving the gift of love's fulness, whereby we are inwardly united in allegiance to the mind of Christ, may be the crisis of an hour or a moment; but resolving and controlling those conflicts that from time to time arise in the area of the natural instincts are processes that require constant, prayerful, and intelligent direction. The same Paul who said, "Put off the old man," declared, "I keep under my body." The first may be thought of as a deliverance; the second must be thought of as a discipline. The language which Paul uses, as when he speaks of bringing the body into subjection, indicates conflict. It speaks of tension. I see no point in denying it. Only let it be remembered that the conflict found its solution—its practical management if you will—in continuous sublimation and self-control.[88]

It can now be said that sin affected the human nature in two ways. First, it separated man from God and destroyed his fellowship with God with the result that he lost the integrating presence of the Holy Spirit. His moral nature became corrupted. In redemption fellowship is restored, the Holy Spirit again fills the heart, and, in entire sanctification, the moral depravity is completely removed, and perfect love restored. In Wesley's terms this is the full restoration of moral likeness to God, or holiness.

But sin also did something else. It brought death to the physical nature of man. The body is broken and corruptible. Also the mental faculties and natural traits of man, though not destroyed, are marred and faulty. In redemption this human nature is assisted and controlled, but it is not restored to its original perfection until after death. The entirely sanctified have need of constant vigilance and discipline.

D. Carnal or Human

Often in this investigation it has been suggested that there is a difference between moral and natural likeness to God. The lack of the first is sin while the lack of the second is infirmity. The problem of determining this difference is very evident and occasioned considerable controversy for Wesley and his successors. While one may say the difference is made clear by using the terms "inward" and "outward," or "infirmity" and "sin," or "carnality" and "humanity," or even "soul" and "body," yet, on further thought, the problem remains and the line between the two is vague. A static theological distinction may break down in the existential situation.

Granted that carnality is not humanity but a depravity or disordering of humanity, one should be able to separate the disease from the substance. In life, however, how can one know when a natural urge or desire clamoring for satisfaction is different from the moral desire? In temptation, how is one to distinguish between the sex urge for a wrong object and the "deeper down" moral inclination? How does one know that the natural desire for a wrong satisfaction is not also a moral one? To say there is a difference is one thing; to experience the difference in a life situation is another thing! Is the desire or instinct carnal, or only human?

It is possible to quote statements from Wesley that seem to mean not only a perfection of love in the source of actions, but also the accomplishment of a perfect act. Especially some of his pointed questions appear to mean that much.

> Do you find no interruption or abatement at any time of your joy in the Lord? Do you continually see God; and without any cloud, or darkness, or mist between? Do you pray without ceasing, without ever being diverted from it by anything inward or outward? Are you ever hindered by any person or thing? by the power or subtlety of Satan, or by weakness or disorders of body, pressing down the soul? Can you be thankful for every thing without exception? And do you feel all working together for good? Do you do nothing, great or small, merely to please yourself? Do you feel no touch of any desire or affection but what springs from the pure love of God? Do you speak no words but from a principle of love, and under the guidance of his Spirit?[39]

Or in the "Character of a Methodist" the questions are statements of fact:

> All the commandments of God he accordingly keeps, and that with all his might. For his obedience is in proportion to his love, the source from whence it flows. . . . All the

157

talents he has received, he constantly employs according to his Master's will; every power and faculty of his soul, every member of his body....

He cannot join in or countenance any diversion which has the least tendency to vice of any kind. He cannot "speak evil" of his neighbor, anymore than he can lie either for God or man. He cannot utter an unkind word of any one; for love keeps the door of his lips....

He is inwardly and outwardly conformed to the will of God, as revealed in the written word. He thinks, speaks, and lives, according to the method laid down in the revelation of Jesus Christ....[40]

If these were the only statements read from Wesley, it could be said he left no place for mistakes, infirmities, or human failures!

While the Christian, or "Methodist," does perform in this manner as far as the motivation in love, intent, and pure desire is concerned, it cannot mean that he has succeeded in an objective performance that is perfect either in his own eyes or in those of others. Actually Wesley has two goals in mind. The one is a perfect performance just as he described it in these above words, and the other is a perfect love that prompts the striving, the desire, and the purpose to perform. The first goal no one can possibly attain in this life, as has already been indicated; the second goal is attainable for all. That this conclusion is a true judgment of Wesley can be found in his answer to a criticism of "The Character of a Methodist," which was written in 1767 and quoted in a letter:

"Five or six and twenty years ago, a thought came into my mind, of drawing such a character myself, only in a more scriptural manner, and mostly in the very words of Scripture: This I entitled 'The Character of a Methodist,' believing that curiosity would incite more persons to read it and also that some prejudice might thereby be removed from candid men. But that none might imagine I intended a panegyric either on myself or my friends, I guarded against this in the very title-page saying, both in the name of myself and them, 'Not as though I had already attained, either were already perfect.' To the same effect I speak in the conclusion, "These are the principles and practices of our sect; these are the marks of a true Methodist; i.e., a true Christian, as I immediately after explain myself: 'By these alone to those who are in dirision so called *desire* to be distinguished from other men.' 'by these marks do we *labour* to distinguish ourselves from those whose minds or lives are not according to the Gospel of Christ.' "[41]

By disclaiming the kind of perfection drawn in "The Character of a Methodist" both for himself and others, Wesley made it the final goal toward which the pure in heart aim. Perfect love is to be found in the *"desire"* that causes one to *"labour"* for this "character" rather than in the perfect performance desired. There are those who insist that Wesley personally denied his attainment of Christian perfection by his denial of attaining the "character of a Methodist."[42] He emphatically wrote, "I have told all the world I am not perfect. . . . I tell you flat, I have not attained the character I draw." He denied that any Methodist attained this character.[43] Yet all these works, though they fall short of the perfect goal, are made holy and acceptable to God by a "pure and holy intention."[44]

Wesley recognized there were such things as "animal joy" and "natural love."[45] He considered it natural for him to be free of worry and to have no weight upon his mind.[46] On the other hand, he claimed that anger was natural to him, even "irregular, unreasonable anger." He wrote, "I am naturally inclined to this, as I experience every day."[47] Yet in another place Wesley wrote, "A man strikes me. Here is a temptation to anger. But my heart overflows with love. And I feel no anger at all; of which I can be as sure, as that love and anger are not the same."[48] What does Wesley mean by claiming to "experience" a natural anger every day and yet in temptation when love overflows he feels "no anger at all"? It can be wished that Wesley had made himself more clear at this point. Did he mean that, as a natural instinct, anger was his besetment, and in temptation he could experience it as unreasonable and irregular? But in his heart where love was pure and overflowed, did he feel no anger, and did this perfect love give complete victory over the temptation to anger? It would seem so. He experienced natural anger while he felt no sinful anger. A blind, natural instinct was enticed by satanic temptation, but the heart, full of love, recoiled and gave no moral response. The holy love, or intent, in the moral nature gave no place to the evil impulse and kept the natural anger from becoming an evil temper.

Is this distinction between temptation and corruption, between sinful and natural, between carnal and human, valid? That Wesley held such a distinction must be admitted. He believed that in general one could distinguish between temptation to anger, pride, or lust on the one hand, and corruption of heart on the other. Sometimes, however, it took the direct witness of the Spirit.[49]

> Truth and falsehood, and so right and wrong tempers, are often divided by an almost imperceptible line. It is more difficult to distinguish right and wrong tempers, or passions, because, in several instances, the same motion of the blood and animal spirits will attend both one and the other. Therefore, in many cases, we cannot distinguish them, but by the unction of the Holy One. In the case you mention, all self-complacency or self-approbation is not pride. Certainly there may be self-approbation, which is not sin, though it must occasion a degree of pleasure.[50]

Wesley further taught that there could be an "ebb and flow" to "heartfelt joy" while there was a constant "humble, gentle, patient love." He was willing to sum up the latter in the one word "resignation."[51] The distinction between a troubled nature and a perfect heart to Wesley's mind seemed clear:

> One may start, tremble, change colour, or be otherwise disordered in body, while the soul is calmly stayed on God, and remains in perfect peace. Nay the mind itself may be deeply distressed, may be exceeding sorrowful, may be perplexed and pressed down by heaviness and anguish, even to agony, while the heart cleaves to God by perfect love, and the will is wholly resigned to him.[52]

Certainly if there is such a thing as total commitment to God, as a pure love for Him, as a pure heart and resigned will, then some such distinction as Wesley made is valid. Even some such distinction must be made for the perfect Son of God in His earthly career.

J. R. Brooks was willing to admit that there is a degree of "vagueness and indefiniteness" about this distinction between natural and carnal, but insisted such is true about many doctrines of Scripture.[53] The "morbid and abnormal" can be eliminated while the "blind appetites and passions" are "controlled through the Christ life" in us.[54]

> All thoughtful men realize the difficulty of distinguishing certain virtues and vices—the innocent and sinful expressions of some of our natural affections, propensities, etc. For example, the line of demarcation between innocent self-love and selfish-

plainness of apparel. One should not wear expensive clothing, nor should his dress be "gay, airy or showy."[62]

> Wear no gold (whatever officers of State may do; or Magistrates, as the ensign of their office,) no pearls, or precious stones; use no curling of the hair, or costly apparel, how grave soever. I advise those who are able to receive this saying, Buy no velvets, no silks, no fine linen, no superfluities, no mere ornaments, though ever so much in fashion. Wear nothing, though you have it already, which is of a glaring colour, or which is in any kind gay, glistering, or showy; nothing made in the very height of fashion, nothing apt to attract the eyes of the by-standers.[63]

Wesley taught his people to eat "plain, cheap, wholesome food, which most promotes health both of body and mind." Their conversation should be "calculated to edify" and to build up "faith, or love, or holiness." Relaxation is necessary. "We need intervals of diversion from business." Some diversions, Wesley thought, are clearly wrong, such as "cock fighting, bear baiting, and other foul remains of Gothic barbarity." The "English theatre," with its "profaneness and debauchery," was condemned. Public dancing was frowned upon. Other diversions, such as plays, novels, cards, hunting, even if innocent, were not the best. Why not cultivate gardens, visit the needy, read history, good poetry, philosophy, or else play music? Wesley sought the "more excellent way."[64]

Wesley had much to say about riches. He feared the love of money more than any other evil. Money is necessary for paying debts, providing for necessities—not "delicacies" or "superfluities"—and for carrying on worldly business. Riches alone are not wrong but the desire for riches is sin. One should not seek happiness in riches nor trust in them.[65] Wesley believed that many Methodists had fallen and many more would fall because they did not heed his warnings on the danger of money.[66] It is all right to gain all one can and to save all one can provided that he gives all he can. Wesley felt that he could not personally lay up any treasure for himself on earth. He must have nothing left at the end of each year. Wesley was almost obsessed with the fear that riches were ruining the Methodist revival![67]

Why did Wesley feel this way toward the natural things of human life? He was earnest in his desire to conform the whole man to the image of God. He knew the subtlety in temptation and the dangers in the things of nature. He felt that costly attire "engenders pride," "tends to breed and to increase vanity," "naturally tends to beget anger" and "tends to create and inflame lust." Furthermore, to spend money on oneself needlessly prevents the ability to feed the poor and clothe the naked. Even if one could be as humble in expensive clothing as in cheap attire, yet he could not be as beneficent since he would have spent more money than necessary on himself.[68]

Was Wesley's asceticism a defect in his concept of perfection, as Flew thinks?[69] It can readily be admitted that an extreme emphasis on his view does lead to false views of Christianity. Too many have made holiness to consist of "negatives" and have measured one's grace by his self-denials. But the opposite view that gives free course to nature's desires has never led to holiness of life nor New Testament Christianity. Discipline and self-denial are obviously lasting ingredients of the Christian life and essential to the perfect ideal. Wesley was human and likely erred in an overemphasis upon certain factors. However, who will deny that certain discipline was needed then, and now?

Wesley wanted holy men. He knew the depravity of the race and the weaknesses of the human nature. He also knew the power of God's grace to redeem the individual and the race. But he believed man's cooperation was needed, both in the purifying of his own heart and in the discipline of his human nature. The most rapid and sure way to let perfect love exert itself was by the discipline of self-denial. This was not a sour note from Wesley; it was his concept of the way to the greatest happiness.

What can these entirely sanctified people be expected to do with the world in which they live? It is clear that they are not to withdraw from the world. They are part of the world though certainly possessed by a different spirit. What are the social implications? Can they be expected to make this evil world into a new one?

Wesley did not envision a utopian society. His principles require a changed person before a changed society. The task is to make better individuals before society can be better. Wesley placed no barrier to the power of grace to transform the individual. Not a thing could keep him from loving God perfectly, and his neighbor. But this person with perfect love needed all his years on earth to let this perfect love *emerge* into outward acts of piety and charity. But these could never be perfect. Even the most holy of men could not create a perfect society.[70]

In his sermon on "The Mystery of Iniquity," Wesley pointed out the evil "leaven" that has continually harassed the Church. The "mystery of iniquity" was present in the New Testament Church.[71] It showed up again and again in the days of Tertullian, Cyprian, and Constantine. From Constantine to the Reformation, the state of the Church was deplorable.[72] In the Reformation manners were not reformed, and apostasy was universal. Wesley wrote that "the whole world never did, nor can at this day, show a Christian country or city."[73] Wesley had hope for the future, but not until both "moral and natural corruption" are removed, and sin and pain are no more.[74] Obviously there must be a change in human existence before a perfect society can be seen. It is clear in Wesley that evil society cannot keep individual Christians from being "holy and unblameable."

Can there be a holy Church? Yes, Wesley believed the Church is holy because its members are holy.[75] No one is a true member of the Church unless he has been born anew. True believers are initially sanctified, so therefore holiness has begun in them. Thus all members are holy although only holy in degrees. Within this holy Church there are schisms and heresies. These are caused by evil tempers in true church members who are not sanctified wholly.[76] Wesley never had much hope of many Christians ever reaching Christian perfection very long before death. The Church is largely composed of believers who have yet the "remains of sin" in them.[77]

But if all the members of a church were entirely sanctified, would that church be perfect? If such a church ever existed, it would be unusual, but it would have its own peculiar problems. Even those who are "really perfect in love" are still "encompassed with infirmities."

> They may be dull of apprehension; they may have a natural heedlessness, or a treacherous memory; they may have too lively an imagination: and any of these may cause little improprieties, either in speech or behaviour, which, though not

sinful in themselves, may try all the grace you have: especially if you impute to perverseness of will, (as it is very natural to do,) what is really owing to defect of memory, or weakness of understanding;—if these appear to you to be voluntary mistakes, which are really involuntary. So proper was the answer which a saint of God (now in Abraham's bosom) gave me some years ago, when I said, "Jenny, surely now your mistress and you can neither of you be a trial to the other, as God has saved you both from sin." "Oh, sir," said she, "if we are saved from sin, we still have infirmities enough to try all the grace that God has given us."[78]

It is apparent that the gap between the perfect love in the heart of a Christian and the perfected outward holiness in everyday living is sufficiently great to require a lifetime of growth and Christian development. Obviously the social order would be improved if all men were Christians. It would be much better still if all Christians were perfect in love. But even then such a society of holy beings in this world would leave much to be desired. They could be holy, but their world would be imperfect.

Is it possible to live a perfect life in an imperfect world? Need we be reminded that Christ did? Christ was made in the "likeness of the fallen creatures" and was made a "real man."[79]

> Yet, even here, we must be careful to make clear what we mean. Christ only lived a perfect life in the sense that He always acted with a perfect motive. He did not always do what a perfect man would do in a perfect world. In the latter, for instance, there would have been no whip for the Temple traders, no "woes" for the Pharisees, no tribute money for the foreign conqueror. Nor would He have gone to the cross.[80]

Nor is it valid to say we are not perfect because we are involved in the sins of society. In that sense Jesus would have been imperfect too. This involvement in "social sins" is an unfortunate consequence of "immoral society," but it need not destroy the possibility of perfect love.

Wesley preached against the violations of justice which he saw. He opposed the oppression of widows and orphans and the living in luxury while there are needs in the world. He called for repentance for the evils caused by one's nation. He pleaded for peace by the ending of war and contention.[81] At the same time Wesley taught that the man of the world who fears not God was to be avoided. There should be no close attachment nor intermarriage with evil men.[82] The Christian must refuse close association with wicked or ungodly men.[83]

Wesley's pessimism concerning the recovery of a wicked world should not blind one to his passion to relieve suffering. His first interest was the spiritual welfare of men, but in his great work man's material needs were remembered.

> Some historians have said that the leaders of the Evangelical Revival of the eighteenth century had no interest in the bodies of men—but it is not hard to rebut this criticism. They had the deepest interest in men's bodies. They fostered a hundred philanthropies—orphanages, hospitals, dispensaries, homes for the aged poor, loan societies and many kindred works of mercy. They fought slavery, smuggling, intemperance, the evil conditions of our prisons, and every form of vice which they recognized as such. It is true that it was mostly social salvage work—even with the great Lord Shaftesbury, who gladly traced his inspiration to John Wesley. But to complain that these men were not communally constructive, and had no great Christian sociology, is to lose all time-sense and accuse them for not being born a century or two later than they were.[84]

For Wesley holiness was both inward and outward. Inward holiness is heart purity or perfect love and is the true essence of pure religion. This inward holiness is accompanied by outward holiness, but these outward acts of piety are limited by human frailty. At the source of one's action he is perfect in motive and intention; in the act itself as it finds expression in outward performance there are limitations and imperfections. These imperfections are found both in the individual, who is perfect in love, and in his social environment. The entirely sanctified person is to discipline himself and bring his powers into subjection to the perfect love, and he is to reveal his love by improving the social order. The imperfect society and the limited human nature are testing grounds for the purity of the heart love. It is in such an environment that perfect love shines.

CHAPTER VI

"SINS" OF THE SANCTIFIED

When one speaks of the sins of the sanctified, it is necessary that he define his meaning. Wesley believed that one fact about the sin problem is settled when the sinner is regenerated. The one born of God does not commit sin. The youngest and weakest child of God is finished with this kind of sin. As long as he possesses this living faith, he does not willfully transgress a known law of God. The only way the believer could ever again sin in this sense is to backslide and lose his justifying faith.

Nor do the sins of the sanctified mean that sinfulness which remains in the believer after justification, but which is purged in the experience of entire sanctification. The "sin in believers" for Wesley was very real and needed the cleansing Blood. This kind of sin is present in the initially sanctified but it no longer remains in the entirely sanctified. The entirely sanctified may lose his state of grace and revert back to the sinfulness of the believer, but so long as he maintains this "second grace" he is free from this second kind of sin.

But Wesley saw a third kind of sin which he variously called "sins" of ignorance, or "sins" of infirmity, or mistakes. These sins are consistent with perfect love and are experienced constantly by the entirely sanctified. From these sins no saint is ever delivered in this life. Wesley opposed any who made perfection include freedom from these sins. To make perfection higher than a perfect love compatible with an earthly and corruptible body is to "sap the foundation of it, and destroy it from the face of the earth."[1]

> I still say, and without any self-contradiction, I know no persons living who are so deeply conscious of their needing Christ both as prophet, priest, and king, as those who believe themselves, and whom I believe, to be cleansed from all sin; I mean, from all pride, anger, evil desire, idolatry, and unbelief. These very persons feel more than ever their own ignorance, littleness of grace, coming short of the full mind that was in Christ, and walking less accurately than they

might have done after their Divine Pattern; are more convinced of the insufficiency of all they are, have, or do, to bear the eye of God without a Mediator; are more penetrated with the sense of the want of him than ever they were before.

Here are persons exceeding holy and happy; rejoicing evermore, praying always, and in everything giving thanks; feeling the love of God and man every moment; feeling no pride, or other evil temper . . . "But are they not sinners?" Explain the term one way, and I say, Yes; another, and I say, No.[2]

Wesley, along with most leaders in the Christian Church, taught that the holiest saint is yet a sinner. Obviously he is not a sinner in the same sense that he was before regeneration nor even in the same sense as before entire sanctification. But that he is yet a sinner in the sense of abhorring himself, and of being penitent, should not be disallowed.[3] An emphasis on Wesley's clear-cut definition of sin as a "wilful transgression of a known law" must not blind us to this clearly defined aspect of sin also found in Wesley's thought.

A. SINS OF IGNORANCE

These sins of the sanctified may be hidden to the consciousness of the person. Here again one must proceed cautiously. To mix the idea of an "unconscious sin" which is of an innocent nature with those deceptive sins which blind men's hearts because of a lack of awakening by the Spirit is to bring confusion. It is at this point that both Flew and Sangster wrongly accuse Wesley.[4] Wesley recognized unconscious, hidden springs of action in the human heart that only the Spirit could uncover. No one was sanctified until this kind of sin was uncovered, and cleansed by the Holy Spirit. Wesley knew that the heart of man was deceitful.[5]

But there are other kinds of sin that are not of this deceitful branch, yet are sins of ignorance. Wesley longed for his people to have more knowledge so they would be more stable.[6] He saw the close connection between right judgment and right action. If a person because of ignorance judged wrongly, he would necessarily act wrongly.[7] This means that an entirely sanctified person who is still deficient in knowledge wrongly judges his path of duty and so acts in a wrong manner. And yet all the time he will believe he is doing the right thing unless new knowledge comes to him. This sin because of ignorance could be serious and needs the atoning merit of Christ. Yet for the entirely sanctified this faulty act is prompted by perfect love and by a pure heart that is ready and willing for more light. Such a person may be deceived by his own ignorance, but he cannot be an egoist, "quarrelsome," or "selfish" while perfect love rules his motives. Ignorance and wicked deceit are not the same. The entirely sanctified may be ignorant and act in ignorance and thus unconsciously do wrongly, but within himself there cannot be any selfish or wicked motivation.

It must be remembered that the profession of this Christian perfection does not make one holy. Because a man testifies that his heart is pure does not make it so. It is possible for deception to be present in one's mind when he thinks he is pure, when in reality he is not. Such false professions bring reproach on any teaching, but counterfeits do not destroy the true. It is wrong to discount all heart holiness because many claims to it are false. Nor should every unconscious wrong action of a person so professing be interpreted to mean a self-deceived heart.

Wesley knew there were dangers in this high profession of grace, and constantly warned those who made the high claim.[8] On the other hand, the saint needs "simplicity," a grace "which cuts the soul off from all unnecessary reflections upon itself." It is possible to become so sensitive about oneself as to yield to satanic suggestion and lose confidence in God's work in the soul.[9] Wesley sought a proper balance between a sincere heart searching on the one hand, and on overcautious, unreasonable sensitivity on the other. The secret was earnest and simple dependence upon the mercy of God.

Failure to recognize the limitations in knowledge is disastrous to anyone who claims perfect love. To claim a possession of greater knowledge leads to pride, the first enemy of all perfect love. The entirely sanctified know that they are weak, ignorant, and utterly dependent on Him who is their Sanctifier. One of the first marks of pure love is the absence of any pride of knowledge or attainment. The sanctified are aware that they act often out of ignorance, for which reason they are yet sinners in this sense.

B. Bodily Infirmities

That there are infirmities of the body no one should deny. The question is as to whether these infirmities should be called sins. Calvin had no hesitancy to call them sins, and he believed that Augustine laid the groundwork for such appellation, although Augustine seemed to make a distinction between sin and infirmity. Speaking of Augustine, Calvin wrote:

> Between him and us, this difference may be discovered—that while he concedes that believers, so long as they inhabit a mortal body, are so bound by concupiscence that they cannot but feel irregular desires, yet he ventures not to call this disease by the name of sin, but, content with designating it by the appellation of infirmity, teaches that it only becomes sin in cases where either action or consent is added to the conception or apprehension of the mind, that is, where the will yields to the first impulse of appetite. But we, on the contrary, deem it to be sin, whenever a man feels any evil desires contrary to the Divine law; and we also assert the depravity itself to be sin, which produces these desires in our minds. We maintain, therefore, that sin always exists in the saints, till they are divested of the mortal body; because their flesh is the residence of that depravity of concupiscence, which is repugnant to all rectitude. Nevertheless, he has not always refrained from using the word *sin* in this sense; as when he says, "Paul gives the appellation of sin to this, from which all sins proceed, that is, to carnal concupiscence. This, as it respects the saints, loses its kingdom on earth, and has no existence in heaven." In these words he acknowledges that believers are guilty of sin, inasmuch as they are the subjects of carnal concupiscence.[10]

This problem of the difference between sin and infirmity which created a tension in Augustine's mind and was set aside by Calvin as having no significance was at least partially solved by Wesley. Clearly Wesley, in agreement with Augustine, did not call the infirmities resulting from a mortal body sins in the proper sense. They could become sins only when "action or consent is added," and the "will yields." Furthermore, Wesley did not make "irregular desires" which are a part of the corruptible body to be moral depravity. Irregular desires are only "bodily depravity" unless there is a corresponding disposition of the will to yield to the wrong desires. This wrong disposition of the moral nature is the sinful, or moral, depravity, or "carnal concupiscence."

With Augustine, but against Calvin, Wesley distinguished between "irregular desires" and "wilful transgression." Against both Augustine and Calvin he distinguished between "innocent infirmities" and "carnal concupiscence."

Wesley never hesitated to call the "moral depravity," or, in Calvin's terms, "carnal concupiscence," by the name of sin. This depravity is the "sin in believers," the evil tempers and desires, and it is purged in entire sanctification. But what about the innocent infirmities, the "irregular desires" of the body? Are they also sins? Yes, in a certain sense, they are also sins.

These "parts in the animal machine" are the basis for considerable satanic attack which God permits.[11] The body "is liable to" many "evils" every day and hour. Temptations will constantly beset a man who "dwells in this corruptible body."[12] There will be "grief," "sorrow," and "heaviness connected with this earthly existence."[13] There is a "degree of anger" which is not a "sinful anger" nor an opposite of love and compassion.[14] This anger which is not sinful "is often attended with much commotion of the animal spirits." Only with God's light can it be well distinguished from sinful anger.[15] This "house of clay" has the power of "dulling or darkening the understanding" and of "damping and depressing the soul, and sinking it into distress and heaviness." It is possible in this condition for "doubt and fear" to "naturally arise," and for Satan to "disturb" the cleansed heart, though he cannot "pollute" it.[16]

Furthermore, there can be a "wandering" of the thoughts and many other "deficiencies" without a break in the pure love.[17] A mother may have little children and "worldly care" and a "weak body," and for a time have "no joy at all" but much "sorrow and heaviness," yet be a possessor of great grace.[18] One may speak "sharply or roughly" with an apparent "want of meekness." Such a situation is hard to reconcile with perfection but one should not condemn "whom God has not condemned."[19] One could add to these statements from Wesley many more where he allows for the human infirmity that grows out of the weakness in present existence. These infirmities Wesley held were not willful sins, nor were they necessarily marks of a moral depravity. Yet all of them were sins in a certain sense and needed the atoning Christ.[20]

Sins in this third sense are not removed from the entirely sanctified, and it is wrong to speak of "eradication" in relation to them. Many who have taught Christian perfection have been misled at this point, and expected freedom from troubling dreams, human passions, faulty temperaments, worry, and even timidity.[21] In speaking of dreams Daniel Steele wrote that the "most peaceable, quarrel; the most gentle and tender, commit murder; the most contented with life, plot suicide; the temperate, become drunken; the most pure, become impure."[22]

Obviously it is wrong to accuse Wesley of teaching a perfection that is freedom from all sin when this third kind of sin is meant. Wesley would have agreed with Luther when Luther wrote:

> Brother, it is not possible for thee to become so righteous in this life, that thou shouldest feel no sin at all, that the body should be clear like the sun, without spot or blemish; but thou hast as yet wrinkles and spots, and yet art thou holy notwithstanding.[23]

Wesley's quarrel with Luther was in his failure to distinguish between the sin that is a "spot or blemish" in the body and the sin of an evil temper or disposition of the will. One in this life can be "so righteous" as to be free from the latter, but not the former. Nonetheless, these "wrinkles and spots" in the corruptible body, for Wesley, need the atoning sacrifice. In that sense they are yet called sins.

C. Social Sins

Because of the "sins of ignorance" and the "bodily infirmities," the entirely sanctified will have mistakes and failures in their social relationships. One must be careful not to judge Wesley by the standards of social consciousness developed in the last century. However, it is interesting to observe Wesley's principle of perfect love as it is related to social behavior. It has already been pointed out that the performance of the entirely sanctified does not measure up to the same standard as the love itself. One may have perfect love without the ability to express that love perfectly. As long as one is in the body he will come short of what he would be. There will be "numberless defects," and the imperfection of one's "best actions and tempers."[24]

173

As already observed, the holiest of men fail the perfect law of God. No man is able to keep a law where he is required to "always think, always speak, and always act precisely right." It is as "natural for man" since the Fall "to mistake as to breathe." No man can perform what the Adamic law requires nor is he obliged to do so. Man is now under a new law—"the law of faith." Faith produces the love which fulfills the law of God.[25]

But does one fail in this law of love? Before God there is no failure because all action is prompted by pure love which sanctifies the act performed. However, since the person so prompted commits mistakes, he fails to respond in his social acts as it would seem that he ought to when prompted by love. It is in this failure that even the entirely sanctified fail the law of love.

> "The best of men need Christ as their Priest, their Atonement, their Advocate with the Father; not only as the continuance of their every blessing depends on his death and intercession, but on account of their coming short of the law of love. For every man living does so. You who feel all love, compare yourselves with the preceding description. Weigh yourselves in this balance, and see if you are not wanting in many particulars.
>
> "But if all this be consistent with Christian perfection, that perfection is not freedom from all sin; seeing sin is the transgression of the law: and the perfect transgress the very law they are under. Besides, they need the atonement of Christ; and he is the atonement of nothing but sin."[26]

To come "short of the law of love" might mean that love is not as warm at one time as another.[27] Also imperfections in "thought, words, and actions" mean that one does not come "up to standard."[28] Consequently one sins in his social behavior every day, not because he does not have perfect love, but because he cannot act as perfectly as he should.

It is only natural, then, for even the holiest of people to offend others in their conduct. Even when all actions spring from love, one is not infallible.

> "For neither love nor the 'unction of the Holy One' makes us infallible: Therefore, through unavoidable defect of understanding, we cannot but mistake in many things. And these mistakes will frequently occasion something wrong, both in our temper, and words, and actions. From mistaking his character, we may love a person less than he really deserves."[29]

Obviously this kind of mistake is not only a defect within the person making it, but it is a social failure. The person fails to treat another person as well as he should. This is a social sin and as such needs the "atoning blood."[30] These mistakes are "short-comings," "omissions" and "defects of various kinds." These mistakes are both "in judgment and practice." They are "deviations from the perfect law." They are not sins in the proper, scriptural sense, but they are sins "improperly so called." They are "involuntary transgressions" which follow naturally from ignorance and mortality. Wesley refused to use the term "sinless perfection" because of this kind of transgression; yet these transgressions, for him, were not truly sins. What Wesley means is that they are not sins in the same sense and kind with willful transgressions and with corrupt, sinful depravity. Yet they do involve a person in wrong actions.[31]

Why did Wesley refuse to call these defects "sins" in the proper sense? He was afraid that if "any sins" were allowed to "be consistent with perfection, few would confine the idea to those defects concerning which only the assertion could be true."[32] In other words, if the term "sin" is used to describe certain failures in the Christian life, it is easy for undiscerning m i n d s to allow for more than innocent failures. If mistakes and failures are called sins, what shall we call the acts of wicked and rebellious men? When both kinds of actions are called sins, the history of doctrine reveals the haziness of any distinction. As in Calvin, sin is sin, if only a mistaken judgment.

However, there is danger in the opposite position. When mistakes and failures are not called "sins," but are named innocent infirmities and weaknesses, two possibilities occur. Either proper sins are classified as mistakes and innocent failures, and thus excused, or innocent failures are minimized and excused with the result that they are not corrected. In either case there are serious social implications.

Wesley saw that a perfectly sanctified person could love a person less than he should, or his love for a person might cause him to think that person better than he is.[33] In this we have the basis for conflict in a person's decisions and conduct. Here is a father who loves his child. This love leads him to overindulge his love and thus to fail in proper

175

discipline. On the other hand, in his desire to train properly his child he wrongly judges and administers wrong punishment. In either case the father "sins" against his child even though out of pure love. This is just one area in which the sanctified may commit "social sins." To call them innocent and insignificant is dangerous. To believe that they need not the atonement is irreligious. However, to say that these sins are the same as those that grow out of an evil heart and selfish desire would be equally dangerous.

There are social sins of which all are guilty and in which all have sinned. Wesley saw the involvement of individual citizens in national sins. He called for a national repentance.[34] But he did not see this involvement as opposed to his doctrine of perfect love. If all individuals possessed perfect love, there still would be imperfect judgment leading to wrong actions. For instance, a person's wrong action at the polls might help elect a representative whose later vote would lead to war. Yet the person and his representative may have acted out of pure love, but with poor judgment. On the contrary, to have acted otherwise in trying to prevent war might have encouraged an aggressor against their own country and homes. In either case a form of guilt is incurred from which a person cannot free himself. It must be remembered that even Jesus was involved in this kind of social sin, although He always acted out of perfect love.

To widen the meaning of sin to include "social sins" and the meaning of perfection to include "redemption of social life" need not destroy the Wesleyan idea of perfect love.[35] The redemption of society is dependent on the redeemed individual. No matter how one feels about his failures in the social order, he can still be filled with pure love and order his conduct accordingly. "There are situations in which we must hold the makers of mistakes blameable for their mistakes," and surely the perfect in heart *wants* to bear his responsibility. Maybe "no high ideal" is reached where blunders do not harm others so far as social conduct is concerned, but it is a "high ideal" attained when a person so blundering acts out of love and exerts himself to correct his mistakes. It is wrong to criticize Wesley's concept of perfection without recognition of these facts.[36]

Holy Christians know that they make mistakes. They

are "afflicted with a sense of failure in their labors."[37] Though these mistakes will not condemn one before God, yet they "cannot bear the rigour of God's justice" and so need "the atoning blood." "None feel their need of Christ like these; none so entirely depend upon him."[38] In humility the entirely sanctified may recognize their blunders and failures, even those that cause harm to others, and seek divine and human forgiveness; they should endeavor to correct their behavior when possible and to maintain perfect love continuously.

D. BACKSLIDINGS

One problem to the minds of many who are not in agreement with Wesley's view on perfection has been that of sinning again. To them it has seemed impossible for the entirely sanctified to yield to temptation. Interestingly enough this seeming impossibility was not a problem to Wesley. His was of an opposite nature—how to keep the entirely sanctified from backsliding. Never did he see the perfection he taught as being a state of impeccability, unless it was in the early years of his life. Christ was holy and He was tempted. Adam was holy; he was tempted and fell. The entirely sanctified are holy, but they are tempted and may fall.

Why Wesley could believe that the most holy man was in danger of falling becomes understandable when it is remembered that the perfection he taught is not absolute or final. It is not a resurrection perfection. The pure love consequent to a complete cleansing of the believer is an experience. This experience is not a static one, but it must be maintained daily. The absence of sin from the pure heart comes with the glorious presence of the indwelling Holy Spirit. If that Spirit is grieved, the light from Him is withdrawn, at least partially, and the "shadows" return. For Wesley one must live in full yieldedness to the Spirit to maintain his purity.

Wesley was critical of those who with censorious minds questioned the testimonies of those claiming perfect love. Rather than doubting whether "the gift really be given," it is wiser, Wesley thought, to believe an honest man's claim. Do not observe him to see "whether he *has* such a blessing, but whether he will *keep* it."[39]

I know several of these were in process of time, moved from their steadfastness. I am nothing surprised at this: it was no more than might be expected: I rather wonder that more were not moved. Nor does this in any degree, alter my judgment concerning the great work which God then wrought.[40]

Obviously Wesley believed it is easy to lose this high state of grace. In fact he held that, though many receive the gift, only a few, "so exceeding few, retain it one year; hardly one in ten; nay, one in thirty."[41] Wesley passed this judgment in 1770 after he had observed his converts for many years. Apparently for Wesley the most common sin of the sanctified was the failure to keep the gift. He could not believe that one who was sinning, or who had sinful tempers, was perfect in love. The "doctrine of the necessity of sinning" is "subversive of all holiness."[42] Any diversion from a perfect commitment in one's loyalty forfeited the grace of perfect love. By all means this did not mean that all grace was forfeited!

One cause of backsliding, or at least a mark of it, was the decrease in attendance at daily devotions. Wesley placed great importance upon rising early in the morning, even in winter, and zealously pursuing spiritual exercises.[43] He saw little holiness apart from rugged and stern discipline. In contrast any holiness in "soft," modern America seems only a faint reflection of what Wesley had in mind. However that may be, perfect love can be maintained only by continual prayer and faithful watching with a constant, unbroken, and full commitment to the Giver of all holiness.

If the holiest of men can fall, as Wesley believed, how is it brought about? Temptation of the sanctified will be discussed in the next section, and it has an important place in the process of backsliding. It can here be stated that the entirely sanctified are tempted and may by God's grace not sin. However, there is a point in the temptation, if not fully resisted, when one "gives way, in some degree" and the "holy Spirit is grieved," and "his love of God grows cold." Anyone continuing in such relationship to God would have lost his perfect holiness. This sin would not yet be "wilful sin," because such can be committed only by those who have entirely lost both love and faith.[44]

Wesley never believed that those who had lost their

entire sanctification had also necessarily lost their justification. In the process of backsliding love grows cold before it is lost; faith weakens before it ceases. It is possible, though not necessary, and certainly not common, for those slipping away from an experience of perfect holiness to lose completely their faith.[45] Wesley's observations and belief were such that holy men did slip and willfully commit sin. When they did, he classified them as lost, because he knew of no justification or sanctification consistent with willful sinning. Furthermore, he knew of no complete holiness consistent with evil tempers and desires which are opposites of love.

Even though lost, sanctifying grace may be regained, even with gain over the earlier experience. Sometimes those who had also lost their justifying grace had recovered both justifying and sanctifying grace in one moment. Usually, however, Wesley noted those who, having failed to maintain their perfect love for a season, had recovered their lost blessing with "increase."[46] In Wesley's view it was not so serious to lose the full glow in one's love as it was to remain indifferent and not press on for more. In his many letters he urged those to whom he was writing to seek for more love and not to grow cold in the active search for more of God's love in their lives.

Wesley pictured the "sins of omission" as the first steps away from perfect love. There may be neglect of private prayer, neglect of reproving or warning another of his sin, failure to "stir up the gift of God," the being careless or slothful.[47] The continued permitting of these omissions appears to be the mark of coldness in love. Are those who are entirely sanctified, and who maintain their perfect love, ever conscious of these omissions? Unquestionably they are, and often they are awakened to having allowed such neglect. But on being awakened they make correction, but they are conscious of having failed. They confess their failures and seek divine assistance for their weaknesses while perfect love is maintained. These "sins" of the sanctified are always present, but, when "indulged" purposely or carelessly, they take away the purity of the love. Wesley insisted on the mercy and patience of God in His dealing with man's weakness.[48]

Though Wesley allowed a certain degree of human weakness and failure to be consistent with his ideal of perfect love, he drew a line, if imaginary, between the failure occasioned by the frailty and the failure allowed by the will. His insistence that sin, strictly speaking, is voluntary leaves one with the idea that the beginning of willing consent to a weakness or failure is the beginning of sin for the entirely sanctified.[49] A neglect occasioned by weakness, though sin in a certain sense, is not sin in the proper sense. However, when a person is awakened to his neglect, and then partly consents to allow it without correction, the omission becomes a sin in the proper sense. The first neglect is not contrary to perfect love; the second is.

If this appraisal of Wesley is correct, then "sin in the proper sense" as used above is not the same as the "wilful sinning" of the unbeliever. The difference is probably in degree. In the believer there is a partial yielding to weakness or temptation. Only in the unbeliever can the yielding be complete.[50]

The sins of the sanctified in relation to backsliding are twofold. First, all who are entirely sanctified constantly make mistakes and are aware of failures and omissions in their daily lives. These involuntary sins do not grieve the Spirit nor destroy the purity of love. Secondly, if and when the sanctified person gives a degree of consent to these omissions, they become sin in the proper sense, and love has a rival. A person so slipping may recover his lost blessing, but he has sinned in losing it.

E. TEMPTATIONS

If to be tempted were to sin, or if the basis for any temptation were the moral depravity of man, then it is useless to talk about either perfect love or freedom from sin. To believe that temptation is sin, one needs to teach that there was a moral depravity in Adam before his temptation, and, worse still, that such depravity was in the Christ when He was tempted, or else insist that Christ's temptation was not real, and that He was without sin, must hold a possible temptation apart from any sinfulness.

Wesley did not believe that temptation was sin nor that strong temptation was a mark of sinfulness. In fact corruption of heart and temptation are not identical.[51] But he taught that human frailties are the occasions for temptations. The human body with its weakness, sickness, and disorders, along with pain, implies temptation. The understanding, with its confused and inaccurate apprehensions and false judgments, is a source of temptation. Temptations may come from wicked men in the world, and from Christians, even the entirely sanctified. Furthermore, "Satan and his angels" constantly seek to lead men away from God.[52]

The entirely sanctified, therefore, are not free from temptation. There is no perfection on earth that lifts a person above temptation.[53] Actually the very things that cause temptation—disease, pain, afflictions—are not a loss for men, but they make men to be "infinite gainers" in the end.[54] In the long run temptation bestows a positive good on men by increasing the glory of their heavenly crown.

Luther looked upon sin in the believer in about the same way as Wesley saw temptation.

> Thus impurity by its attack renders the soul all the more chaste. Pride makes it all the more humble. Indolence makes it all the more industrious. Avarice makes it all the more generous. Anger makes it all the more gentle. Gluttony makes it all the more obedient. In this way temptation turns out to be a great blessing. Sin indeed rules over our mortal body if we yield to it; but we must resist it and make it our servant.[55]

In this passage Luther came close to identifying temptation and sinfulness, and one gets the impression that he believed temptation to pride to be pride. Wesley taught that one could be tempted to pride without possessing any pride.[56] The presence of sin in the heart does not make a Christian humble. Pride exalts one in his own eyes, while its destruction makes one lowly.[57] However, a person may be humble and calm even though tempted to pride and anger. One need not be proud in order to be tempted to pride.

Is Wesley correct when he distinguishes between pride and the temptation to pride? Sangster appears to disagree. He claims that he has never met anyone claiming entire cleansing who "never experiences a stab of jealousy, or a mood of irritation, or a sense of pride, or a lustful thought." When any one of these evils appear, "it is already 'me' in the moment of my first awareness." There is no chance to say, "Yes," or "No." "It stabs *in* me. *I*, for that moment, am vain. In the first split second of awareness, it is possession. Repudiation is eviction, for it is already in."[58] Actually, what Sangster does here is make the temptation to pride to be a "sense of pride." He, with Luther, makes the presence of the wrong feeling in temptation to be sin.

Must it be conceded that the "lust" or desire made attractive in temptation really is sin? Should one conclude that a "stab of jealousy, or a mood of irritation, or a sense of pride, or a lustful thought" is sin in the proper moral sense? Cannot a person distinguish between a "sense of pride" and a consent to pride? Might there be a jealousy in which the will participates, at least partially, as over against a "stab of jealousy" occasioned by temptation? In the moment one is aware of the passion awakened in temptation is he the possessor of "evil" because the passion is not good?

The answer to these questions is not simple. To claim as does Sangster that these feelings are sins would necessitate convicting Christ of sin. For surely Jesus was tempted by natural desires. Was the desire, which Jesus saw as a satanic suggestion, sin because it was the "I" in the first moment of awareness? Certainly it was Christ's own desire that Satan allured. Furthermore, one must believe that He felt the pull of the desire to the wrong thing. Yet He was without sin.

With fallen men, even for the entirely sanctified, discernment is slow and knowledge of self is very limited. In the moment of temptation satanic influence may not be readily detected and, consequently, the attracted desire or awakened passion may continue for a period of time. However, there must be a moment in temptation when the wrong impulse is resisted or yielded to by the will. No matter how long or attractive the enticing desire may be, even though it is my desire, it need not gain any approval from the moral nature. If it does not, it cannot be sin in the proper, or strict, sense.

> We think it is precisely at that point where the soul is conscious of a disposition to yield to what it supposes to be sin, that is discovered sinfulness, and the beginning of sin. And our doctrine is that a soul may be so completely dead to sin and alive to God, that however attractive the object of evil may be to nature, the soul will have no corresponding movement toward it. The natural appetite or passion may feel the blind impulse, but the moral nature feels it not at all, but turns away from it with recoil.[59]

What is it in the Christian that turns away from a blind impulse for a wrong object? Carnell's observation is interesting:

> Our moral struggle is a wretchedly complex affair. We seem to have two wills, in fact (though there is but one); one which assents affectionately to the word and will of God, and another which assents affectionately to the persuasions of sin. . . . A man often comes to the very edge of sinfulness, confessing that his reigning affections lie on the side of righteousness and that he hates both himself and his actions; yet finally yielding to the lure of the minor will by capitulating to the temptation. This ambivalence is experienced every day in the hearts of all who are struggling with a besetting sin. And whom does this category exclude? Never once do we triumph over sin but what we glance over our left shoulder with a very slight—but nevertheless real—regret that we cannot remain holy before God and enjoy our sin, too.[60]

Carnell, a Calvinist, is describing here the Christian who still has a divided loyalty and therefore an imperfect love. But there is in his description a truth for the entirely sanctified. For them there is not a divided will; there is nothing but complete abhorence at the thought of indulging a wrong desire. There is no "regret" in their victory! However, even for them there is the attractive appeal that pulls toward the forbidden object. It is at this point one is tempted. When that enticing desire becomes a sinful one is not easily determined.

Steele wrote that when the "will indulges the desire, or even fosters it against the remonstrance of the conscience," sin is present.[61] The term "desire" here is used as something apart from the will. Peck argued that the subject of temptation sins "when the temptation begets in the mind a desire for the forbidden object." A "perfectly formed desire" in the mind "is positive proof of an alienation of the affections from God."[62] The term "desire" here is used as something in the mind or will. It would appear in these theologians that a blind impulse or desire in the animal nature is not the same as a "desire" in the mind, or as a "movement" of the will.

Wesley had some such concept when he discussed the steps in losing one's sanctifying grace. David, he claimed, loved God perfectly. But a time came when he *felt* a temptation—a thought which tended to evil. Here is a sanctified person feeling a pull toward evil. Then, Wesley added, David "yielded in some measure" to the temptation which began to prevail over him.[63] In discussing Jas. 1:14, Wesley saw that the desire which is "drawn out" is one's own desire.

> In the beginning of temptation, *he is drawn away*, drawn out of God, his strong refuge, *by his own desire*—We are therefore to look for the cause of every sin in (not out of) ourselves. Even the injections of the devil cannot hurt, before we make them our own. And every one has desires arising from his own constitution, tempers, habits, and way of life; *and enticed*—In the progress of the temptation, catching at the bait; so the original word signifies.[64]

Quite obviously a person cannot be tempted to do something for which he has no inclination or desire. The basis for every temptation must be found in the passions, instincts, drives, urges, and desires of the human nature. If in the moment of the first awareness of such desires heart sin is present, then there is no such gift as perfect love. However, if the wrong desire is not admitted into the heart, there is no committing of the evil in the heart (Matt. 5:28). The pure heart repels the temptation of the enticing natural desire. An awakened mind of the entirely sanctified will repel the evil passions and keep itself wholly reliant upon God.

However, the boundary line between the natural instincts or impulses and the desires flowing from perfect love is not clear because of limited understanding. The entirely sanctified need the constant guidance of the Spirit and His searching eye. They should recognize their peril and wholly rely on the merits of Christ. Any involvement in the moment of temptation calls for humble confession and faith on the part of the pure in heart.

F. Moment by Moment

Wesley pleaded again and again that the holiness he preached was a "moment by moment" life. He never saw perfection as an attainment of grace wherein the person became the source of his own holiness. Perfection is not a light in the heart maintained by resources within the individual, but it is light streaming from the only Source of light, and the individual's holiness is wholly dependent on that Source. For this reason Wesley ever insisted that one is holy, or pure, or perfect, only so long as that holiness is derived from God. He insisted on an inherent holiness, but only in the sense that a person has righteousness truly in himself but never of himself. Man, and this means the wholly sanctified man, is ever dependent upon the only true Source of his holiness.

Sangster believes that Wesley's plea for the "moment by moment" life is sustained by investigation and is scriptural.[65] On this point he is in agreement with the Reformed position on the Christian's sense of unworthiness. He did not teach a sanctification that "is bound to produce an insidious self-esteem."[66] His was a holiness that produces humility and a sense of complete unworthiness. One without these qualities had no such holiness.

A person is sanctified by faith, but the purity attained is maintained by faith.[67] No state attained by faith becomes the basis for faith, or for the assurance of acceptance with God. The life of holiness is carried on daily by good works.[68] One cannot live on what God did in the past. God comes today and every day to destroy the tendencies to evil.[69] One is to go on from faith to faith if entire holiness is maintained.[70]

There is a daily growth in knowledge.[71] The entirely sanctified need to know more so they can better exemplify the Christ they follow. They should daily use the grace God gives, and seek constantly more grace.[72]

> Yea, suppose God has now thoroughly cleansed our heart, and scattered the last remains of sin; yet how can we be sensible enough of our own helplessness; our utter inability to all good, unless we are every hour, yea, every moment, endued with power from on high? Who is able to think one good thought, or to form one good desire unless by that almighty power which worketh in us to will and to do of his good pleasure? We have need, even in this state of grace, to be thoroughly and continually penetrated with a sense of this, otherwise we shall be in perpetual danger of robbing God of his honour, by glorying in something we have received, as though we had not received it.[73]

Wesley insisted on the need of a steady will. There is no state of sanctification without a "will steadily and uniformly devoted to God." The "heart and life is entirely devoted to God."[74] In speaking of the sanctified Wesley wrote that they "continually" presented their souls and bodies in sacrifice.[75] Obviously Wesley never intended for holiness to be thought of as attained in a crisis experience in which commitment is so complete that further presentation is unnecessary. One can reach a point where no reservations are retained in his consecration, but this consecration is maintained by a daily and continuous offering. Why is this so? Is not a gift, presented unreservedly, given in such a way that further presentation is impossible? For certain kinds of gifts, yes, but the nature of man's gift to God is such that a daily yielding is necessary. It is a *living* sacrifice carried out in a continuous consecration.

In Wesley's view the entirely sanctified need daily the atonement of Christ. None feel their need of Christ more than they. The life from Christ is "in and with himself" and not separate from Him.

> "In every state we need Christ in the following respects, (1) Whatever grace we receive, it is a free gift from him. (2) We receive it as his purchase, merely in consideration of the price he paid. (3) We have this grace, not only from Christ, but in him. For our perfection is not like that of a tree, which flourishes by the sap derived from its own root, but, as was said before, like that of a branch which, united to the vine, bears fruit; but, several from it, is dried up and withered. (4) All our blessings, temporal, spiritual, and eternal, depend on his intercession for us, which is one branch of his priestly office, whereof therefore we have always equal need. (5) The best of men still need Christ in his priestly office, to atone for their omissions, their short-comings, (as some not improperly speak,) their mistakes in judgment and practice, and their defects of various kinds. For these are all deviations from the perfect law, and consequently need an atonement."[76]

Wesley saw no inconsistency between perfection and the daily need of the atonement. If he had to, Wesley preferred to give up perfection as a doctrine than to teach a perfection without continual atonement, but, he said, "we need not give up either the one or the other."

> "The holiest of men still need Christ, as their Prophet, as "the light of the world." For he does not give them light, but from moment to moment: the instant he withdraws, all is darkness. They still need Christ as their King; for God does not give them a stock of holiness. But unless they receive a supply every moment, nothing but unholiness would remain.

186

> They still need Christ as their Priest, to make atonement for their holy things. Even perfect holiness is acceptable to God only through Jesus Christ."[77]

This atonement in Christ for the sanctified is not only for the supplying of needed grace, and the maintaining of a present victory and holiness, but also for daily forgiveness.

> In speaking from these words, "In many things we offend all," I observed, 1. As long as we live, our soul is connected with the body: 2. As long as it is thus connected, it cannot think but by the help of bodily organs: 3. As long as these organs are imperfect, we are liable to mistakes, both speculative and practical: 4. Yea, and a mistake may occasion my loving a good man less than I ought; which is a defective, that is, a wrong temper: 5. For all these we need the atoning blood, as indeed for every defect or omission. Therefore, 6. all men have need to say daily, "Forgive us our trespasses."[78]

Although Wesley found only a very few in his day who taught that perfection ended the need for daily forgiveness, apparently Wesley has not been followed in this sense by some of the modern "holiness" advocates. Unwillingness to offer prayers of confession was not found in Wesley, whatever his successors may have done.[79] Turner insists that Wesley was inconsistent in teaching that sins of ignorance need repentance and forgiveness. "In this case, however, the forgiveness needed was for the effects, not the intent."[80] But one must remember that between the "intent" and the "effects" there is that involvement of one's weak and fallen human nature for which one needs mercy and forgiveness. Certainly this "forgiveness" is not quite on the same level as that received for willful transgressions, but it is a true forgiveness. There is a sense in which repentence is in order. One needs to be convinced and convicted of his errors. When seen, they bring humiliation and confession. Also there is a forsaking of these "sins" in the sense that one corrects all he can. Our failures in performance do need the forgiveness of God.

Wesley understood that involuntary transgressions did not bring condemnation before God. One is not under a curse when he blunders.[81] Rather than being condemned, he is convicted.[82] This being "convicted" awakens one to his utter need of Christ, of discipline, and of mercy. Failure to see a constant need for the atoning Christ, and for forgiveness from Him, is itself a serious blunder. It can lead to a false holiness that discredits the true work of God.

There are many dangers that lie in the path of utter abandonment to God. Wesley warned against pride into which one can slide unawares, especially if he thinks there is no danger. He feared "enthusiasm," by which he meant the supposing that one has special knowledge from God. There is constant danger of satanic deception. One's desire to grow in grace may lead a person into desires for gifts of a new kind. He warned against sins of omission, against schism, against self-indulgence. The holiest men are continually facing perils to their souls. They must be zealous and active and desire nothing but God.[83]

In view of these admonitions of Wesley, one must conclude that in Christian perfection there is no place for boasting except in Christ. No one has anything of himself in the highest attainment of grace for which he can be proud. All he has is from Christ and in Christ and of His great mercy. No testimony of any grace attained should include more than witness of Christ's great work in the soul. Thus all self-exaltation is excluded.

Are Sangster and Flew correct in saying that none should make the claim that he is free from sin? Certainly they are correct if the sins included in that claim were the involuntary transgressions. No one is free from them. But, as has been shown, Wesley did not mean the involuntary sins. May the claim be wisely made that sin in the proper, moral sense, is cleansed? Wesley thought so. But he believed that a person making such claim should know what he is doing.

Obviously any testimony that bears witness to God's mighty grace in the heart is in order. But one must watch against spiritual pride. The emphasis should be upon, not man's *sinlessness,* but Christ's fullness within him. Rather than saying, "I am entirely sanctified," which makes the "I" the "springboard of the announcement," one should testify, "Christ is now, by faith, my Sanctifier."[84] When one knows God has wrought a great work in his life, he wants all glory to be the Christ's. He will not take the glory that belongs to another. In fact he cannot while he depends "moment by moment" on his Lord, and while he knows that, apart from Christ, there is no goodness in himself.

CHAPTER VII

SUMMARY AND CONCLUSION

In this investigation of Wesley's concept of perfection an earnest attempt has been made to discover and examine the main problems that any doctrine of perfection encounters. There has been no intentional evasion of any difficulty that the teaching faces. Wesley's ideas as they were expressed by him in his wide experience with people have been gathered and related to his special teaching on perfect love. These ideas were expressed by him in various terms. These terms, however, must be understood in the light of Wesley's meanings and according to his definitions. To attack his doctrine on the basis of an alleged meaning of the term or terms which Wesley used gives no light in the discussion. Wesley knew that verbal terms conveyed different meanings. He tried to express what he understood the Bible writers taught and was always ready to be corrected by the Scriptures. He concluded that "perfect love" expressed best what he believed "Christian perfection" meant. There has been found no reason to set aside this conclusion.

A. SUMMARY OF WESLEY'S DOCTRINE

Wesley's teaching is a doctrine of grace. Following traditional thought he believed in the total corruption of man's nature. He could describe the Fall in the blackest of terms. Against this corruption Wesley set the prevenient grace of God which is given to every man. This grace actually redeems the race in the sense that any racial guilt is removed, a degree of freedom is restored to every individual, a beginning of divine light is present in every soul, and all men are made salvable. In reality no person is in the mere state of nature, but already salvation has begun in every human being.

This prevenient grace lifts everyone to the place where he can choose or refuse more grace. By choosing more grace a person can be led to repentance and faith, the conditions of justification. Any works preceding faith are of grace, and the faith is of grace. The ability to cooperate is of grace. In this sense the *sola gratia* is retained in Wesley. Also justification, and hence salvation, is by faith alone. No work, even that which is of grace, can justify. The immediate condition of justification is faith. Without this faith no one is justified; with it a person is justified. In this sense Wesley maintained the *sola fide*.

Wesley believed in a universal atonement and held that grace is given to all men. From this grace comes a "gracious ability" by which anyone can cooperate with God. No man will be sent to hell because he has no grace, but because he fails to use the grace he has. By grace works are performed, both before and after faith. These works are essential because no one can come to faith, or maintain faith, without them. This is synergism, but a synergism born of monergism—God works, therefore man is enabled to work.

Sin for Wesley may be considered in one of two ways. Original sin was the sin of Adam and, by his representation, it became the sin of the race. This sin accounts for the natural weaknesses and evils inherent in the human race. However the guilt for this sin is removed for all men in prevenient grace, though the unfortunate and evil results remain. From this fallen nature flow the corruptions and evil tendencies in the sons of Adam. But into this evil nature also flows the grace of God, which fact changed Wesley's definition of sin. Since man has grace, it is the refusal of this grace that becomes the condemning sin.

Wesley's definition of a proper sin is clear and distinct. It is a voluntary transgression of a known law. Man in his refusal of free grace goes on in his sins and by this refusal he has become a "wilful sinner." For these sins he will suffer eternal death unless he repents and believes. The person who by grace is convicted of sin, repents, and believes, ceases to sin in this sense. He cannot commit sin so long as he has faith. It is clear that Wesley did not mean by this kind of sin the evil tempers and desires in the heart of the believer, nor the unfortunate and involuntary wrongs that flow from a fallen human nature. He meant the personal sins of an individual who willingly goes his own way apart from any real faith in Christ.

Salvation, perfection, and holiness have the same meaning for Wesley. They begin in a sense with that early dawning of light in prevenient grace. When a person is justified he is also regenerated and initially sanctified. The justification is complete in that he is forgiven and accepted as a child of God, although continuation of forgiveness is dependent on continued faith. Regeneration is complete in that new life begins, and all the graces of God are implanted in the soul. At regeneration there are also a breaking of the power of sin and a cleansing of the pollution of the heart. The cleansing is sanctification, but it is incomplete. Entire sanctification comes in a later stage of perfection.

Wesley saw sanctification as both gradual and instantaneous. When sanctification was viewed as a cleansing, it began in regeneration, continued in the believer until by faith entire cleansing, or full purity, came. The point of completion was a crisis, or special experience, in which the Holy Spirit finished the cleansing of sin He had begun. When sanctification was viewed as a growth, it was a process that began when love and other graces were planted in the heart of the believer. These graces continue to grow, both before and after entire sanctification. No point is ever reached beyond which the graces cannot grow. In this sense is sanctification gradual.

In Wesley, then, there were two perfections. One is reached when the heart is made pure and love alone reigns. This is Christian perfection, or perfect love. The other perfection is the goal ever ahead of the Christian and is never attained in this life, though growth and improvement are experienced. The first has to do with the moral corruption that remains in the heart of the believer; the second is concerned with the growth of the graces and their emergence in the daily conduct of the Christian.

To understand the difference between being perfect in the one sense and not perfected in the other sense, it has been necessary to make a unique distinction between two kinds of sin in the believer. The sin that is cleansed or destroyed at entire sanctification is a moral depravity. This depravity is a wrong disposition of the will, an evil temper, a self-will, or evil moral desire, that is opposed to love for God and man. It is not identical with the weaknesses, infirmities, or natural instincts, which are part of a fallen, human existence. This evil in the heart opposed to God and love is gone when one loves God perfectly. This perfect love is not a perfect performance but a pure intention. In entire sanctification the believer's moral likeness to God is fully restored.

This perfect love, or Christian perfection, is the only perfection possible in this present life. It is a purity that sets the will free from inclinations to evil. It is freedom from the sinful depravity of the heart or will. It comes in an experience that may be called the fullness of the Spirit, and it is accomplished by the Spirit in response to the faith of the believer. For Wesley it is a scriptural concept and is attainable here and now by all believers. It enables one to fulfill the law of Christ. It is not perfection in the Adamic or angelic sense. Nor is perfect love resurrection perfection. There is much ahead for those whose love is made perfect.

Obviously there are human limits to this present perfection. Finite existence is such that perfect love must never be thought of as infinite perfection. In man's fallen state he is pressed down by a corruptible body and must act through a faulty mind. With limited knowledge and human frailty, no man, however perfect in love, can perform perfectly. Although every act is prompted by perfect love, the imperfect reactions of a faulty body and mind create all kinds of imperfections. These human imperfections must never be confused with an evil moral nature, although the line between the two may not always be clear.

These imperfections that flow from a weakened human nature are consistent with pure love. That they are not deviations from the law of love is clear; that they are deviations from the perfect law given to Adam is equally clear. With the reformers Wesley agreed that these deviations from the perfect law are sins. But they are not sins in the same sense as deviations from the law of love. Since Wesley made this distinction, he could speak of freedom from the sin that is a deviation from pure love. He felt that this is the freedom from sin taught in the Scriptures. The greater freedom from all sins, including the failures to perfectly keep the perfect law, must await the resurrection.

This area of imperfection between a perfect love and a perfect performance was not passed over lightly by Wesley. There were times when he had no hesitancy in calling these shortcomings "sins." That he did not always call them sins was because people would confuse them with the other kinds of sins. Yet he believed that these "sins" of infirmity needed the atoning Blood, and that one should daily pray for forgiveness. The life of holiness was a moment-by-moment reliance upon the priesthood of Christ.

B. Perfection in American Methodism

This message of holiness was proclaimed by Wesley without intermission. It is true that there were times of questioning. But these questions were not as to whether perfection was the message to preach—Wesley was certain on this point. He sought for clearer ways to preach it and he attempted to avoid the dangers. Raising the question of the possibility to "let it drop" only intensified Wesley's proclamation. Any changes Wesley made in the doctrine were in the direction of clarity and earnest exhortation to seek the "blessing." No one can read Wesley and conclude that Christian perfection was only a "pet" theory for him. It was the main drive in his ministry.

In 1777 Wesley wrote the following words:

> But you will naturally ask, what is Methodism? . . . Methodism, so called, is the old religion, the religion of the Bible, the religion of the primitive church, the religion of the Church of England. This old religion, (as I observed in the "Earnest Appeal to Men of Reason and Religion,") is "no other than love, the love of God and of all mankind; the loving God with all our heart, and soul, and strength, . . . and the loving every soul which God hath made, every man on earth, as our own soul."[1]

Here Wesley saw Methodism and holiness as standing for the same thing. He had great confidence in the success of the Methodist revival and associated it with the teaching of pure religion, which for him was heart holiness. He never intended that Methodism should be a church apart from the Church of England.[2]

In answering the question as to why God raised up the Methodists, Wesley said, "Not to form any new sect; but to reform the nation, particularly the Church: and to spread scriptural holiness over the land." His answer to the question, "What was the rise of Methodism?" was given in a revision in 1791:

> In 1729, two young men, reading the Bible, saw they could not be saved without holiness, followed after it, and incited others so to do. In 1737 they saw holiness comes by faith. They saw likewise, that men are justified before they are sanctified; but still holiness was their point. God then thrust them out, utterly against their will, to raise a holy people. When Satan could no otherwise hinder this, he threw Calvinism in the way; and then Antinomianism, which strikes directly at the root of all holiness.[3]

In 1790 he wrote that "full sanctification" as a doctrine "is the grand depositum which God had lodged with the people called Methodists; and for the sake of propagating this chiefly he appeared to have raised us up."[4]

How well has Methodism retained the conviction of its founder? Laying aside Wesley's opinion that Methodists should remain in the Church of England, since before his death he did allow the organization of Methodism in America as a church, one is interested in the outcome of the "grand depositum." As this investigation reveals, Christian perfection has very close ties with total depravity, atonement in Christ, prevenient grace, justification by faith, regeneration, and good works. Neglect of any of these will distort the teaching on holiness.

Several valuable investigations have revealed interesting data on the question of perfectionism in American Methodism. Robert Clark studied the history of the doctrine in Methodism up to the year 1845. He claims that the standards inherited from Wesley provided a constant unity in Methodism on the doctrine of Christian perfection, from which there was no deviation from the original principles.[5] In the early years of Methodism in America the great camp meetings for which Methodism became famous were set up. These camps later became known as "Holiness Camp Meetings."[6] Robert Clark thinks, however, that from the year 1840 and on "there was a general decline of the presentation of the doctrine by the clergy of the church, and as a result a smaller group in the church sought and professed this grace." Nevertheless the only controversy during this earlier period was "over the practice and presentation of this doctrine in the church, and not over the doctrine itself."[7]

Leland Scott's study of Methodist theology in the nineteenth century in America suggests several interesting trends. The early Methodists in America had little time or concern for reflection on their theology. Even Asbury felt that little learning was needed for one to speak and write for simple people.[8] By the middle of the century need for original and independent theological work was felt.[9] In the 1840's attempt was made to safeguard the teaching on holiness by Timothy Merritt and Phoebe Palmer because, they feared, there was a drift away from the doctrine. During this time important transitions were occurring. There was a declining stress on experiential "moments" of redemptive grace. Evangelical conversion, witness of the Spirit, and full sanctification lost somewhat their vitality, according to Scott. There was a growing concern in the church over excess in revivals. With this came an increasing emphasis on the nurture of the child.[10]

During the latter part of the century changes in theology began to appear. Daniel Whedon stressed free agency and the power of contrary choice.[11] William Warren and John Miley, according to Scott, contributed to these changes. Miley emphasized moral choice but neglected the doctrines of original sin and prevenient grace.[12] On the other hand men like Daniel Steele and Thomas Summers stressed recapturing the Methodist doctrinal heritage by a renewal of "experiential concomitants" of that heritage.[13] In spite of the transition, Scott argues, Methodist theology in the nineteenth century sustained a "formalistic allegiance" to the evangelical outlines of Wesleyanism.[14] However there is evidence of a gradual decline in emphasis on the Wesleyan doctrines of conversion, witness of the Spirit, instantaneous entire sanctification, and the urgency of salvation.[15]

Elmer Gaddis, who wrote on the history of the perfectionist movement in America, attributes great importance to the "introduction of the Wesleyan strain of perfectionism" into America by the Methodists.[16] He claims that the "extent of the Methodist perfectionists in shaping the principles and procedure of the frontier sects perhaps can never be accurately appraised, but this influence was very great."[17]

The Methodists, says Gaddis, were "equipped to spread the gospel of superlative piety far and wide."[18]

Yet it seems that there was a neglect of the doctrine of holiness in the first half of the nineteenth century on the part of the American Methodist. John Peters finds little in the literature of this period to justify any claim that holiness was greatly emphasized.[19] Before 1805 the earliest American Methodist considered themselves "sons of Wesley" and in the conference of 1781 they agreed that they would preach the "old Methodist doctrine" and follow Wesley's teachings.[20] By 1812, according to Peters, "events conspired to bring about an almost opposite effect." The Doctrinal Tracts were removed from the *Discipline* for convenience' sake, and these writings of Wesley were not again published until 1832. Little was written about the doctrine of holiness in the principal denominational journals between 1832 and 1840. During these years, Peters says, this doctrine was "not seriously questioned nor generally preached." When expounded or defended, it was in strict Wesleyan terms, but "Christian Perfection seems not to have been a vital ingredient in general Methodist thought and life during this period.[21]

What were the reasons for this neglect of Wesley's "grand depositum"? Several reasons have been suggested. Peter thinks the frontier in America helped to make conversion the principal theme in Methodist preaching. The War of 1812 may have contributed to the neglect, although the peace afterwards was not marked by a resumption of interest in holiness. The rising national prosperity in which Methodists shared did not, according to Peters, "provoke deepening piety."[22] Delbert Rose, speaking of the period before the Civil War, attributes the decline in holiness emphasis in the Methodist church to the "growth between denominations, religious fanaticisms in the name of perfection, and reactions to the autocratic character of the Methodist episcopacy."[23]

Whatever causes may have contributed to the decline or neglect of emphasis on holiness during the first half of the nineteenth century, the doctrine was not lost. Timothy Smith's investigation reveals a renewal of emphasis and interest as early as 1825. In that year Timothy Merritt published his *Treatise on Christian Perfection,* a very influential handbook for many years. The bishops of the Methodist church called for a revival of holiness in the General Conference of 1832. In 1835 the famous Tuesday Meeting in New York City came under the leadership of Phoebe Palmer, and four years later the monthly magazine, the *Guide to Holiness,* was launched by Timothy Merritt.[24]

It is not intended in the conclusion of this study on Wesley's doctrine to trace in detail the success or failure of this teaching on the American scene. For detailed studies of this kind the reader is referred to the works already mentioned of Elmer Gaddis, Delbert Rose, Timothy Smith, Claude Thompson, and John Peters. The general conclusions of these men who studied perfection teaching in America should be helpful in the forming of some general opinion as to how much Wesley's special doctrine has been emphasized.

Timothy Smith is convinced that the doctrine of perfection held an important place in the mid-nineteenth-century revivals.[25] These revivals became acceptable to many denominations, including Baptist, Presbyterian, Congregational, Lutheran, and Episcopalian.[26] These revivalists of the mid-century were not sectarian and they gave strength to interfaith fellowship.[27] The Palmers, who were Methodists and strong advocates of Wesleyan perfection, were used in revival campaigns supported by other churches.[28] If Smith is correct in his conclusions, the doctrine of holiness was widely held by the revivalists of this period. This should not be taken to mean, however, that Wesley was always followed, although most writers on Christian perfection in this period quote him at length.[29]

That this revival movement and holiness emphasis of the 1850's were not shared by all Methodists is indicated by Rose. By 1860, Methodist church papers were earnestly discussing the propriety of wholly abandoning the camp meetings. Also for several years prior to 1867 there was a growing opposition to the subject of entire sanctification. In some places this opposition became very violent.[30] Rose produces evidence to show that there was a sustained witness to Wesleyan perfection throughout the "period of Methodism's drastic reaction to her own doctrine." He discusses at length the influence of Phoebe Palmer and her husband upon many Methodist preachers and bishops.[31] It would appear that within Methodism by 1860 there were two distinct groups. The one group was becoming more and more strong in advocating holiness while the other tended to oppose. Probably between the two extremes were many who neglected the doctrine but did not oppose it.

What happened after the Civil War has not yet been fully written. A history of the National Holiness Association would assist in finding an answer.[32] After the increased interest in holiness created by the Palmers and other revivalists, there grew a desire on the part of many to create a camp meeting designed to promote the teaching on holiness. The first such camp was held in Vineland, N.J., in 1867 and was called "The National Camp-Meeting Association for the Promotion of Christian Holiness." The purpose of this association was to revive the work of holiness in the churches.[33] All holiness advocates did not favor such a movement because of dangers involved, but others were favorable.[34] The leadership of this organization has been largely from the Methodist church. These leaders frowned upon schism and sect-formation, and encouraged a continuing witness within the denominations. This association, though with changes in structure of organization and in name, has continued to the present time. It is acclaimed as "modern-Wesleyan emphasis within Methodism and her family of smaller denominational and undenominational offspring."[35]

Although the National Holiness Association leaders did not want to encourage schism within Methodism, it ultimately came. John Peters produces evidence from various periodicals and journals that with increasing momentum a controversy was waged within Methodism in the last three decades of the nineteenth century. The holiness advocates emphasized instantaneous entire sanctification while others insisted on a sanctification identified with regeneration, or on a gradual sanctification only.[36]

During this period of controversy over Wesley's doctrine of entire sanctification, the holiness advocates formed independent camp meeting associations and began to hold property. Many evangelists became active in these camps, and some of them were unwilling to be controlled by the Methodist leadership. The bishops naturally feared excesses and gave warnings. With the growth of the number of these independent camp meetings and evangelists the threat of schism arose. Publishing houses arose for the purpose of exclusive publication of holiness materials. There were four such houses in 1888 and 27 holiness journals. By 1892 there were 41 such journals. It is not surprising that adverse reaction to such a program arose.[37]

While the holiness advocates increasingly insisted upon traditional views and sometimes "took refuge in obscurantism and appalling dogmatism," the other extreme sought haven in the new liberalism which was inspired by German rationalism, Darwinism, and the new social reform movement. The theological positions of the two separate camps were fast becoming "mutually incomprehensible."[38] One sector of the church was intent upon revival of the traditional emphasis while the other "sector was restive under that tradition." The first appeared unconcerned with the society of which it was a part; the latter was intent on establishing new bases of interpretation for the Christian faith. A demand for peace arose, but the group insisting on entire sanctification was unwilling to make any concession. The result was withdrawal by many from the Methodist church in the 1890's and the organization of various sects.[39]

> Thus as the century drew to its close, the doctrine of Christian perfection was presented in differing fashion by two Methodistic groups, both claiming Wesleyan authority for their positions. In the sects it was an abbreviated Wesleyanism—in many respects characteristic of his unmodified 1760 views, stressing his instantaneous teaching and neglecting in large part his emphasis on the gradual. In the church it was an uncertain Wesleyanism—in many respects characteristic of his 1745 views, mildly hopeful of the efficacy of a gradual approach but ignoring for the most part his emphasis on the instantaneous.[40]

Robert Cushman passes the judgment that "modern Methodism has reverted to and settled for the religion of John Wesley prior to 1738," but that they do not possess the same zeal for good works which he had.[41] However that may be, it does appear that the emphasis upon holiness in Methodism by and large ceased with the nineteenth century.

> Vital holiness was passing out of Methodist faith and practice. Finally, all traces of the doctrine were carefully eliminated from the songs of the church in the hymnal published in 1935. For example, in Charles Wesley's great hymn, "Love

Divine, All Loves Excelling," which has appeared in all the hymn books since 1747, a line in the second stanza reading "Let us find *that second* rest" was altered by the hymnal commission to "let us find *the promised* rest." Nothing was allowed to remain that might remind Methodists that their church had ever endorsed a *second* work of grace![42]

Although the investigators Gaddis, Elmer Clark, Thompson, and Peters agree in the general conclusion that the holiness agitation within Methodism in the last three decades of the nineteenth century resulted in the formation of the holiness sects and that these holiness sects make a specialty of entire sanctification,[43] it must not be concluded that the Methodist church has repudiated the Wesleyan doctrine of Christian perfection. All of the presidents of the National Holiness Association until 1952, w i t h the exception of three, have been Methodist ministers.[44] There is a revival of interest among contemporary Methodist in Wesley's doctrine of holiness as is evidenced by the studies of Flew, Sangster, Lindstrom, Cannon, Thompson, and Peters. That a large number of Methodists did not repudiate this doctrine is indicated by Rose.[45] It is probable that a Methodism which tried to keep up with the contemporary changes of a half-century ago is now, along with other churches, trying to recapture some of its lost heritage.

From this relatively brief and limited survey of studies made of perfection in American Methodism, one may suggest a general summary. The early Methodists in America were closely tied to Wesley and determined to follow his doctrines and instructions. By the beginning of the nineteenth century, however, frontier conditions led to a general neglect of Wesley's special teaching on entire sanctification for two or three decades. By 1835 there was a renewed interest in this doctrine on the part of some leaders, who used various means of emphasizing the teaching. This interest reached considerable proportion by 1858. At the same time of this renewed interest others in Methodism began to oppose the holiness teaching as it was developing. After the organizing of the National Holiness Association in 1867, and during the rapid increase of holiness camps, periodicals, and evangelists following this date, the controversy became so great that, by the close of the nineteenth century, many holiness sects were formed, and the special emphasis on entire sanctification suffered an eclipse in the Methodist church. However, there has been a continuing interest on the part of some within Methodism in the twentieth century, with a revival of new interest in the last two decades being evident.

C. AMERICAN HOLINESS SECTS

It is impossible in this conclusion to give any detailed account of the various sects that claim to teach entire sanctification. Methodism is directly or indirectly responsible for over fifty of the existing sects in America. All of these "may be called perfectionist so far as their official doctrines are concerned, and at least thirty of them still make sanctification one of their central principles."[46] Many of these were created at the height of the holiness controversy in the 1890's. By 1900, Peters declares, "the greater part of the outspoken advocates of holiness—by which was meant principally Christian perfection in its entire-sanctification aspect—had withdrawn from or been encouraged to leave American Episcopal Methodism."[47] According to Gaddis these sects clamored for the restoration of primitive Methodism.[48]

Reference here will be made to only three of these many holiness groups. The Wesleyan Methodist church came out of a break with the Methodist Episcopal church over the question of slavery and episcopacy. When it was formed in 1843, holiness was not an issue. Later the Wesleyan Methodist church took its stand on Christian perfection as a distinct holiness church by the insertion of the following statement in the *Discipline*.

> Entire sanctification is that work of the Holy Spirit by which the child of God is cleansed from all inbred sin through faith in Jesus Christ. It is subsequent to regeneration, and is wrought when the believer presents himself a living sacrifice, holy and acceptable unto God, and is thus enabled through grace to love God with all the heart and to walk in His holy commandments blameless.[49]

This church has continued its ministry for over a century and takes its definite stand for the doctrines of John Wesley. Gaddis claims that the Wesleyan Methodists are constantly seeking to restore "true" Wesleyanism in doctrine as well as "primitive" ideals in organization.

201

There is probably no existing denomination more loyal to the primitive Wesleyan interpretation of Christian perfection, more devoted to the central ethical purpose of the doctrine and more free from emotional and enthusiastic extremes than the Wesleyans.[50]

In the very early stages of the holiness controversy within Methodism, a schism occurred in the New York area. This resulted in the formation of the Free Methodist church in 1860. In this break holiness was definitely an issue, although occasioned by misunderstanding. This church formed a clear statement on the entire-sanctification phase of Christian perfection and considered itself a distinct holiness church.[51] This did not mean that the Methodist church had already abandoned at this early date the teaching on holiness. It did mean that discipline was important to the Methodist bishops.[52]

The Church of the Nazarene was formed out of a number of independent holiness churches created out of Methodism at the close of the century. Dr. Bresee organized the first church in California in 1893. This church along with others united with related groups in 1907 and 1908 to form the Church of the Nazarene.[53] It is the largest of the holiness groups. "To advance perfectionism was the sole excuse for the existence of this sect." Elmer Clark thinks the Nazarenes are already losing some of their distinctiveness as a holiness church. They have removed the term "holiness" from the names of their institutions. "Not one institution of the denomination now exposes its doctrinal character in its name."[54] However, this change of name may be best explained by the popular ascription of the term "holiness" to all the Pentecostal churches. The Nazarenes, as well as other churches claiming the Wesleyan doctrines, do not want to be confused with the "tongues" movement.

These three churches, along with the Pilgrim Holiness, "a smaller edition of the Nazarenes,"[55] and many other smaller sects, attempted to carry on the tradition of Wesley's doctrine of perfect love. How well they have succeeded is not easy to determine. The sect-formation shows that the doctrine will not die. However, it seems probable that the teaching would have fared better if it had been favorably retained in the Methodist church. That there have been extremes in the holiness groups is readily admitted; "not all movement has been forward and upward." There have been "retrogressions and embarrassments as well as successes and advances" in the "course of this modern-Wesleyan emphasis."[56]

In these "moderate holiness groups," as Gaddis calls them, has there been the retention of the Wesleyan message?[57]

> Modern Methodists who are embarrassed by the "second blessing" holiness teachings put forth by the small sects of Methodist derivation, are inclined to deny that Wesley gave any support to such interpretations. In this their wishes prevail over their historical judgments. Wesley gave full support to the "second blessing" or "second work of grace" principle and technique; and the small holiness sects, whether for better or for worse, are far more "Wesleyan" than their critics.[58]

Robert Clark insists that all the sects from Methodism return to the principle of Christian perfection. They "incite their followers to go all the way in seeking this grace" much in the same way that Wesley urged his people "when the Methodist Church was considered a sect by the established denominations."[59] He believes that the holiness sects have been true to Wesley's teaching.

> When one reads a discourse of one of these modern holiness clergymen, and then compares it with some of the messages preached by our early church fathers in the Methodist Church, the similarity is so great that one cannot deny the common source of their ideas.[60]

It is not well to compare the perfectionist teachings of these holiness sects with those of Wesley unless there has been careful investigation of their methods, sermons, and writings. It seems to be the opinion of Gaddis and Robert Clark that similarity does exist. Further investigation, however, would be needed to determine the degree of deviation from Wesley's ideal. It would seem that separation into small groups would easily lead to extremes that might have been avoided in a larger church. Wesley opposed independence on the part of his preachers and urged continuance in the Church of England. Bitter controversy and independent action are contrary to Wesley's spirit and teaching.

Even if it could be proved that Wesley's doctrine of perfection was retained in some of the holiness churches, there is still the problem of communication. When groups become isolated in their activity and are no longer in active contact with the larger Christian community, any helpful contribution they can make in ecumenical discussion is lost, and they are no longer influenced and corrected by the larger group. Such groups are in danger of fanatical extremes and obscurantism.

A word should be said about the modern Pentecostal movement. There is much confusion in the popular mind, and even in scholars' minds, as to any distinction between those groups that endeavor to maintain the Wesleyan heritage and those who place stress on the "gifts" of the Spirit. Horton Davies in an article on Christian sects uses the words holiness, Pentecostal, and adventist rather indiscriminately. He appears to see in holiness sects emphasis upon the Holy Spirit and emotional experience.[61] Obviously a clearer understanding is needed.

It is admitted that the earlier Pentecostal churches grew out of the holiness revivals of the last decades of the nineteenth century. It is possible that the emphasis of the holiness movement on the baptism of the Spirit as a Pentecostal experience could lead to overemphasis on emotional experience and the "spiritual gifts." With the "movement" getting into the hands of independents without proper church oversight, extremes were inevitable. When the more conservative holiness advocates saw these extremes, they acted against them.[62]

The "moderate" holiness advocates reacted against the extremes that developed in Pentecostalism. The elimination of the word "Pentecostal" from the Nazarene name is one evidence for this.[63] There is practically no place for the Pentecostal groups in the modern Holiness Association.[64] The emphasis on "tongues" or "healing" leaves something wanting in any doctrine of holiness. When it is remembered that Wesley's doctrine is inward religion and perfect love, not outward manifestations, it becomes clear why holiness as he taught it should not be confused with emotional experiences.

In contrast to the non-Wesleyan Pentecostal groups of the twentieth century, there are the sanctification, or "higher life," movements which have developed out of a Calvinistic background. The German "Sanctification Movement" received its inspiration largely from one man, Theodor Jellinghaus. He received his doctrine from Robert P. Smith, who founded the "Keswick Movement" in England.[65] Interestingly enough, Phoebe Palmer and her husband, and other holiness advocates from America, were greatly instrumental in laying the foundation work for the Keswick Movement.[66] Since the Palmers were directly influenced by Wesleyan doctrine in America, one can see the common origin of all these groups.[67]

But into this same movement went a non-Wesleyan influence. Charles Finney and Asa Mahan had Congregational backgrounds and Westminster phraseology.[68] Finney's teachings also affected the Keswick and sanctification movements in Europe.[69] D. L. Moody, Evan Roberts, R. A. Torrey, Wilbur Chapman, and "Gypsy" Smith, all of non-Wesleyan churches, entered into the revivals from which came these movements.[70] One would expect in these movements outside Methodist tradition a different interpretation of holiness from that of Wesley. When Warfield ascribes to Wesleyan teaching what he discovers in the sanctification movements, he is not wholly correct.[71]

The non-Wesleyan sanctification movements, though retaining considerable holiness terminology and emphasis, and though making place for a real work of God's grace in the soul, even in the "second blessing" sense, fall short of Wesley's idea of a pure heart. Their conception of sin is such that the sanctifying grace is not a purification.[72] They stop short of a real cleansing from all sin.[73] Their doctrine is such, though related to the Wesleyan doctrine, that they could not subscribe to the statement of holiness in the National Holiness Association.[74] Though the difference is largely one of definition, basically their concepts of grace, sin, and "positional holiness" place them closer to a Calvinistic doctrine of sanctification.[75]

D. CONCLUSION

It is highly improbable that the successors to a great thinker like John Wesley would be able to hold without change the great ideals and spirit of such a man. In fact one like Wesley would expect time and experience to modify his methods, terminology, and ideas. He was aware of some changes in himself and his people during his lifetime. However, his basic concept of perfection did not change, according to his own testimony.

It is not argued here that there are not deviations from Wesley's mature views among holiness advocates. Wesley's opinions were too complex for many to follow him wholly. Nor should one disregard the possibility of new insights into the experience of perfect love, and new expressions of the same truth, found in the exponents of Christian perfection in the nineteenth and twentieth centuries. Also it is wrong to judge a doctrine by some of the popular opinions or actions of adherents to the teaching. Wesley would not have wanted to be judged on the basis of some opinions of his followers! Neither should it be required of those who claim to follow Wesley in his doctrine of Christian perfection that they also follow him in his views on the church, on politics, or economics, or t h a t they consider sacrosanct his terms, methods, or practices.

It would appear that American frontier life, the agitation over slavery and the Civil War, and the controversies over sanctification in Methodism during the nineteenth century did result in modifications of Wesley's view on holiness. In the heat of controversy it is very easy to emphasize one truth to the neglect of others. John Peters is apparently correct in his conclusion that the holiness movement of the nineteenth century in its emphasis upon instantaneous sanctification and testimony neglected Wesley's equal insistence upon the gradual aspect, and his cautions about testimony.[76] Also Wesley's broad and liberal spirit was forgotten by many in the heated conflict.

It is impossible to evaluate accurately the present status of perfection teaching in the Methodist church or the holiness sects without further investigation. A close examination of the methods and teachings of these groups would need to be made in their Sunday schools, prayer meetings, youth services, pastoral ministry, devotional literature, and other means of Christian nurture, as well as their theological treatises. Before any true evaluation could be given, the Christian testimony and lives of people professing the experience of entire sanctification would need to be studied. If such a study as this were made, it might shed some light on the question as to how much of Wesley's concepts of perfection has been retained and practiced.

The results of this survey of Wesley's concept of perfection likely reveal certain areas of weakness in the modern holiness message, and a few suggestions may serve as correctives. In the first place, Wesley's concept of prevenient grace attributed a power to God's free grace that is often overlooked. Wesley saw that a person might be acceptable to God with the faith of a servant *before* evangelical faith was given. In other words, there may be many people who are not "under wrath" who have not yet experienced knowingly the new birth in saving faith. They are still "under law" but do possess the beginnings of faith, though it is weak.

A second corrective in Wesley is found in his insistence that the justified are sanctified initially and are made holy in degrees. This sanctification increases gradually as a process until the moment of entire sanctification. Wesley never held that a believer could be indifferent at this point of gradual sanctification and expect to reach perfect love. There must be intense, earnest, and continual seeking, sometimes for years, before the faith for complete holiness is given. And for Wesley this faith for entire sanctification, as for justification, is a gift. Then, after the attainment of perfect love, the work of progressive, or gradual, sanctification on the whole of one's life continues. There is no true holiness without growth and discipline.

Another suggested corrective in Wesley may be in his disapproval of the demand for the "second blessing" as a requirement for heaven. He held that no one could get to heaven without complete holiness, as all churches teach, but he did not hold that all who did not consciously enter the experience in life were lost. In fact he held the opposite view—only a few of the believers reach entire sanctification until shortly before death. He opposed the method of urging believers into entire holiness by threats of punishment. It was possible for men to walk in the "lower way," not attain the higher level of Christian life, and yet be accepted with God.

The recognition of the human limits to perfection was vitally important to Wesley. The difference between two perfections—perfection in love and perfection in performance —must be understood. To expect perfection in the natural powers here and now was misleading. The perfect *desire* to become perfect in act was Christian perfection; the becoming perfect in the second sense must await the resurrection.

These human limits leave a large area in the sanctified person where confession is necessary and humility must be shown. The entirely sanctified are in constant danger of losing their special grace. It is not a grace, once given, that will maintain itself. Moment-by-moment reliance upon Christ is essential. The failures and mistakes of the holiest people are serious and need the efficacy of Christ's atonement. There is no place for boasting in one's attainment. The greatest of humility is necessary in any testimony. A continual feeling of unworthiness and dependence increases with a pure heart. When these "sins" of the sanctified are recognized, the holiness advocate can better understand his Calvinist brother who feels himself still a sinner.

Neglect of Wesley's emphasis upon the moment-by-moment life may easily lead to a pharisaical attitude toward sin. When Wesley's concept of willful sin is emphasized without his corresponding emphasis on sinfulness in the believer and weakness and failure in the entirely sanctified, an imagined state of holiness may be professed without the essential sense of unworthiness and the necessary dependence upon the continuing merits of Christ. However, true holiness of heart destroys any boasting in any goodness obtained and causes the believer to feel deeply his constant need of the atonement in Christ. Without this latter emphasis, there is no true holiness.

Wesley was determined to speak to the Christian Church of his day. His was not an isolated message. He put his message in terms understood by the people in the eighteenth century. He did not expect favor, but he did get a hearing. There is great loss to any truth that is hidden in isolated groups. If the message of Wesley is valid, it needs to be heard in the mainstream of Christian churches. Wesley not only wanted his message of holiness *retained* in Methodism but also *communicated* to all. One of the greatest weaknesses resultant from sect-formation is the inability to speak with a united voice.

Wesley does have a contribution to make to ecumenical discussion. His influence u p o n modern Protestantism has been too great for his voice not to be heard. Controversies, schisms, and extremes must not blind Christian leaders to the value of Wesley's thought on redemption in Christ. The central truth of Wesley's theology should not be left for isolationists or extremists alone. This truth properly understood and proclaimed is the possession of the Church Universal.

One great contribution of Wesley is found in his emphasis upon universal grace. This was not new in Wesley by any means, but he made the idea come alive in Protestantism. Christ died for all men. His grace is operating in every man. Every man by this grace can, if he will, be saved. He is saved by faith which is God's gift, yet a gift everyone can have if he uses the grace he has. Salvation is all of grace and yet by faith. It is synergism in the framework of monergism. It is a grand synthesis of the universal free grace of God with the salvation of the elect by faith.

Wesley's distinctions in the definition of sin, though possibly not as clear as they might be, should be recognized. Certainly the "sins" which the sinner commits in rebellion and defiance of God are not the same as the "sins" in the life of the believer whose heart has been changed. And this difference is not just in God's attitude toward the "sins." Basically there has been a change in the believer's will so that no longer is he committing voluntary sins knowingly. Such "sins" are impossible to one who is trusting in God. The believer is not in rebellion against God.

Also there is a difference between deviations from perfect or pure love and deviations from a standard of perfect conduct or performance. In the first is found divided loyalty; in the second is found involuntary failure. Whether one agrees with Wesley that one can experience a perfect love for God, he must agree that a pure love is not the same as perfection in carrying out that love. If this distinction is grasped, Wesley's idea of Christian perfection has meaning.

Wesley's emphasis upon a real change in the individual has great significance. This "real change" is inward and is discovered in the love motivation. The new life in regeneration is the love "shed abroad in the heart" by the Holy Spirit. This love becomes perfect when its rivals in the self are destroyed. But it may abound more and more. In this concept Wesley's holiness is not only a righteousness "reckoned" to be the believer's because of Christ's, but is actually a love possessed by the believer. Yet it is not a natural love but a gift of God that is communicated by constant union with Christ.

Should one deny the validity of Wesley's concept of perfect love? Since this love is a gift of God, it cannot be the natural development of a human love. Since it is given by God, should it not expel all its enemies in the self? No one should deny the power of God to create a heart totally loyal to God. This basic fact of a pure love is the Christian message and becomes the foundation for all Christian unity. It is a drastic fact and calls for changed and loyal wills, but it describes New Testament Christianity correctly. Wesley's doctrine of perfection has a clear relevance for this modern world.

It is *perfection*—a perfection in the love motive. It is *holiness*—a holiness derived from Christ and totally dependent on Him. It is *salvation* from sin, but it is from the sin of rebellion, pride, and selfishness. It is *purity*—a purity in the desire and loyalty of a heart wholly devoted to God. It is *humility* born of a conviction of personal worthlessness and of Christ's all-sufficiency. These for Wesley describe the pure religion which he called Christian perfection.

FOOTNOTES

CHAPTER I

1. *The Works of John Wesley,* authorized edition published by the Wesleyan Conference, London, 1872 (14 vols.; photo offset edition; Grand Rapids: Zondervan Publishing House, 1958), VI, 1.

2. *Ibid.,* VIII, 300.

3. *Ibid.,* XII, 387.

4. George A. Turner, *The More Excellent Way* (Winona Lake, Ind.: Light and Life Press, 1952), p. 38.

5. R. Newton Flew, *The Idea of Perfection in Christian Theology* (London: Oxford University Press, 1934), pp. 114-17.

6. *Works,* VII, 178.

7. Claude Holmes Thompson, "The Witness of American Methodism to the Historical Doctrine of Christian Perfection" (unpublished Ph.D. dissertation, Drew University, 1949), pp. 112-26.

8. Flew, *op. cit.,* p. 123.

9. *Ibid.,* p. 130.

10. *Ibid.,* pp. 193-94.

11. *Ibid.,* pp. 208-9.

12. *Ibid.,* p. 244.

13. *Ibid.,* pp. 158-59.

14. Wallace R. Haines, "A Survey of Holiness Literature," *Heart and Life Magazine,* XXX, No. 2 (1943), 12.

15. Rufus M. Jones, *Spiritual Reformers in the 16th and 17th Centuries* (London: MacMillan and Co., Ltd., 1914), p. 336.

16. Elmer Merrill Gaddis, "Christian Perfectionism in America" (unpublished Ph.D dissertation, University of Chicago, 1929), p. 58.

17. Flew, *op. cit.,* pp. 275-76.

18. Gaddis, *op. cit.,* pp. 60-61.

19. *Works,* I, 114-40.

20. Benjamin B. Warfield, *Studies in Perfectionism* (2 vols.; New York: Oxford University Press, 1931), I, 305-15.

21. Elmer T. Clark, *The Small Sects in America* (New York: Abingdon-Cokesbury Press, 1949), p. 53.

22. Gerrit C. Berkouwer, *Faith and Sanctification* (Grand Rapids: Wm. B. Eerdmans Publishing Company, 1952), p. 55.

23. Clark, *op. cit.,* p. 55.

24. *Works,* XIII, 272.

25. Umphrey Lee, *John Wesley and Modern Religion* (Nashville; Cokesbury Press, 1936), pp. 39-57. See also Maximin Piette, *John Wesley in the Evolution of Protestantism* (New York: Sheed and Ward, 1937), pp. 218-25.

26. Ernest J. Rattenbury, *The Conversion of the Wesleys* (London: The Epworth Press, 1938), pp. 48-49.

27. Lee, *op. cit.,* pp. 30-32.

28. *Works,* I, 93-95.

29. *Ibid.,* XII, 250.

30. Rattenbury, *op. cit.,* p. 51.

31. *Works,* XI, 366-69.

32. Lee, *op. cit.*, p. 178.

33. Piette, *op. cit.*, p. 480.

34. *Works*, XII, 239.

35. Rattenbury, *op. cit.*, p. 173.

36. *Works*, I, 114-40.

37. *Ibid.*, VI, 263.

38. John L. Peters, *Christian Perfection and American Methodism* (Nashville: Abingdon Press, 1957), pp. 67-132. Also Gaddis, *op. cit.*, pp. 164-202.

39. Warfield, *op. cit.*, II, 567.

40. Clark, *op cit.*, p. 59.

41. Delbert R. Rose, *A Theology of Christian Experience* (Wilmore, Ky.: The Seminary Press, 1958), p. 54.

42. Warfield, *op. cit.*, I, 3-302.

43. Francis McConnell, *John Wesley* (New York: The Abingdon Press, 1939), p. 192.

44. George Croft Cell, *The Rediscovery of John Wesley* (New York: Henry Holt and Co., 1935), p. 347.

45. *Ibid.*, pp. 265-66.

46. *Ibid.*, pp. 341-42.

47. Franz Hildebrandt,, *From Luther to Wesley* (London: Lutterworth Press, 1951), pp. 15, 80-81.

48. Turner, *op. cit.*, p. 15.

49. Rose, *op. cit.*, p. 78.

50. Hildebrandt, *op. cit.*, pp. 108-9.

51. Karl Barth, *The Christian Life* (London: Student Movement Press, 1930), pp. 25-30.

52. Berkouwer, *op. cit.*, pp. 75-76.

53. *Ibid.*, pp. 48-53.

54. *Ibid.*, pp. 9-12.

55. William E. H. Lecky, *A History of England in the Eighteenth Century* (London: D. Appleton and Co., 1879), p. 631.

56. John Wesley Bready, *England: Before and After Wesley* (London: Hodder and Stoughton, Ltd., 1938), p. 13.

57. Lee, *op. cit.*, p. 5.

58. William R. Cannon, *The Theology of John Wesley* (Nashville: Abingdon-Cokesbury Press, 1946), pp. 13-14.

59. Harald Lindstrom, *Wesley and Sanctification* (London: The Epworth Press, 1946), p. 1.

60. J. Ernest Rattenbury, *Wesley's Legacy to the World* (Nashville: Cokesbury Press, 1929), p. 9.

61. Lee, *op. cit.*, p. 5.

62. Robert Burton Clark, "The History of the Doctrine of Christian Perfection in the Methodist Episcopal Church in America up to 1845" (unpublished Th.D. thesis, Temple University, 1946), p. 13.

63. *Works*, X, 353.

64. Piette, *op. cit.*, p. 201.

65. Hildebrandt, *op. cit.*, p. 15.

66. Rattenbury, *The Conversion of the Wesleys*, *op. cit.*, p. 183.

67. Piette, *op. cit.*, p. 478.

68. Rattenbury, *The Conversion of the Wesleys*, *op. cit.*, p. 240.

69. Cell, *op. cit.*, p. 17.

70. Lee, *op. cit.*, pp. 83-109, 321.

71. Cannon, *op. cit.*, pp. 89-90.

72. *Ibid.*, pp. 244-45.

73. Timothy L. Smith, *Revivalism and Social Reform* (Nashville: Abingdon Press, 1957), pp. 114-47.

74. Peters, *op. cit.*, p. 11.

75. Lindstrom, *op. cit.*, p. 15.

76. *Ibid.*, p. 16.

77. Turner, *op. cit.*, p. 11, where Albert Knudson writes the Foreword.

78. *Ibid.*, pp. 13-14.

79. Flew, *op. cit.*, pp. 332-34.

80. W. E. Sangster, *The Path to Perfection* (Nashville: Abingdon-Cokesbury Press, 1943), p. 72.

81. Lee, *op. cit.*, pp. 185-87.

82. Warfield, *op. cit.*, I, 113-18.

83. McConnell, *op. cit.*, pp. 192-94.

84. Berkouwer, *op. cit.*, pp. 48-53.

85. *Works,* XI, 300, 364-65.

CHAPTER II

1. James C. Spalding, "Recent Restatements of the Doctrines of the Fall and Original Sin" (Ph.D. thesis, Columbia University, University Microfilms, Ann Arbor, 1950), p. 2.

2. Leo G. Cox, "John Wesley's Concept of Sin" (unpublished M.A. thesis, State University of Iowa, 1957). The reader is referred to this detailed account of Wesley's doctrine of sin. In this paper on perfection only the relevant matters will be discussed.

3. *Works,* VI, 269-70, 352-53.

4. *Ibid.*, IX, 341. See also VI, 242-43.

5. *Ibid.*, VI, 272.

6. *Ibid.*, p. 223.

7. *Ibid.*, IX, 283. See R. S. Foster, *Studies in Theology* (New York: Eaton and Mains, 1899). VI, 123.

8. David Cairns, *The Image of God in Man* (New York: Philosophical Library, 1953), pp. 125-26, 131-37.

9. *Works,* VI, 63.

10. *Ibid.*, IX, 270-71.

11. *Ibid.*, VI, 68.

12. *Ibid.*, IX, 285-86.

13. John Miley, *Systematic Theology* (2 vols.; New York: The Methodist Book Concern, 1892), I, 521-33.

14. Cox, *op. cit.*, pp. 167-69.

15. *Works,* IX, 256.

16. *Ibid.*, pp. 318, 428.

17. Cox, *op. cit.*, pp. 170-72. See Foster, *op. cit.*, II, 180, 238.

18. *Works,* IX, 315.

19. *Ibid.*, IX, 393-94.

20. *Ibid.*, X, 222-24.

21. *Ibid.*, V, 7.

22. *Ibid.*, VI, 511-12.
23. *Ibid.*, I, 427.
24. *Ibid.*, VI, 347.
25. *Ibid.*, X, 204.
26. *Ibid.*, XIV, 356.
27. *Ibid.*, IX, 103.
28. *Ibid.*, XII, 323.
29. *Ibid.*, VIII, 289.
30. *Ibid.*, VII, 373-74.
31. *Ibid.*, pp. 373-86.
32. Cannon, *op. cit.*, p. 90.
33. *Works*, VI, 512.
34. Foster, *op. cit.*, VI, 123. Also see Miley, *op. cit.*, II, 432.
35. *Works*, VIII, 277.
36. *Ibid.*, IX, 315.
37. *Ibid.*, VI, 509.
38. *Ibid.*, V, 110.
39. *Ibid.*, pp. 59-60.
40. *Ibid.*, VII, 345.
41. Cannon, *op. cit.*, p. 100.
42. *Works*, VII, 187-88.
43. Lee, *op. cit.*, p. 124. See also John W. Prince, *Wesley on Religious Education* (New York: Methodist Book Concern, 1926), p. 34.
44. *Works*, VI, 512.
45. Lee, *op. cit.*, pp. 125-26.
46. Cannon, *op. cit.*, p. 208.
47. *Works*, X, 358-60.
48. Miley, *op. cit.*, II, 165-69.
49. *Works*, V, 239.
50. *Ibid.*, pp. 55-56.
51. *Ibid.*, p. 62.
52. *Ibid.*, X, 318-22.
53. Charles Hodge, *Systematic Theology* (2 vols.; Grand Rapids: Wm. B. Eerdmans Publishing Company, 1952), II, 472.
54. *Works*, V, 240.
55. *Ibid.*, X, 318-22.
56. Hodge, *op. cit.*, II, 548.
57. *Works*, VIII, 277.
58. Miley, *op. cit.*, II, 241-48.
59. *Works*, V, 236-40.
60. Hodge, *op. cit.*, II, 493-94.
61. *Works*, X, 325-26.
62. *Ibid.*, IX, 489.
63. *Ibid.*, VII, 313.
64. *Ibid.*, p. 512.
65. *Ibid.*, VIII, 277-78.
66. Lindstom, *op. cit.*, pp. 71-72.
67. Miley, *op. cit.*, II. 248-53.
68. Cell, *op. cit.*, p. 245.
69. *Ibid.*, pp. 251-52.

70. *Ibid.*, p. 256.

71. *Ibid.*, pp. 263-65.

72. *Ibid.*, p. 271.

73. Robert E. Chiles, "Methodist Apostasy: From Free Grace to Free Will," *Religion in Life,* XXVII, No. 3 (1958), 438-39.

74. *Ibid.*, p. 448.

75. Leland Scott, "Methodist Theology in America in the Nineteenth Century" (unpublished Ph.D. dissertation, Yale University, 1954), pp. 48-52.

76. *Ibid.*, pp. 193-225.

77. Peters, *op. cit.*, p. 151.

78. *Ibid.*, p. 225.

79. Prince, *op. cit.*, p. 19.

80. Lee, *op. cit.*, p. 125.

81. Warfield, *op. cit.*, II, 608.

82. Reinhold Niebuhr, *The Nature and Destiny of Man* (New York: Charles Scribner's Sons, 1943), II, 175.

83. Turner, *op. cit.*, p. 129.

84. Pope, *op. cit.*, II, 78-80.

85. Spalding, *op. cit.*, p. 22. He refers there to Adolph von Harnack, *Lehrbuch der Dogmengeschichte* (Funfte Auflage, Tubingen: J. E. B. Mohn, 1932), III, 195 ff.

86. Pope, *op. cit.*, II, 86.

87. *Works*, X, 350.

88. *Ibid.*, V, 104.

89. *Ibid.*, X, 392.

90. *Ibid.*, p. 231.

91. *Ibid.*, p. 468.

92. *Ibid.*, XII, 4-5.

93. *Ibid.*, VII, 228-29.

94. *Ibid.*, X, 235.

95. *Ibid.*, XIII, 96.

96. *Ibid.*, X, 360.

97. *Ibid.*, p. 234.

98. *Ibid.*, VI, 512.

99. *Ibid.*, X, 478.

100. *Ibid.*, V, 233.

101. Martin Luther, *A Compend of Luther's Theology,* ed. Hugh T. Kerr (Philadelphia: The Westminster Press, 1943), p. 90.

102. John Calvin, *A Compend of the Institutes of the Christian Religion by John Calvin,* ed. Hugh T. Kerr (Philadelphia: Presbyterian Board of Christian Education, 1939), p. 51.

103. *Ibid.*, p. 53.

104. Cannon, *op. cit.*, p. 93.

105. *Ibid.*, p. 115.

106. Lindstrom, *op. cit.*, p. 50.

107. *Works*, V, 405-13.

108. *Ibid.*, VI, 511-13.

109. Emil Brunner, *The Divine Imperative* (New York: The Macmillan Company, 1942), pp. 57, 68-71.

110. Miley, *op. cit.*, II, 305.

111. Clyde Manschreck, *Melanchthon, The Quiet Reformer* (New York: Abingdon Press, 1958), pp. 293-302.

112. Martin Luther, *Commentary on the Epistle to the Romans* (Grand Rapids: Zondervan Publishing House, 1954), p. 99.

113. *Ibid.*, p. 152.

114. Martin Luther, *Commentary on St. Paul's Epistle to the Galatians* (Grand Rapids: Wm. B. Eerdmans Publishing Company, 1930), p. 114.

115. *Works,* V, 57.

116. Calvin, *Compend, op. cit.*, p. 53.

117. Brunner, *op. cit.*, pp. 30, 199.

118. Warfield, *op. cit.*, I, 113-14.

119. Barth, *op. cit.*, pp. 12-13. See the detailed account of the Lutheran and Reformed position as analyzed by Berkouwer, *op. cit.*, pp. 71-75.

120. Hodge, *op. cit.*, II, 190. See also Abraham Kuyper, *The Work of the Holy Spirit* (Grand Rapids: Wm. B. Eerdmans Publishing Co., 1946), pp. 263-67.

121. Charles Hay, *The Theology of Luther* (Philadelphia: Lutheran Publication Society, 1897), II, 465-67.

122. Lindstrom, *op. cit.*, p. 44.

123. *Works,* V, 72.

124. *Ibid.*, pp. 98-111.

125. *Ibid.*, pp. 81-82.

126. See sections on *"Sola Gratia"* and "Atonement in Christ" in this chapter.

127. Foster, *op. cit.*, p. 183. See also *Works,* VI, 512; VII, 228.

128. *Works,* V, 163-64.

129. *Ibid.*, XI, 395.

130. *Ibid.*, IX, 286.

131. *Ibid.*, VII, 490.

132. *Ibid.*, V, 58.

133. *Ibid.*, XII, 239.

134. *Ibid.*, IX, 312.

135. *Ibid.*, p. 275.

136. *Ibid.*, VI, 270.

137. *Ibid.*, p. 512.

138. *Ibid.*, V, 227-28.

139. *Ibid.*, p. 231.

140. *Ibid.*, pp. 106-8.

141. *Ibid.*, VII, 235-36. See Lee, *op. cit.*, p. 97.

142. Flew, *op. cit.*, p. 333.

143. *Works,* V, 99.

144. *Ibid.*, VII, 490; XII, 239.

145. *Ibid.*, V, 108-9.

146. *Ibid.*, pp. 318-27.

147. F. R. Tennant, *The Concept of Sin* (Cambridge: University Press, 1912), pp. 104-5.

148. Sangster, *op. cit.*, p. 76.

149. *Ibid.,* p. 113.

150. *Works,* V, 146.

151. *Ibid.,* p. 149.

152. *Ibid.,* p. 153.

153. Foster, *op. cit.,* VI, 239.

154. Miley, *op. cit.,* I, 511.

155. *Works,* I, 222.

156. Berkouwer, *op. cit.,* pp. 56-60.

157. Edward Sugden, ed., *Standard Sermons by John Wesley* (London: Epworth Press, 1921), I, 262-63.

158. *Works,* VI, 263.

159. Cell, *op. cit.,* pp. 361-62. Flew, *op. cit.,* pp. 256-57. Rattenbury, *Conversion, op. cit.,* p. 199.

160. Berkouwer, *op. cit.,* p. 74.

161. *Works,* V, 148.

162. *Ibid.,* p. 155.

163. *Ibid.,* p. 92.

164. *Ibid.,* p. 96.

165. *Ibid.,* p. 161.

166. *Ibid.,* VI, 45, 84-85, 413.

167. Sangster, *op. cit.,* pp. 72, 76.

168. Luther, *Romans, op. cit.,* p. 84. See E. LaB. Cherbonnier, *Hardness of Heart* (Garden City: Doubleday & Company, Inc., 1955), pp. 89-90.

169. Warfield, *op. cit.,* II, 582-83.

170. Hodge, *op. cit.,* III, 245-50.

171. *Works,* I, 17.

172. *Ibid.,* p. 74.

173. Rattenbury, *Conversion, op. cit.,* p. 71.

174. *Works,* I, 103.

175. Lee, *op. cit.,* pp. 77-78.

176. Martin Luther, *Works of Martin Luther,* 6 vols. (Philadelphia: A. J. Holman Company, 1932), VI, 451-52.

177. Hildebrandt, *op. cit.,* pp. 23-25.

178. *Ibid.,* p. 24. See Lindstrom, *op. cit.,* p. 16.

179. *Works,* VII, 204.

180. *Ibid.,* X, 279.

181. *Ibid.,* V, 63-64.

182. *Ibid.,* XII, 342.

183. *Ibid.,* pp. 359-60, 387.

184. *Ibid.,* p. 447.

185. Rattenbury, *Conversion, op. cit.,* p. 71.

186. *Works,* VII, 198-99.

187. *Ibid.,* pp. 235-36.

188. *Ibid.,* I, 77, 100-101. See Lee, *op. cit.,* pp. 90-100.

189. *Works,* V, 213.

190. *Ibid.,* p. 9.

191. *Ibid.,* I, 106, 117.

192. *Ibid.,* pp. 257, 276.

193. *Ibid.,* p. 117; VI, 526-27; XIII, 62.

217

194. *Ibid.*, V, 85-86; VIII, 276-77.

195. *Ibid.*, VII, 261; X, 73.

196. *Ibid.*, XII, 78-79.

197. *Ibid.*, VI, 49-54; VII, 236-38. In this last reference Wesley made quite clear that the faith of a child is hindered by doubts and fears, but, when it becomes strong, then full sanctification occurs.

198. Berkouwer, *op. cit.*, p. 17.

199. *Ibid.*, p. 52.

200. *Ibid.*, pp. 73-75.

201. *Ibid.*, pp. 76-78.

202. Cherbonnier, *op. cit.*, pp. 95-97.

203. *Works*, I, 333-34.

204. *Ibid.*, pp. 315-16.

205. *Ibid.*, II, 142.

206. *Ibid.*, VII, 204.

207. Niebuhr, *op. cit.*, II, 175.

208. Gordon Rupp, *The Righteousness of God* (New York: Philosophical Library, Inc., 1953), p. 46.

209. Luther, *Galatians, op. cit.*, p. 117.

210. Berkouwer, *op. cit.*, p. 27.

211. Hay, *op. cit.*, II, 438-58.

212. Barth, *op. cit.*, pp. 17-20.

213. *Ibid.*, pp. 47-49.

214. Brunner, *op. cit.*, pp. 70-71.

215. Berkouwer, *op. cit.*, pp. 168-73.

216. *Ibid.*, pp. 51-52.

217. *Works*, VI, 48.

218. *Ibid.*, VIII, 47, 428-29; V, 213-14.

219. *Ibid.*, XI, 493-94.

220. *Ibid.*, p. 494.

221. *Ibid.*, VII, 411.

222. *Ibid.*, VI, 49.

223. *Ibid.*, p. 50.

224. Cannon, *op. cit.*, p. 146.

CHAPTER III

1. *Works,* XI, 449.

2. *Ibid.*, p. 450.

3. *Ibid.*, p. 444.

4. *Ibid.*, III, 369.

5. *Ibid.*, XI, 451.

6. Sangster, *op. cit.*, p. 146.

7. Flew, *op. cit.*, p. 52.

8. *Works*, VIII, 21-22.

9. *Ibid.*, VI, 411-23.

10. *Ibid.*, VI, 1-22, 411-23; VIII, 248-49, 340-41, 373-74; XI, 374-76; XIII, 132-33.

11. *Ibid.*, VI, 6.

12. *Ibid.*, pp. 417-18, 492.

13. *Ibid.*, I, 172.

14. *Ibid.*, VIII, 290.

15. *Ibid.*, XI, 451.
16. *Ibid.*, XII, 208.
17. *Ibid.*, III, 273; XI, 417-18.
18. *Ibid.*, XII, 131.
19. Lee, *op. cit.*, pp. 90-91.
20. *Works,* I, 99-102.
21. *Ibid.*, pp. 103-5.
22. Carl F. Eltzholtz, *John Wesley's Conversion and Sanctification* (New York: Eaton and Mains, 1908), pp. 5-41.
23. *Works,* I, 222.
24. *Ibid.*, p. 46.
25. *Ibid.*, pp. 70-71.
26. *Ibid.*, XII, 71.
27. *Ibid.*, VI, 44.
28. Lindstrom, *op. cit.*, p. 113.
29. *Works,* VIII, 46-47.
30. *Ibid.*, V, 239.
31. *Ibid.*, p. 57.
32. *Ibid.*, p. 13.
33. *Ibid.*, VIII, 276.
34. *Ibid.*, p. 373.
35. *Ibid.*, V, 56.
36. *Ibid.*, p. 57.
37. *Ibid.*, I, 321; VIII, 47.
38. *Ibid.*, VI, 263.
39. Cannon, *op. cit.*, pp. 244-45.
40. Berkouwer, *op. cit.*, pp. 27-28.
41. *Works,* VI, 44.
42. Hay, *op. cit.*, II, 438-39.
43. Calvin, *Compend, op. cit.*, p. 110.
44. *Ibid.*, pp. 96-98.
45. *Works,* V, 223-24.
46. *Ibid.*, VI, 71.
47. *Ibid.*, pp. 66-70.
48. *Ibid.*, pp. 74-75; VII, 205-6.
49. *Ibid.*, I, 172.
50. Cannon, *op. cit.*, pp. 119, 223-24.
51. *Works,* VIII, 285.
52. *Ibid.*, IX, 343.
53. *Ibid.*, X, 271-83.
54. Berkouwer, *op. cit.*, pp. 94-97.
55. *Ibid.*, pp. 50-51.
56. Cannon, *op. cit.*, pp. 224-25.
57. Rattenbury, *Conversion, op. cit.*, pp. 28 29.
58. *Works,* VI, 6-7.
59. Cannon, *op. cit.*, p. 252.
60. *Works,* VI, 16.
61. *Ibid.*, V, 223-24.
62. *Ibid.*, pp. 214-19.
63. Brunner, *op. cit.*, p. 77.

64. *Ibid.*, p. 103.

65. Robert E. Cushman, "Karl Barth on the Holy Spirit," *Religion in Life*, XXIV, No. 4 (1955), pp. 566-78.

66. Miley, *op. cit.*, II, 356-62.

67. *Works*, V, 220-21.

68. *Ibid.*, VI, 45.

69. *Ibid.*, p. 74.

70. *Ibid.*, VII, 237.

71. Jesse T. Peck, *The Central Idea of Christianity* (Boston: Henry V. Degen, 1856), pp. 15-16.

72. *Works*, VI, 489.

73. Samuel Chadwick, *The Call to Christian Perfection* (Kansas City: Beacon Hill Press, 1943), p. 28.

74. Asbury Lowrey, *Possibilities of Grace* (Chicago: The Christian Witness Co., 1884), p. 204.

75. *Works*, X, 203.

76. Kuyper, *op. cit.*, pp. 469-73.

77. *Ibid.*, pp. 450-51.

78. Warfield, *op. cit.*, I, 117; Berkouwer, *op. cit.*, p. 97.

79. Turner, *op. cit.*, p. 88.

80. Peters, *op. cit.*, p. 107.

81. *Ibid.*, pp. 102-3.

82. *Ibid.*, pp. 192-93.

83. Sangster, *op. cit.*, p. 143.

84. *Works*, VI, 46.

85. *Ibid.*, p. 91.

86. *Ibid.*, pp. 5-6.

87. *Ibid.*, VI, 509.

88. *Ibid.*, XII, 340, 350-51, 363-64, 374.

89. *Ibid.*, VII, 27-34.

90. *Ibid.*, XII, 333-34.

91. Rattenbury, *Conversion, op. cit.*, p. 199.

92. *Works*, VII, 489.

93. *Ibid.*, XII, 255.

94. *Ibid.*, VII, 205-6.

95. J. A. Wood, *Purity and Maturity* (Boston: Christian Witness Co., 1899), pp. 186-89.

96. *Ibid.*, pp. 145-47.

97. *Works*, XIII, 351-52.

98. *Ibid.*, VI, 46; VIII, 285.

99. John Fletcher, *The Works* (New York: B. Waugh and T. Mason, 1835), II, 632-33.

100. Luther, *Compend, op. cit.*, pp. 244-46; Hay, *op. cit.*, II, 551.

101. Warfield, *op. cit.*, II, 582-83.

102. John Calvin, *Institutes of the Christian Religion* (Grand Rapids: Wm. B. Eerdmans Publishing Co., 1949), I, 658.

103. *Works*, XI, 367.

104. *Ibid.*, pp. 368-71.

105. *Ibid.*, VI, 490.

106. *Ibid.*, p. 491; XIV, 261-62.

107. Peters, *op. cit.*, pp. 30-31.

108. Rattenbury, *Conversion, op. cit.*, p. 193.

109. *Works*, VIII, 328-29.

110. *Ibid.*, VI, 491.

111. Rattenbury, *Conversion, op. cit.*, p. 197.

112. Edward John Carnell, *A Philosophy of the Christian Religion* (Grand Rapids: Wm. B. Eerdmans, 1954), p. 418.

113. *Works*, VIII, 286-90.

114. *Ibid.*, VI, 526; XII, 389.

115. *Ibid.*, VII, 28-29.

116. *Ibid.*, XIV, 261-63.

117. *Ibid.*, VII, 202.

118. John Wesley, *Explanatory Notes upon the New Testament* (New York: Eaton and Mains, n.d.), p. 512.

119. *Ibid.*, VII, 237.

120. Rattenbury, *Conversion, op. cit.*, p. 199.

121. Kuyper, *op. cit.*, p. 450.

122. Luther, *Galatians, op. cit.*, pp. 164-65.

123. Calvin, *Institutes, op. cit.*, I, 660.

124. David E. Roberts, *Psychotherapy and a Christian View of Man* (New York: Charles Scribner's Sons, 1953), pp. 122-23.

125. Flew, *op. cit.*, p. 398.

126. *Works*, VIII, 290.

127. *Ibid.*, VI, 412.

128. *Ibid.*, pp. 2-6.

129. *Ibid.*, XII, 207.

130. *Ibid.*, III, 273.

131. *Ibid.*, XII, 227.

132. *Ibid.*, pp. 229-30.

133. *Ibid.*, XI, 377-78.

134. *Ibid.*, VI, 418.

135. *Ibid.*, VII, 482.

136. *Ibid.*, p. 483.

137. Luther, *Galatians, op. cit.*, p. 304.

138. Luther, *Romans, op. cit.*, p. 84.

139. Barth, *op. cit.*, pp. 17-25.

140. Niebuhr, *op. cit.*, I, 251-54.

141. *Ibid.*, pp. 117-19.

CHAPTER IV

1. Henry E. Brockett, *Scriptural Freedom from Sin* (Kansas City: Kingshiway Press, 1941), p. 24.

2. Warfield, *op. cit.*, II, 451.

3. *Ibid.*, pp. 453-54.

4. McConnell, *op. cit.*, pp. 193-94.

5. Martin Foss, *The Idea of Perfection in the Western World* (Princeton: Princeton University Press, 1946), pp. 8-9.

6. *Works*, VI, 16-20.

7. Thompson, *op. cit.*, p. 45. See Turner, *op. cit.*, pp. 202-3.

8. Thomas Benjamin Neely, *Doctrinal Standards of Methodism* (New York: Fleming H. Revell Co., 1918), p. 274.

9. *Works,* XI, 444-46.

10. W. E. Sangster, "The Church's One Privation," *Religion in Life,* XVIII, No. 4 (1949), 493-507.

11. Sangster, *Path to Perfection, op. cit.,* pp. 51-52.

12. Gerald O. McCulloh, "Evangelizing the Whole of Life," *Religion in Life,* XIX, No. 2 (1950), 236-44.

13. Leslie F. Church, *The Early Methodist People* (London: The Epworth Press, 1948), p. 130.

14. *Works,* XI, 424-26.

15. Roberts, *op. cit.,* pp. 124-27.

16. *Ibid.,* pp. 129-32.

17. Sangster, *Path to Perfection, op. cit.,* p. 68.

18. Niebuhr, *op. cit.,* II, 175.

19. *Works,* VI, 53.

20. Niebuhr, *op. cit.,* II, 173-74.

21. Sangster, *Path to Perfection, op. cit.,* p. 81.

22. Warfield, *op. cit.,* I, 278-79.

23. *Works,* VI, 7.

24. Sangster, *Path to Perfection, op. cit.,* p. 54.

25. Turner, *op. cit.,* p. 38.

26. *Ibid.,* p. 113.

27. *Works,* VIII, 294.

28. *Ibid.,* p. 296.

29. *Ibid.,* XII, 257.

30. *Ibid.,* XI, 373.

31. Robert E. Cushman, "Landmarks in the Revival Under Wesley," *Religion in Life,* XXVII, No. 1 (1957), 105-18.

32. Henry Bett, *The Spirit of Methodism* (London: The Epworth Press, 1937), pp. 111-12.

33. Randolph S. Foster, *Philosophy of Christian Experience* (New York: Hunt and Eaton, 1890), pp. 10-11.

34. *Ibid.,* pp. 21-25.

35. Cell, *op. cit.,* p. 72.

36. Bett, *op. cit.,* pp. 93-94.

37. *Ibid.,* p. 96.

38. Cell, *op. cit.,* pp. 135-36.

39. W. J. Townsend, *A New History of Methodism* (London: Hodder and Stoughton, 1909), I, 55-56.

40. Lee, *op. cit.,* p. 69.

41. *Works,* VIII, 110-12.

42. *Ibid.,* p. 14.

43. *Ibid.,* I, 249.

44. J. Baines Atkinson, *The Beauty of Holiness* (New York: Philosophical Library, 1953), p. 73.

45. Hay, *op. cit.,* II, 441-58.

46. Henry C. Thiessen, *Introductory Lectures in Systematic Theology* (Grand Rapids: Wm. B. Eerdmans Publishing Company, 1951), p. 379.

47. Warfield, *op. cit.,* II, 582-83.

48. John Murray, *Redemption—Accomplished and Applied* (Grand Rapids: Wm. B. Eerdmans Publishing Company, 1955), p. 177.

49. Cecil Northcott, "The Great Divide: Experience Versus Tradition," *Religion in Life*, XX, No. 3 (1951), 396-402.

50. Douglas V. Steere, "The Meaning of Mysticism Within Christianity," *Religion in Life*, XXII, No. 4 (1953), 515-26.

51. *Works*, VI, 52-54.

52. *Ibid.*, II, 528.

53. *Ibid.*, p. 530.

54. *Ibid.*, XII, 30.

55. *Ibid.*, VIII, 297.

56. *Ibid.*, I, 476.

57. *Ibid.*, VI, 490-91.

58. *Ibid.*, pp. 526-27.

59. Murray, *op. cit.*, pp. 196-98.

60. *Works*, V, 278-80.

61. *Ibid.*, p. 432.

62. *Ibid.*, III, 75.

63. Wood, *op. cit.*, p. 26.

64. Harry E. Jessop, *Foundations of Doctrine* (Chicago: The Chicago Evangelistic Institute, 1938), pp. 131-32.

65. *Works*, VI, 19.

66. *Ibid.*, X, 367.

67. *Ibid.*, XII, 413.

68. *Ibid.*, V, 326-27.

69. *Ibid.*, XI, 400-402.

70. *Ibid.*, V, 165.

71. Pope, *op. cit.*, II, 68.

72. Turner, *op. cit.*, p. 249.

73. Warfield, *op. cit.*, II, 582-83.

74. Sangster, *Path to Perfection*, *op. cit.*, pp. 115-16.

75. *Ibid.*, p. 190.

76. Flew, *op. cit.*, pp. 332-33.

77. *Ibid.*, p. 335; Sangster, *op. cit.*, p. 113.

78. Cell, *op. cit.*, pp. 274-75.

79. Turner, *op. cit.*, p. 213.

80. Flew, *op. cit.*, p. 333.

81. *Works*, V, 161.

82. *Ibid.*, p. 165.

83. Flew, *op. cit.*, p. 333.

84. Brockett, *op. cit.*, p. 54.

85. McConnell, *op. cit.*, p. 198.

86. Brockett, *op. cit.*, p. 122.

87. Cannon, *op. cit.*, p. 241.

88. *Works*, XII, 398-400.

89. *Ibid.*, XIV, 270-71.

90. *Ibid.*, XII, 257.

91. *Ibid.*, V, 283.

92. *Ibid.*, p. 328.

93. McConnell, *op. cit.*, p. 194.

94. *Works*, XI, 367-69.

95. McConnell, *op. cit.*, p. 195.

96. Luther, *Compend, op. cit.,* pp. 67-73.

97. Kuyper, *op. cit.,* p. 21.

98. Berkouwer, *op. cit.,* p. 78.

99. Murray, *op. cit.,* p. 97.

100. Nels F. S. Ferre, "The Holy Spirit and Methodism Today," *Religion in Life,* XXIII, No. 1 (1953), 36-46.

101. *Works,* V, 30.

102. *Ibid.,* VII, 515.

103. *Ibid.,* VIII, 49.

104. *Ibid.,* p. 106.

105. *Ibid.,* XII, 71.

106. Calvin, *Compend, op. cit.,* pp. 89-90.

107. Charles Ewing Brown, *The Meaning of Sanctification* (Anderson, Indiana: The Warner Press, 1945), pp. 104-15.

108. Asbury Lowrey, *op. cit.,* pp. 344-49; D. Shelby Corlett, *The Meaning of Holiness* (Kansas City: Beacon Hill Press, 1944), pp. 70-72; S. A. Keen, *Pentecostal Papers* (Chicago: Christian Witness Co., 1895); Wood, *op. cit.,* pp. 72-73; E. T. Curnick, *A Catechism on Christian Perfection* (Chicago: The Christian Witness Co., 1885), pp. 58-61.

109. *Works,* V, 38.

110. *Ibid.,* I, 117-18.

111. *Ibid.,* III, 116.

112. *Ibid.,* XII, 416; VI, 10-11; Sangster, *Path to Perfection, op. cit.,* p. 83.

113. Fletcher, *op. cit.,* pp. 630-33.

114. Peters, *op. cit.,* p. 107.

115. Adam Clarke, *The Holy Bible with a Commentary and Critical Notes* (New York: Abingdon-Cokesbury Press), V, 682-83.

116. Peters, *op. cit.,* pp. 188-91.

117. *Works,* V, 133-34.

118. *Ibid.,* XI, 420.

119. *Ibid.,* VI, 47.

120. *Ibid.,* VI, 52-53.

121. *Ibid.,* XI, 420.

122. Sangster, *Path to Perfection, op. cit.,* p. 130.

123. *Works,* XI, 397-98.

124. Flew, *op. cit.,* p. 336.

125. *Ibid.,* p. 337.

126. *Works,* XI, 420.

127. Flew, *op. cit.,* p. 333.

128. *Works,* XI, 394, 443.

129. Sangster, *Path to Perfection, op. cit.,* p. 87.

130. *Ibid.,* p. 165.

131. *Works,* XI, 398.

132. *Ibid.,* V, 117.

133. *Ibid.,* p. 118.

134. Townsend, *op. cit.,* I, 31-32.

135. *Ibid.,* pp. 28-29.

136. Flew, *op. cit.,* pp. 329-30.

137. Cell, *op. cit.,* p. 181.

138. *Works*, V, 435-37.
139. *Ibid.*, pp. 438-39.
140. *Ibid.*, pp. 443-44.
141. *Ibid.*, p. 445.
142. *Ibid.*, p. 67.
143. *Ibid.*, pp. 68-69.
144. *Ibid.*, p. 70.
145. *Ibid.*, pp. 452-53.
146. *Ibid.*, pp. 455-57.
147. *Ibid.*, p. 460.
148. *Ibid.*, p. 462.
149. Lindstrom, *op. cit.*, p. 173.
150. *Ibid.*, p. 174.
151. Fletcher, *op. cit.*, II, 494-95.
152. *Ibid.*, p. 493.
153. Sangster, *Path to Perfection*, *op. cit.*, p. 147.
154. *Works*, VII, 495.
155. *Ibid.*, pp. 298-99.
156. *Ibid.*, pp. 46-49.
157. *Ibid.*, p. 57.
158. Lindstrom, *op. cit.*, pp. 174-75.
159. *Works*, XII, 235-36.
160. *Ibid.*, pp. 238-39.
161. *Ibid.*, IX, 292-93.
162. Lindstrom, *op. cit.*, pp. 179-80.
163. *Works*, VIII, 474.

CHAPTER V

1. McConnell, *op. cit.*, p. 198.
2. *Works*, VI, 149-67.
3. Graham Ikin, "Sin, Psychology and God," *Hibbert Journal*, XLVIII, 368.
4. *Ibid.*, p. 369.
5. McConnell, *op. cit.*, p. 198.
6. *Works*, VI, 215.
7. *Ibid.*, pp. 216-18.
8. *Ibid.*, pp. 64-65.
9. *Ibid.*, VII, 347.
10. *Ibid.*, pp. 345-46.
11. *Ibid.*, p. 348.
12. *Ibid.*, XI, 419.
13. *Ibid.*, XII, 278-79.
14. H. A. Baldwin, *Holiness and the Human Element* (Louisville: Pentecostal Publishing Company, 1919), pp. 88-89.
15. *Ibid.*, p. 89.
16. John R. Brooks, *Scriptural Sanctification* (Nashville: Publishing House of the M.E. Church, South, 1899), p. 15.
17. *Works*, VI, 477-78.
18. Sangster, *Path to Perfection*, *op. cit.*, p. 114.
19. *Works*, VI, 477.
20. *Ibid.*, XII, 340.

21. Prince, *op. cit.,* p. 24.
22. *Works,* VII, 228.
23. *Ibid.,* XI, 419.
24. *Ibid.,* p. 415.
25. *Ibid.,* VII, 226-27.
26. *Ibid.,* VI, 477-78.
27. *Ibid.,* XI, 374.
28. *Ibid.,* VI, 30-31.
29. *Ibid.,* p. 94.
30. *Ibid.,* pp. 95-97.
31. Quoted in Jessop, *op. cit.,* p. 129.
32. Brockett, *op. cit.,* p. 48.
33. *Ibid.,* p. 49.
34. Paul S. Rees, "Our Wesleyan Heritage After Two Centuries, *Asbury Seminarian,* II, No. 2 (1948), p. 56.
35. Paul F. Abel, "Human Nature," *Asbury Seminarian,* III, No. 3 (1948), p. 114.
36. *Ibid.,* pp. 114-15.
37. *Ibid.,* pp. 120-21.
38. Rees, *op. cit.,* pp. 56-58.
39. *Works,* XII, 217-18.
40. *Ibid.,* VIII, 345-47.
41. *Ibid.,* III, 273.
42. Peters, *op. cit.,* p. 202.
43. *Works,* III, 273.
44. *Ibid.,* V, 328.
45. *Ibid.,* I, 330.
46. *Ibid.,* pp. 481-82.
47. *Ibid.,* IX, 273.
48. *Ibid.,* XI, 419.
49. *Ibid.,* p. 419.
50. *Ibid.,* XII, 443.
51. *Ibid.,* XIII, 130-31.
52. *Ibid.,* XI, 399.
53. Brooks, *op. cit.,* pp. 321-23.
54. *Ibid.,* p. 372.
55. *Ibid.,* p. 355.
56. Richard S. Taylor, *A Right Conception of Sin* (Kansas City: Nazarene Publishing House, 1939), pp. 96-97.
57. *Works,* V, 283.
58. *Ibid.,* pp. 298-99.
59. *Ibid.,* pp. 307-8.
60. Cannon, *op. cit.,* pp. 222-23.
61. *Ibid.,* pp. 234-36.
62. *Works,* XI, 467.
63. *Ibid.,* p. 468.
64. *Ibid.,* VII, 32-35.
65. *Ibid.,* V, 367-72.
66. *Ibid.,* VI, 334.
67. *Ibid.,* VII, 9-11.

68. *Ibid.*, pp. 17-21.
69. Flew, *op. cit.*, p. 338.
70. *Works*, VI, 479.
71. *Ibid.*, pp. 255-60.
72. *Ibid.*, pp. 261-62.
73. *Ibid.*, pp. 263-64.
74. *Ibid.*, p. 267.
75. *Ibid.*, p. 400.
76. *Ibid.*, p. 403.
77. *Ibid.*, pp. 478-79.
78. *Ibid.*, p. 479.
79. *Notes*, pp. 508-9.
80. Sangster, *Path to Perfection*, *op. cit.*, pp. 176-77.
81. *Works*, VII, 404-8.
82. *Ibid.*, VI, 454-58.
83. *Ibid.*, p. 473.
84. Sangster, *Path to Perfection*, *op. cit.*, p. 89.

CHAPTER VI

1. *Works*, XIII, 49.
2. *Ibid.*, XII, 366.
3. Atkinson, *op. cit.*, pp. 78-79.
4. Flew, *op. cit.*, pp. 411-12; Sangster, *Path to Perfection*, *op. cit.*, pp. 135-39.
5. *Works*, VII, 341-42.
6. *Ibid.*, III, 420.
7. *Ibid.*, XII, 287.
8. *Ibid.*, p. 219.
9. *Ibid.*, pp. 483-84.
10. Calvin, *Institutes*, *op. cit.*, I, 659.
11. *Works*, XII, 483-84.
12. *Ibid.*, VI, 477.
13. *Ibid.*, VI, 94-96.
14. *Ibid.*, XII, 290-91.
15. *Ibid.*, pp. 390-91.
16. *Ibid.*, p. 292.
17. *Ibid.*, p. 385.
18. *Ibid.*, p. 379.
19. *Ibid.*, p. 334.
20. *Ibid.*, XI, 419.
21. Sangster, *Path to Perfection*, *op. cit.*, p. 116; Baldwin, *op. cit.*, pp. 78-79; Randolph S. Foster, *Christian Purity* (New York: Eaton and Mains, 1897), pp. 66-69.
22. Daniel Steele, *Love Enthroned* (New York: Phillips and Hunt, 1881), pp. 86-87.
23. Luther, *Compend*, *op. cit.*, pp. 87-88.
24. *Works*, XII, 495.
25. *Ibid.*, XI, 414-15.
26. *Ibid.*, pp. 417-18.
27. *Ibid.*, XII, 385.
28. *Ibid.*, pp. 278-79.

29. *Ibid.*, XI, 417.
30. *Ibid.*, III, 68-69.
31. *Ibid.*, XI, 395.
32. *Ibid.*, pp. 396-97.
33. *Ibid.*, pp. 396-97, 419.
34. *Ibid.*, VII, 406-8.
35. Sangster, *Path to Perfection, op. cit.*, pp. 183-84.
36. McConnell, *op. cit.*, p. 195.
37. Steele, *op. cit.*, pp. 88-89.
38. *Works*, XI, 394-96.
39. *Ibid.*, III, 136.
40. *Ibid.*, pp. 105-6.
41. *Ibid.*, XII, 375-76.
42. *Ibid.*, XI, 453.
43. *Ibid.*, IV, 269-70.
44. *Ibid.*, V, 230.
45. *Ibid.*, VI, 525-26.
46. *Ibid.*, p. 526.
47. *Ibid.*, pp. 80-82.
48. *Ibid.*, pp. 83-84.
49. *Ibid.*, XII, 394.
50. *Ibid.*, V, 232.
51. *Ibid.*, XI, 419.
52. *Ibid.*, VI, 477-80.
53. *Ibid.*, p. 5.
54. *Ibid.*, VII, 348.
55. Luther, *Romans, op. cit.*, pp. 88-89.
56. *Works*, XI, 419.
57. *Ibid.*, X, 327-28.
58. Sangster, *Path to Perfection, op. cit.*, pp. 136-37.
59. Foster, *Purity, op. cit.*, pp. 73-74.
60. Carnell, *op. cit.*, pp. 424-25.
61. Steele, *op. cit.*, pp. 325-26.
62. Peck, *op. cit.*, p. 436.
63. *Works*, V, 231-33.
64. *Notes*, p. 598.
65. Sangster, *Path to Perfection, op. cit.*, p. 112.
66. Berkouwer, *op. cit.*, p. 129.
67. *Works*, X, 333.
68. *Ibid.*, VIII, 337-38.
69. *Ibid.*, XII, 276.
70. *Ibid.*, XIII, 62.
71. *Ibid.*, III, 420.
72. *Ibid.*, XII, 323.
73. *Ibid.*, VI, 398.
74. *Ibid.*, XII, 398,400.
75. *Ibid.*, VI, 526.
76. *Ibid.*, XI, 395-96.
77. *Ibid.*, p. 417.
78. *Ibid.*, III, 68-69.

79. Spalding, *op. cit.*, pp. 45-46.
80. Turner, *op. cit.*, p. 238.
81. *Works*, XII, 227-28.
82. *Ibid.*, p. 276.
83. *Ibid.*, XI, 427-32.
84. Rees, *op. cit.*, III, 12.

CHAPTER VII

1. *Works*, VII, 423-24.
2. *Ibid.*, pp. 425-29.
3. *Ibid.*, VIII, 300.
4. *Ibid.*, XIII, 9
5. Robert Clark, *op. cit.*, p. 214.
6. *Ibid.*, p. 65.
7. *Ibid.*, pp. 238-40.
8. Scott, *op. cit.*, pp. 29-30.
9. *Ibid.*, p. 143.
10. *Ibid.*, pp. 161-65.
11. *Ibid.*, pp. 193-225.
12. *Ibid.*, pp. 265, 464.
13. *Ibid.*, p. 403.
14. *Ibid.*, p. 499.
15. *Ibid.*, p. 504.
16. Gaddis, *op. cit.*, p. 141.
17. *Ibid.*, p. 221.
18. *Ibid.*, p. 164.
19. Peters, *op. cit.*, pp. 188-89.
20. *Ibid.*, pp. 87, 90.
21. *Ibid.*, pp. 98-101.
22. *Ibid.*, p. 101.
23. Rose, *op. cit.*, p. 21.
24. Smith, *op. cit.*, pp. 115-16.
25. *Ibid.*, pp. 135-47.
26. *Ibid.*, p. 62.
27. *Ibid.*, p. 85.
28. *Ibid.*, pp. 67-68.
29. *Ibid.*, pp. 146-47.
30. Rose, *op. cit.*, p. 21.
31. *Ibid.*, pp. 22-35.
32. *Ibid.*, p. 13.
33. *Ibid.*, pp. 36-37.
34. *Ibid.*, pp. 47-48.
35. *Ibid.*, pp. 52-54.
36. Peters, *op. cit.*, pp. 175-76.
37. *Ibid.*, pp. 136-46.
38. *Ibid.*, pp. 143-44.
39. *Ibid.*, p. 192.
40. *Ibid.*, pp. 192-93.
41. Cushman, "Landmarks in the Revival," *op. cit.*, p. 118.
42. Elmer Clark, *op. cit.*, p. 58.
43. Gaddis, *op. cit.*, pp. 321-23; Thompson, *op. cit.*, pp. 709-10.

44. Rose, *op. cit.*, p. 53.
45. *Ibid.*, pp. 76–77.
46. Elmer Clark, *op. cit.*, p. 59.
47. Peters, *op. cit.*, p. 150.
48. Gaddis, *op. cit.*, p. 268.
49. *Discipline of the Wesleyan Methodist Church of America* (Syracuse: Wesleyan Methodist Publishing Association, 1951), p. 17.
50. Gaddis, *op. cit.*, pp. 299–301.
51. Peters, *op. cit.*, pp. 130–31.
52. Smith, *op. cit.*, pp. 129–30.
53. Peters, *op. cit.*, p. 149.
54. Elmer Clark, *op. cit.*, p. 75.
55. Gaddis, *op. cit.*, p. 376.
56. *Ibid.*, p. 54.
57. Gaddis, *op. cit.*, p. 353.
58. *Ibid.*, p. 99.
59. Robert Clark, *op. cit.*, pp. 215–16.
60. *Ibid.*, pp. 236–37.
61. Horton Davies, "Centrifugal Christian Sects," *Religion in Life,* XXV, No. 3 (1956), 323–58.
62. Smith, *op. cit.*, pp. 60, 86.
63. Elmer Clark, *op. cit.*, p. 75.
64. Rose, *op. cit.*, pp. 192–93.
65. Warfield, *op. cit.*, I, 345.
66. Wall, *op. cit.*, pp. 404–6.
67. Rose, *op. cit.*, pp. 29–33.
68. Gaddis, *op. cit.*, p. 227.
69. Warfield, *op. cit.*, II, 213.
70. Rose, *op. cit.*, p. 32.
71. Warfield, *op. cit.*, II, 567.
72. *Ibid.*, pp. 582–83.
73. Norman Grubb, *The Law of Faith* (London: Lutterworth Press, 1947), pp. 79–93.
74. Peters, *op. cit.*, p. 162.
75. H. Orton Wiley, *Introduction to Christian Theology* (Kansas City: Beacon Hill Press, 1946), pp. 305–6.
76. Peters, *op. cit.*, pp. 191–92.

BIBLIOGRAPHY

WORKS BY JOHN WESLEY

WESLEY, JOHN. *The Works of John Wesley*. An edition of the complete and unabridged *Works* reproduced by the photo offset process from the authorized edition published by the Wesleyan Conference Office in London, England, in 1872. 14 vols. Grand Rapids: Zondervan Publishing House, 1958.

————. *Explanatory Notes upon the New Testament*. New York: Eaton and Mains, n.d.

————. *Standard Sermons*. Edited by E. H. Sugden, 2 vols. London: The Epworth Press, 1921.

————. *The Journal of the Rev. John Wesley, A.M.* Edited by Nehemiah Curnock. 8 vols. London: Epworth Press, 1938.

————. *The Letters of the Reverend John Wesley, A.M.* Edited by John Telford, 8 vols. London: Epworth Press, 1931.

————. and WESLEY, CHARLES. *Poetical Works*. Collected and arranged by G. Osborn, 1868-72.

————. *A Calm Address to Our American Colonies*. Edited by Thomas Kepler. Cleveland: World Publishing Co., 1954.

————. *Survey of the Wisdom of God in the Creation*. Lancaster, Pa.: Hamilton, 1810.

————. *A Compend of Wesley's Theology*. Compiled by Robert Burtner and Robert Chiles. New York: Abingdon Press, 1954.

WORKS ABOUT WESLEY

BAKER, FRANK. *A Charge to Keep*. London: The Epworth Press, 1947.

BOWEN, MARJORIE. *Wrestling Jacob*. London: Watts & Co., 1937.

BRAILSFORD, MABEL R. *A Tale of Two Brothers*. New York: Oxford University Press, 1954.

BREADY, JOHN WESLEY. *England: Before and After Wesley*. London: Hodder and Stoughton, Ltd., 1938.

CANNON, WILLIAM R. *The Theology of John Wesley*. New York: Abingdon-Cokesbury Press, 1946.

CELL, GEORGE CROFT. *The Rediscovery of John Wesley*. New York: Henry Holt and Company, 1935.

CLARK, ELMER T. *What Happened at Aldersgate?* Nashville: Methodist Publishing House, 1938.

COX, LEO G. "John Wesley's Concept of Sin." Unpublished master's thesis, University of Iowa, 1957.

CUSHMAN, ROBERT E. "Landmarks in the Revival Under Wesley," *Religion in Life*, XXVII, No. 1, 1958, 105-18.

DOUGHTY, WILLIAM L. *John Wesley: His Conferences and His Preachers*. London: The Epworth Press, 1944.

EDWARDS, MALDWYN. *John Wesley and the Eighteenth Century*. London: George Allen and Unwin, Ltd., 1933.

ELTZHOLTZ, CARL F. *John Wesley's Conversion and Sanctification*. New York: Eaton and Mains, 1908.

ENSLEY, FRANCIS G. *John Wesley Evangelist.* Nashville: Tidings, 1955.

FAULKNER, JOHN A. "Wesley's Attitude Toward Luther," *Lutheran Quarterly,* New Series, XXXVI, 1906, 156-59.

————. *Wesley as Sociologist, Theologian, Churchman.* New York: The Methodist Book Concern, 1918.

FITCHETT, W. H. *Wesley and His Century.* London: Smith, Elder, and Company, 1906.

GREEN, J. BRAZIER. *John Wesley and William Law.* London: The Epworth Press, 1945.

GREEN, RICHARD. *The Conversion of John Wesley.* London: Francis Griffiths, 1909.

HARRISON, G. ELSIE. *Son to Susanna.* Nashville: Cokesbury Press, 1938.

HILDEBRANDT, FRANZ. *Christianity According to the Wesleys.* London: The Epworth Press, 1956.

————. *From Luther to Wesley.* London: Lutterworth Press, 1951.

HUTTON, WILLIAM HOLDEN. *John Wesley.* London: Macmillan and Co., Ltd., 1927.

KROLL, HARRISON. *The Long Quest.* Philadelphia: The Westminster Press, 1954.

LEE, UMPHREY. *John Wesley and Modern Religion.* Nashville: Cokesbury Press, 1936.

LIPSKY, ABRAM. *John Wesley a Portrait.* New York: Simon and Schuster, 1928.

LUNN, ARNOLD. *John Wesley.* London: Cassell and Company, Ltd., 1929.

MACARTHUR, K. W. *The Economic Ethics of John Wesley.* Chicago: University of Chicago Libraries, 1938.

McCONNELL, FRANCIS. *John Wesley.* New York: The Abingdon Press, 1939.

NEELY, THOMAS BENJAMIN. *Doctrinal Standards of Methodism.* New York: Fleming H. Revell Co., 1918.

PIETTE, MAXIMIN. *John Wesley in the Evolution of Protestantism.* New York: Sheed and Ward, 1937.

PRINCE, JOHN W. *Wesley on Religious Education.* New York: Methodist Book Concern, 1926.

RATTENBURY, J. ERNEST. *The Conversion of the Wesleys.* London: The Epworth Press, 1938.

————. *Wesley's Legacy to the World.* Nashville: Cokesbury Press, 1929.

SIMON, JOHN S. *John Wesley the Master Builder.* London: The Epworth Press, 1927.

————. *John Wesley, The Lost Phase.* London: The Epworth Press, 1934.

SIMPSON, W. J. SPARROW. *John Wesley and the Church of England.* New York: The Macmillan Company, 1934.

SOUTHEY, ROBERT. *The Life of John Wesley and the Rise and Progress of Methodism.* 3rd ed. London: Longman, Brown, Green and Longmans, 1846.

TENNEY, MARY ALICE. *Blue Print for a Christian World.* Winona Lake: Light and Life Press, 1953.

THOMPSON, DAVID D. *John Wesley as a Social Reformer.* New York: Eaton and Mains, 1898.

TYERMAN, LUKE. *The Life and Times of the Rev. John Wesley, M.A.* 3 vols. London: Hodder and Stoughton, 1875.

WADE, JOHN D. *John Wesley.* New York: Coward-McCann, Inc., 1930.

WATSON, RICHARD. *The Life of the Rev. John Wesley, A.M.* New York: T. Mason and G. Lane, 1839.

WHITELEY, JOHN H. *Wesley's England: Survey of Eighteenth Century England.* London: The Epworth Press, 1938.

WINCHESTER, C. T. *The Life of John Wesley.* New York: The Macmillan Company, 1916.

YOST, JESSE J. "Plerophoria in the Spiritual Experiences of John Wesley." Unpublished master's thesis, State University of Iowa, 1922.

WORKS ON CHRISTIAN PERFECTION

ABEL, PAUL F. "Human Nature," *Asbury Seminarian,* III, Nos. 2-3 (1948), 62-71, 114-21.

ANDERSON, TONY M. *After Holiness, What?* Kansas City: Nazarene Publishing House, 1929.

ARTHUR, WILLIAM. *The Tongue of Fire.* New York: Eaton and Mains, 1856.

ATKINSON, J. BAINES. *The Beauty of Holiness.* New York: Philosophical Library, 1953.

BALDWIN, H. A. *Holiness and the Human Element.* Louisville: Pentecostal Publishing Co., 1919.

BROCKETT, HENRY E. *Scriptural Freedom from Sin.* Kansas City: Kingshiway Press, 1941.

BROOKS, JOHN R. *Scriptural Sanctification.* Nashville: Publishing House of the M.E. Church, South, 1899.

BROWN, CHARLES EWING. *The Meaning of Sanctification.* Anderson, Ind.: The Warner Press, 1945.

CARRADINE, BEVERLY. *Sanctification.* Syracuse: A. W. Hall, Publisher, 1897.

CHADWICK, SAMUEL. *The Call to Christian Perfection.* Kansas City: Beacon Hill Press, 1943.

CLARK, DOUGAN. *The Theology of Holiness.* Chicago: The Christian Witness Co., 1893.

CLARK, ROBERT BURTON. "The History of the Doctrine of Christian Perfection in the Methodist Episcopal Church in America up to 1845." Unpublished Th.D. dissertation, Temple University, 1946.

CORLETT, D. SHELBY. *The Meaning of Holiness.* Kansas City: Beacon Hill Press, 1944.

CURNICK, E. T. *A Catechism on Christian Perfection.* Chicago: The Christian Witness Co., 1885.

EARLE, RALPH. "The Holiness Teaching of the New Testament." Unpublished Th.D. dissertation, Gordon Divinity School, 1944.

FAIRBAIRN, CHARLES V. *Purity and Power.* Chicago: The Christian Witness Company, 1930.

FLETCHER, JOHN. *The Works.* 4 vols. New York: B. Waugh and T. Mason, 1835.

FLEW, R. NEWTON. *The Idea of Perfection in Christian Theology.* London: Oxford University Press, 1934.

FOSTER, RANDOLPH S. *Christian Purity* or *The Heritage of Faith.* New York: Eaton and Mains, 1897.

———. *Philosophy of Christian Experience.* New York: Hunt and Eaton, 1890.

GADDIS, ELMER MERRILL. "Christian Perfectionism in America." Unpublished Ph.D. dissertation, University of Chicago, 1929.

GREER, GEORGE DIXON. "A Psychological Study of Sanctification as a Second Work of Divine Grace." Unpublished Ph.D. dissertation, Drew University, 1936.

HAINES, WALLACE R. "A Survey of Holiness Literature," *Heart and Life Magazine,* XXX, No. 2 (1943), 10-15.

HINSHAW, CECILE EUGENE. "Perfectionism in Early Quakerism." Unpublished Th.D. dissertation, Iliff School of Theology, 1943.

HUNTINGTON, D. W. C. *Sin and Holiness* or *What It Is to Be Holy.* New York: Eaton and Mains, 1898.

JESSOP, HARRY E. *Foundations of Doctrine in Scripture and Experience.* Chicago: Chicago Evangelistic Institute, 1938.

JONES, E. STANLEY. *Victorious Living.* New York: Abingdon-Cokesbury Press, 1936.

KEEN, S. A. *Faith Papers.* Chicago: The Christian Witness Co., 1919.

———. *Pentecostal Papers.* Chicago: The Christian Witness Co., 1895.

LINDSTROM, HARALD. *Wesley and Sanctification.* London: The Epworth Press, 1946.

LOWERY, ASBURY. *Possibilities of Grace.* Chicago: The Christian Witness Co., 1884.

MALLALIEU, WILLARD F. *The Fullness of the Blessing of the Gospel of Christ.* Chicago: The Christian Witness Co., 1903.

MANIFOLD, ORRIN AVERY. "The Development of John Wesley's Doctrine of Christian Perfection." Unpublished Ph.D. dissertation, Boston University, 1945.

PALMER, PHOEBE. *Faith and Its Effects.* New York: Palmer and Hughes, 1867.

PECK, GEORGE. *The Scripture Doctrine of Christian Perfection.* New York: Lane and Scott, 1850.

PECK, JESSE T. *The Central Idea of Christianity.* Boston: Henry V. Degen, 1856.

PETERS, JOHN LELAND. *Christian Perfection and American Methodism.* Nashville: Abingdon Press, 1956.

REES, PAUL S. "Our Wesleyan Heritage After Two Centuries," *Asbury Seminarian,* III, Nos. 1-3 (1948), 8-12, 54-58, 103-7; IV, Nos. 1-2 (1949), 13-17, 47-54.

RIES, CLAUDE ARDEN. "A Greek New Testament Approach to the Teaching of the Deeper Spiritual Life." Unpublished Th.D. dissertation, Northern Baptist Theological Seminary, 1945.

ROSE, DELBERT R. *A Theology of Christian Experience.* Wilmore, Ky.: The Seminary Press, 1958.

SANGSTER, W. E. "The Church's One Privation," *Religion in Life,* XVIII, No. 4 (1949), 493-507.

———. *The Path to Perfection.* Nashville: Abingdon-Cokesbury Press, 1943.

SCHWAB, RALPH KENDALL. *The History of the Doctrine of Christian Perfection in the Evangelical Association.* Menasha, Wis.: George Banta Publishing Co., 1922.

SMITH, HANNAH WHITALL. *The Christian's Secret of a Happy Life.* New York: Fleming H. Revell Co., 1916.

SMITH, JOSEPH H. *Pauline Perfection.* Chicago: The Christian Witness Co., 1913.

SMITH, TIMOTHY L. *Revivalism and Social Reform.* Nashville: Abingdon Press, 1957.

STEELE, DANIEL. *Love Enthroned.* New York: Phillips and Hunt, 1881.

———. *Steele's Answers.* Chicago: The Christian Witness Company, 1912.

THOMPSON, CLAUDE HOLMES. "The Witness of American Methodism to the Historical Doctrine of Christian Perfection." Unpublished Ph.D. dissertation, Drew University, 1949.

TURNER, GEORGE A. *The More Excellent Way.* Winona Lake: Light and Life Press, 1952.

WALKER, EDWARD F. *Sanctify Them.* Chicago: The Christian Witness Co., 1899.

WOOD, J. A. *Purity and Maturity.* Boston: Christian Witness Co., 1899.

ZEPP, ARTHUR C. *Progress After Sanctification.* Chicago: The Christian Witness Co., 1909.

WORKS RELATED TO SANCTIFICATION

BERKOUWER, GERRIT C. *Faith and Sanctification.* Grand Rapids: Wm. B. Eerdmans Publishing Company, 1952.

COCHRANE, ARTHUR C. "The Doctrine of Sanctification: Review of Barth's *Kirchliche Dogmatik,*" *Theology Today,* XIII, No. 3 (1956), 376-88.

CUSHMAN, ROBERT E. "Karl Barth on the Holy Spirit," *Religion in Life,* XXIV, No. 4 (1955), 566-78.

FOSS, MARTIN. *The Idea of Perfection in the Western World.* Princeton: Princeton University Press, 1946.

KUYPER, ABRAHAM. *The Work of the Holy Spirit.* Grand Rapids: Wm. B. Eerdmans Publishing Co., 1946.

LAW, WILLIAM. *A Serious Call to a Devout and Holy Life.* New York: E. P. Dutton and Co., 1906.

McCULLOH, GERALD O. "Evangelizing the Whole of Life," *Religion in Life,* XIX, No. 2 (1950), 236-44.

NORTHCOTT, CECIL. "The Great Divide: Experience Versus Tradition," *Religion in Life,* XX, No. 3 (1951), 396-402.

STEERE, DOUGLAS V. "The Meaning of Mysticism Within Christianity," *Religion in Life,* XXII, No. 4 (1953), 515-26.

TAYLOR, JEREMY. *Holy Living and Dying.* London: Henry G. Bohn, 1850.

THOMAS A KEMPIS. *The Imitation of Christ.* New York: J. M. Dent and Sons, Ltd., 1910.

WALL, ERNEST. "I commend to you Phoebe," *Religion in Life,* XXVI, No. 3 (1957), 396-408.

WARFIELD, BENJAMIN B. *Studies in Perfectionism.* 2 vols. New York: Oxford University Press, 1931.

ARMINIUS, JAMES. *Works.* 3 vols. London: Longman, Hunt, Rees, Orme, Brown, and Green, 1825.

BERKOUWER, G. C. *The Triumph of Grace in the Theology of Karl Barth.* Grand Rapids: Wm. B. Eerdmans Publishing Co., 1956.

CAIRNS, DAVID. *The Image of God in Man.* New York: Philosophical Library, 1953.

CALVIN, JOHN. *A Compend of the Institutes of the Christian Religion.* Edited by Hugh T. Keer. Philadelphia: Presbyterian Board of Christian Education, 1939.

————. *Institutes of the Christian Religion.* 2 vols. Grand Rapids: Wm. B. Eerdmans Publishing Co., 1949.

CLARKE, ADAM. *Christian Theology.* New York: Waugh and Mason, 1837.

————. *The Holy Bible, with a Commentary and Critical Notes.* New York: Abingdon-Cokesbury Press, n.d.

CURTIS, O. A. *The Christian Faith.* New York: Eaton and Mains, 1905.

FINNEY, CHARLES G. *Systematic Theology.* Oberlin: E. J. Goodrich, 1878.

FOSTER, RANDOLPH S. *Studies in Theology.* 6 vols. New York: Eaton and Mains, 1899.

HAY, CHARLES E. *The Theology of Luther.* 2 vols. Philadelphia: Lutheran Publication Society, 1897.

HILLS, A. M. *Fundamental Christian Theology.* 2 vols. Pasadena, California: C. J. Kinne, 1931.

HODGE, CHARLES. *Systematic Theology.* Grand Rapids: Wm. B. Eerdmans Publishing Co., 1952.

HORDERN, WILLIAM. "The Relevance of the Fall," *Religion in Life,* XX, No. 1 (1951), 99-105.

IKIN, GRAHAM. "Sin, Psychology and God," *Hibbert Journal,* XLVIII, 368-71.

KNUDSON, ALBERT C. *Basic Issues in Christian Thought.* New York: Abingdon-Cokesbury Press, 1950.

LUTHER, MARTIN. *Commentary on the Epistle to the Romans.* Grand Rapids: Zondervan Publishing House, 1954.

————. *Commentary on St. Paul's Epistle to the Galatians.* Grand Rapids: Wm. B. Eerdmans Publishing Company, 1930.

————. *A Compend of Luther's Theology.* Edited by Hugh T. Kerr. Philadelphia: The Westminster Press, 1943.

————. *Works of Martin Luther.* 6 vols. Philadelphia: A. J. Holman Company, 1932.

MACKINTOSH, ROBERT. *Christianity and Sin.* New York: Charles Scribner's Sons, 1914.

McGIFFERT, ARTHUR CUSHMAN. *Protestantism, Thought Before Kent.* New York: Charles Scribner's Sons, 1936.

MILEY, JOHN. *Systematic Theology.* 2 vols. New York: The Methodist Book Concern, 1892.

MURRAY, JOHN. *Redemption—Accomplished and Applied.* Grand Rapids: Wm. B. Eerdmans Publishing Company, 1955.

POPE, WILLIAM BURT. *A Compendium of Christian Theology.* 2 vols. 2nd ed. revised and enlarged. New York: Hunt and Eaton, 1899.

RALSTON, THOMAS N. *Elements of Divinity.* Edited by T. O. Summers. Nashville: Cokesbury, 1924.

RAYMOND, MINER. *Systematic Theology.* 3 vols. Cincinnati: Hitchcock and Walden, 1877.

SMITH, H. SHELTON. *Changing Conceptions of Original Sin.* New York: Charles Scribner's Sons, 1955.

SPALDING, JAMES C. "Recent Restatements of the Doctrines of the Fall and Original Sin." Ph.D. thesis, Columbia University. Ann Arbor: University Microfilms, 1950.

SPERRY, WILLIAM. "Sin and Salvation," *Religion in Life,* XXI, No. 2 (1952), 163-206.

TAYLOR, JOHN. *The Scripture-Doctrine of Original Sin Proposed to Free and Candid Examination.* 3 parts. 3rd ed. Including *A Supplement.* Belfast: John Hay, Bookseller, 1746.

TAYLOR, RICHARD S. *A Right Conception of Sin.* Kansas City: Nazarene Publishing House, 1939.

TENNANT, FREDERICK ROBERT. *The Concept of Sin.* Cambridge: University Press, 1912.

THIESSEN, HENRY CLARENCE. *Introductory Lectures in Systematic Theology.* Grand Rapids: Wm. B. Eerdmans Publishing Company, 1951.

WAKEFIELD, SAMUEL. *Christian Theology.* New York: Hunt and Eaton, 1869.

WATSON, RICHARD. *Theological Institutes.* 2 vols. New ed. New York: Carlton and Porter, 1857.

WILEY, H. ORTON. *Christian Theology.* 3 vols. Kansas City: Nazarene Publishing House, 1941.

WORKS CONCERNING METHODISM

BETT, HENRY. *The Spirit of Methodism.* London: The Epworth Press, 1937.

BUCKLEY, J. M. *A History of Methodists in the United States.* New York: The Christian Literature Co., 1896.

CAMERON, RICHARD M. *The Rise of Methodism.* A source book. New York: Philosophical Library, 1954.

CHILES, ROBERT E. "Methodist Apostasy: From Free Grace to Free Will," *Religion in Life,* XXVII, No. 3 (1958), 438-49.

CHURCH, LESLIE F. *The Early Methodist People.* London: The Epworth Press, 1948.

DANIELS, W. H. *History of Methodism.* New York: Methodist Book Concern, 1880.

FERRE, NELS F. S. "The Holy Spirit and Methodism Today," *Religion in Life,* XXIII, No. 1 (1954), 36-46.

HYDE, A. B. *The Story of Methodism.* Springfield, Massachusetts: Willey and Company, 1888.

LUCCOCK, HALFORD E. and HUTCHINSON, PAUL. *The Story of Methodism.* New York: Methodist Book Concern, 1926.

McLEISTER, IRA F., and NICHOLSON, ROY S. *History of the Wesleyan Methodist Church of America.* Revised edition. Syracuse: Wesleyan Methodist Publishing Association, 1951.

Scott, Leland Howard. "Methodist Theology in America in the Nineteenth Century." Unpublished Ph.D. dissertation, Yale University, 1954.

Simpson, Matthew (ed.). *Cyclopedia of Methodism*. Philadelphia: Louis H. Everts, 1880.

Stevens, Abel. *A Compendious History of American Methodism*. New York: Eaton and Mains, 1868.

Stokes, Mack B. *Major Methodist Beliefs*. Nashville: The Methodist Publishing House, 1955-56.

Sweet, William Warren. "Religion on the American Frontier, 1783-1840." Vol. IV. *The Methodists*. Chicago: The University of Chicago Press, 1946.

Townsend, William John, Workman, H. B., and Eayrs, George. *A New History of Methodism*. 2 vols. London: Hodder and Stoughton, 1909.

Tucker, Robert L. *The Separation of the Methodists from the Church of England*. New York: The Methodist Book Concern, 1918.

Warner, Wellman J. *The Wesleyan Movement in the Industrial Revolution*. New York: Longmans, Green and Co., 1930.

Wheeler, Henry. *History and Exposition of the Twenty-five Articles of Religion of the Methodist Episcopal Church*. New York: Eaton and Mains, 1908.

General Works

Barth, Karl. *The Christian Life*. London: Student Christian Movement Press, 1930.

Bosley, Harold A. *A Firm Faith for Today*. New York: Harper and Brothers Publishers, 1950.

——. *Main Issues Confronting Christendom*. New York: Harper and Brothers Publishers, 1948.

Brightman, Edgar S. *Personalism in Theology*. Boston: Boston University Press, 1943.

Brunner, Emil. *The Divine Imperative*. New York: The Macmillan Company, 1942.

Carnell, Edward John. *A Philosophy of the Christian Religion*. Grand Rapids: Wm. B. Eerdmans, 1954.

——. *Christian Commitment*. New York: The Macmillan Company, 1957.

Chapman, J. B. *A History of the Church of the Nazarene*. Kansas City: Nazarene Publishing House, 1926.

Cherbonnier, E. LaB. *Hardness of Heart*. Garden City: Doubleday and Company, Inc., 1955.

Clark, Elmer T. *The Small Sects in America*. New York: Abingdon-Cokesbury Press, 1949.

Davies, Horton. "Centrifugal Christian Sects," *Religion in Life*, XXV, No. 3 (1956) 323-35.

Discipline of the Wesleyan Methodist Church of America. Syracuse: Wesleyan Methodist Publishing Association, 1951.

Forell, George W. *Ethics of Decision*. Philadelphia: The Muhlenberg Press, 1955.

——. *Faith Active in Love*. New York: The American Press, 1954.

GRUBB, NORMAN. *The Law of Faith.* London: Lutterworth Press, 1947.

HUNT, JOHN. *Religious Thought in England.* London: Strahan and Co., 1873.

JAMES, WILLIAM. *The Varieties of Religious Experience.* New York: Longmans, Green, and Co., 1925.

JONES, RUFUS M. *Spiritual Reformers in the 16th and 17th Centuries.* London: Macmillan and Co., Ltd., 1914.

LECKY, WILLIAM E. H. *A History of England in the Eighteenth Century.* London: D. Appleton and Co., 1879.

LEWIS, EDWIN. *A Christian Manifesto.* New York: The Abingdon Press, 1934.

————. *A Philosophy of the Christian Revelation.* New York: Harper and Brothers Publishers, 1940.

————. *The Practice of the Christian Life.* Philadelphia: The Westminster Press, 1942.

MANSCHRECK, CLYDE LEONARD. *Melanchthon, the Quiet Reformer.* New York: Abingdon Press, 1958.

NIEBUHR, REINHOLD. *The Nature and Destiny of Man.* 2 vols. New York: Charles Scribner's Sons, 1943.

PELIKAN, ·JAROSLAV. *Fools for Christ.* Philadelphia: Muhlenberg Press, 1955.

RALL, HARRIS FRANKLIN. *Religion as Salvation.* Nashville: Abingdon-Cokesbury Press, 1953.

ROBERTS, DAVID E. *Psychotherapy and a Christian View of Man.* New York: Charles Scribner's Sons, 1953.

RUPP, GORDON. *The Righteousness of God.* New York: Philosophical Library, Inc., 1953.

WATSON, PHILIP S. *Let God Be God!* London: The Epworth Press, 1947.

WILLEY, BASIL. *The Eighteenth Century Background.* London: Chatto and Windus, 1940.

————. *The Seventeenth Century Background.* London: Chatto and Windus, 1934.